Intelligence Requirements
for the 1980's:
Covert Action

CONSORTIUM FOR THE STUDY OF INTELLIGENCE

Intelligence Requirements for the 1980's:

Covert Action

Edited by
Roy Godson

Published by
National Strategy Information Center, Inc.

Second Printing, 1985

Intelligence Requirements for the 1980's
NUMBER FOUR
Covert Action

Published by
National Strategy Information Center, Inc.
1730 Rhode Island Avenue, N.W.
Washington, D.C. 20036

Printed in the United States of America

Table of Contents

Chapter Seven
THE NECESSARY MEANS FOR US COVERT ACTION
IN THE 1980's

APPENDICES

Preface

From time immemorial, nations have sought to affect one another's internal affairs, if not by the egregious display of cannon, then by royal marriages and the casuistry of envoys. Sometimes they resort to open threats and blandishments, or foreign aid with strings, both visible and otherwise. In the era of mass media, disinformation has proved a major weapons system. Especially when the stakes are high, statesmen seek secretly to alter subtly the balance of political forces within a rival state or even to suborn political violence.

Historically, Western nations tended to assign such tasks to their diplomatic corps; and, from the fiction of Shakespeare to the reality of Talleyrand, an ambassador was expected to know the arts of Machiavelli as well as the rules of the racquet club. But in our more civilized era, diplomats bargain over the riches of the seabed, while subterranean chores are more often left to intelligence services on the premise that the latter have relevant "assets" in the form of existing networks of secret agents armed with the equipment and training for underground politics.

Americans have coined the prejudicial term "covert action" to refer to "black" propaganda and other clandestine attempts to exert influence abroad. The semantics of our major opponent, however, have no similar connotation of guilt. Reflecting an Oriental and Leninist mentality, for whom psychological warfare is more "natural" than the Western concept of the rule of law, the Soviets speak rather of "active measures." From Moscow's perspective, a covert operation is so conspicuously the "norm" that it would be illogical to seal it off from parallel levers, just as it would be equally illogical to insist that a KGB officer could not live inside the credentials of a TASS reporter, a priest, or one of Dr. Arbatov's "scholars."

In a world of imperfection and ambiguity—let alone the fog of protracted conflict—whether or not one calls a particular activity "covert action" is often an arbitrary decision. Foreign policy is pursued by a variety of means, some made manifest to the press or World Affairs Councils, others restricted to elites. (Does the Secretary of State always announce on the *Today Show* what he really said to Begin and Sadat?) It makes little sense to act—or to expect others to behave—as if there were written in the stars a frozen category of wholly secret activity to be performed exclusively by formally constituted intelligence services. (One gathers from history that 19th century Britain held its empire together in part because extracurricular activities were performed at times by the Board of Trade and Colonial Office as well as by those charged more specifically to play the "great game.")

If "covert action" is regarded as an isolated card, an unsavory joker in an otherwise respectable game, it may embarrass an opponent for one round, but will scarcely prove the winning margin. On the other hand, if it is regarded as being as orthodox a form of influence as the sale of fighter-bombers (and potentially far less lethal), then covert action can have a synergistic impact on the more "conventional" means of diplomacy such as open propaganda, exchange programs or the visit of a carrier to neutral ports.

Before the reader objects that the "unethical" should not be commingled with "legitimate" forms of international intercourse, let us remind ourselves that *clandestine* acts need not be *beastly*. Indeed, many forms of "covert operations" are non-violent and as routine—and as benign—as providing advice and funds to politicians, labor leaders and editors who oppose foreign takeovers in their own countries. It is a curious form of morality that would forbid the West to assist indigenous leaders in the Third World in their political and ideological battles to sustain their own genuine independence. It might improve our critique if we realized that 90% of what we denegrate as "covert action" could be renamed "transnational politics" and would likely consist of little more than techniques familiar to the political scene in many democratic countries where money and talent from one part of the country is used secretly to help elect or defeat politicians elsewhere.

Intelligence services do control certain assets—agents of influence, dossiers on foreign elites, the means to transmit ideas and funds through secret channels—which, combined with more publicized instruments of statecraft, can be employed to safeguard the vital interests of the US and our allies by largely non-military means. A preemptive dose of transnational politics, to avert a totalitarian power-grab of another hapless population, is surely preferable, both in strategy and ethics, to waiting until a "people's militia" has been impressed into further aggression, and the only solution one can think of is to drop napalm. (If this sounds like academic hyperbole, consider that in the Caribbean, the Soviets may have hit upon a method of "pyramiding" low-cost manpower—Cuban proxies assist in the takeover of Nicaragua, so that a Nicaraguan Army can serve as a proxy's proxy in the extension of subversive combat in a theatre that lies close to the oil of Mexico and Venezuela, and through whose waterways transit 75% of US mineral imports.) Thus, to conlcude, "covert action" can be the additive in the battery that drives all the diverse working parts of foreign policy. Conversely, recent American history suggests that when clandestine measures are played as random wild cards, and not fully integrated into overall national security policy, they can invite disaster.

The Consortium for the Study of Intelligence, a project of the National Strategy Information Center, was formed in the Spring of 1979 to provide an institutional focus for a balanced, coherent understanding of the role of intelligence in a free society. From its work, we hope that the teaching and study of intelligence will be furthered, and the values of American civil liberties and US national security will be enhanced.

Frank R. Barnett, President
National Strategy Information Center
July 1981

CHAPTER ONE

Covert Action
An Introduction

Roy Godson

Covert Action is a controversial component of US intelligence. While policymakers, scholars and intelligence professionals generally support US efforts to collect and analyze data, and to engage in a variety of counterintelligence activities, covert action has been questioned in non-governmental circles and by important forces within government. In the mid-1970's, disaffection became so widespread that apparently the US virtually abandoned covert action as an instrument of policy. As a former senior CIA official put it in an earlier volume in this series, by the late 1970's US covert action had "all the appearances of a dying art form."

To help increase understanding of this instrument of foreign policy, the Consortium for the Study of Intelligence convened a two-day colloquium in December 1980. The colloquium examined the logical and historical relationship of covert activities and foreign policy, the record and style of American and Soviet covert activities, and the factors required to provide the US with an effective option for covert activities in the 1980's. This volume, the fourth in the series *Intelligence Requirements for the 1980's*, is the result of a meeting of over sixty academics, current and former intelligence practitioners from the US and abroad, and Congressional specialists on intelligence. This introduction summarizes major conclusions of the volume.

What is covert action and what is its relation to foreign policy and other components of intelligence? Covert action is defined in the US as the attempt by a government to influence events in another state or territory without revealing its involvement. Seeking to influence the politics of other governments and societies is, of course, the stuff of foreign policy. Indeed, it is synonomous with it. Moreover, usually governments do not reveal exactly what they seek to accomplish nor how they intend to do it. They are to one degree or another secretive or covert.

1

Covert action, however, is essentially an American term that came into use after World War II. The term is still uncommon, even in translation, in other states. That is not to imply these states do not engage in what we call covert action—almost all of them at some point seek to exert influence in this way. Yet most states have not developed a special term for these activities. Nor have they consigned to a special bureaucracy responsibility to influence secretly events abroad. Why? Because most states do not make the same sharp distinction between overt and covert behavior. While they may indeed create special components to deal with some aspects of tradecraft, they regard influencing politics abroad, with varying degrees of secrecy, as part of the normal functions of much of the entire foreign policy bureaucracy.

The Soviet Union, for example, employs the term "active measures" to include both overt and covert attempts to influence people or events. The Soviet leadership assigns a role in active measures to the KGB and also a number of other bureaucratic elements, such as the Communist Party's International Department, the Information Department, the Ministry of Foreign Affairs, and their assets. Many Western, as well as non-Western, states also use political action to influence events abroad without indicating fully the objectives or the means that are being used, and while working to keep them secret. Sometimes intelligence services are called upon to assist in accomplishing the objectives, sometimes not. But seeking to influence events abroad without fully showing one's hand is not regarded exclusively as a special activity that is the preserve of an intelligence bureaucracy.

There are, of course, reasons why governments use intelligence services in secret political action. To begin with, effective action requires detailed analysis and understanding of the sensitive pressure points of foreign societies. The collection and analysis of this kind of information is certainly within the province of intelligence services—but not uniquely. Other parts of the foreign affairs bureaucracy also assess the major actors, interests, and the workings of foreign societies. But intelligence officers have singular means at their disposal. As a result of their collection and counterintelligence activities, they possess the tradecraft and have special access to the assets necessary for conducting secret action.

Very often the same individuals recruited to provide information, whether they are in government or important non-governmental sectors, are in a position to influence events. They may be politicians, journalists, military officers or diplomats. Indeed, many of them would be reluctant to provide information unless they believed it to be part of an effort, and one in which they would play a role, to influence events in their societies. While some spy or steal information for money or other base motives, others do so because they agree with the policies of foreign powers. They want to be able to influence events, and they are in positions where these desires can be translated into effective action. Intelligence services are usually best placed to run these kinds of activities—clandestinely.

They are also in a good position to ensure that foreign governments do not neutralize or turn political action to their advantage. The task of the counterintelligence component of an intelligence service is to identify and neutralize the activities of other governments' intelligence services. In this capacity, counterintelligence helps ensure that recruited agents are *bona fide*, that they are carrying out their missions, and that they are not being used by the target nation's intelligence service to manipulate or deceive. The counterintelligence component also can be assigned to assist in secret action by penetrating and deceiving foreign intelligence services. Finally, counterintelligence bureaucracies have many of the skills needed to uncover secret political actions that are not directed specifically by foreign intelligence services, but by other components of foreign governments and groups.

Yet in spite of their special placement, knowledge and access, there are disadvantages which can flow from using intelligence services in the arena of political action. First, because they are adept at clandestine work, they are themselves the long-term targets of foreign intelligence services. One significant penetration by a foreign service will damage not only collection and counterintelligence but also covert action. The damage caused by the penetration and discovery of covert action can have serious corollary effects on other secret activities of the penetrated intelligence service. Indeed, it can be argued that secret political action, because it is undertaken with the hope of tangible, and frequently observable results, is perhaps the most insecure type of activity an intelligence service can undertake. This has led a number of foreign as well as experienced US intelligence officers to argue for separating covert action from what they identify as genuinely clandestine intelligence activities, lest all of them be jeopardized.

While there may be good arguments for using or not using secret intelligence services for political action abroad, little argument can be made for considering covert action *apart* from overall policy. Seeking to influence events abroad secretly is part and parcel of foreign policy. While states may protest that they do not intervene in the internal affairs of other states, this norm among both Western and non-Western states does not, in fact, appear to be standard international behavior.

Another major focus of this volume is the global conditions in the 1980's which present challenges and opportunities that policymakers may wish to address with the means of covert action. There are some who see US covert activities as inevitably defensive. They maintain that our major adversaries are using both overt and covert means to project their power abroad, and that one means of checking this would be covert action. Specifically, they suggest that the Soviet Union and its allies are providing secret paramilitary, political, and propaganda assistance to communists and selected non-communists in various regions of the world in an effort to detach these areas from the US and shift the "correlation of forces" further in their favor. They argue that because many countries, including the Western democracies are vulnerable to covert instruments of policy, the US should focus its own efforts on countering these effects by covert means.

Others, while noting Western vulnerabilities, also seek to identify conditions in adversary states and groups that lend themselves to covert action by the United States. It is not easy, however, to affect the politics of totalitarian states and political organizations. Usually they are skilled at maintaining control of all major institutions and groups. Nevertheless, they also have weak spots and, it is maintained, that there are areas of opportunity. The "masses," governmental institutions, and the Party, at various levels, are all open to outside influence to a degree—as the Soviet leaders constantly warn each other.

The loyalty, however strong or weak, of the people to the Party and the government can be further eroded by a range of mechanisms. For example, there are enormous differences and tensions between workers and Party officials (similar to those in Poland) and between Party officials and people who value their religious faith or ethnic heritage. These divergent interests can be further accentuated. Today radio, and perhaps one day television, can be used to highlight the differences for millions of people. Emigré and other private groups in the West, and perhaps China, can pass and reinforce the message.

The corruption, jealousies, rivalries, and the conspiracies of Party leaders also can be exploited. Exposure of one faction's corruption or machinations could have very serious and potentially paralytic consequences for the power of the Party. Stalin probably needed no prompting by Nazi intelligence services to purge senior officials. But German efforts to discredit Marshall Tukachevsky and other senior military officers probably hastened their demise, as well as weakening Soviet military power in the late 1930's, and, in 1941 almost resulted in the destruction of the Soviet state. More recently in the late 1970's, defectors broadcasting details of corruption and interparty machinations into Bulgaria apparently piqued the sensitivity of the Bulgarian rulers and resulted in retaliatory assassinations in Paris and London.

The Soviet system has vulnerabilities and genuine political, economic and social weaknesses that can be exploited. The US and other Western states could seek, for defensive reasons, to counter at the source Soviet efforts to shift the global balance in its favor. Or the West can more actively, assist in the non-military destruction of the Soviet empire.

Whatever line of action is persued, does the United States have the means? What is needed for an effective covert action capability? Although views differ there may be a consensus on many of the important ingredients.

One set of ingredients concerns the President and overall foreign policymaking. First, in order to be useful, covert action *must* be part of overall policy, characterized by sound direction and continuity. United States covert action it seems has been at its best when integrated in this way. It appears to have been at its worst when used as a quick-fix or as something to be thrown into the breach in an *ad hoc* fashion—or when all else failed.

Second, covert action should be integrated into the bureaucratic structure. That means that all relevant parts of the government must be involved either directly or in supporting roles. Half-hearted efforts or protracted bureaucratic wars between the Department of State and the CIA, or between various elements of the intelligence agencies themselves, can only be damaging. Yet only the President and his senior officials can ensure overall direction and government-wide coordination. If this happens, the US may be able to emulate the success of the Marshall Plan era. If not there will in all probability be a recurrence of the failures in Chile and Angola in the early 1970's, in the aftermath of which the Executive and Legislative branches became locked in a protracted, divisive and debilitating struggle with consequences far beyond the issues themselves.

And thirdly, the President also has responsibility for building public support for the goals of his foreign policies. If he succeeds, both the public and the bureaucracy probably would be ready to understand why covert means are necessary. Consensus on goals would presumably obviate the Congressional battles which characterized so much of our foreign policy in the seventies.

A second set of ingredients pertains to the specific organization in the US government, the Central Intelligence Agency, which is charged with primary responsibility for developing and implementing covert action. As was discussed earlier, successful covert action requires good intelligence collection, counterintelligence, and analysis. Effective covert action is impossible without integrating all the major components of intelligence. Yet covert action frequently has not been integrated even into the rest of CIA's activities. While there may be good organizational reasons for a certain amount of separation, some maintain it has developed into a chasm. It seems necessary to keep and strengthen a special Covert Action Staff (to ensure that covert action specialists receive bureaucratic protection). But it is also necessary to ensure that this staff has ties to and is involved in overall US policymaking and implementation, as well as in various other activities of the intelligence community.

In addition to being considered in the formulation of overall policy which takes place outside the CIA, covert action should also be considered within CIA when collection requirements are set, counterintelligence priorities are considered, and analysis is undertaken. This will ensure that collection requirements for effective covert action have been considered, and that covert action is protected and assisted by counterintelligence. Also, US policy probably will be enhanced if intelligence analysts have considered whether US covert actions can affect global trends, and at the same time if they provide the covert action specialists with the benefit of the analysts' independent review of their activities. With care, the components of the intelligence system can be integrated without impairing the integrity of any single component.

Another necessary ingredient is recruitment and training. Apparently, in the field of covert action, the US has disarmed unilaterally. If the President is to have all instruments of statecraft available to him, the US must rebuild its capabilities as quickly as possible. While there may be a number of short-term options and quick fixes available (such as rehiring some of the best specialists who left in the 1970's), securing the services of effective covert actioneers cannot be effected overnight. Great care and judgment has to be exercised to ensure that we hire either those who already have all the necessary qualities or those who have some of the necessary skills and can be provided, through training, with others.

It is doubtful, however, that these human resources are to be found exclusively in the ranks of recent college graduates—even those from the best schools. It would be difficult enough for the children of the American middle class to understand, to gain the confidence of, and to work covertly with all the major political sectors in our own Western and basically college-educated society. But to dispatch recent Ivy League graduates to work with Islamic, Asian, African, and Latin American military, political, religious, business and trade union leaders with whom they share few experiences, is to invite failure. Such young people would most often require an enormous amount of training before becoming candidates for such assignments. Rather, a well-thought out conscious effort needs to be made to actively recruit Americans (and foreigners willing to work with us) from all walks of life, who already have the requisite skills and experience, or who have special attributes which match special needs. Only then will the US be able to build up the kind of covert action capability it needs to take advantage of the opportunities and meet the threats of the 1980's.

In Western literature on intelligence very little has been written on the relationship between covert action and foreign policy. The first contribution in this volume is by Adda B. Bozeman, Professor Emeritus at Sarah Lawrence College, who has written extensively on the interrelationship of culture and statecraft. Professor Bozeman maintains that US definitions and concepts of intelligence are very different from those in other societies. In most societies today, and indeed throughout world history, secret political intrigue and espionage have been considered part and parcel of the culture, foreign policy, and statecraft. Professor Bozeman insists that American scholars must focus much more attention on comparative studies of statecraft and intelligence, and understand the differences between our own and other cultures if US policymakers are to avoid the repetition of recent intelligence failures and to carry out successful covert action. She illustrates these general propositions with several comparative studies.

The second part of Chapter Two, by Angelo Codevilla, a member of the professional staff of the Senate Select Committee on Intelligence since 1977, also proposes that secret means of influencing foreign societies are a natural constituent part of foreign policy. Dr. Codevilla describes various types of secret means which nations use to influence the decisions of foreign governments, as well as to change the system of government, and indeed, the very nature of foreign societies. He also identifies important vulnerabilities of democracies and authoritarian and totalitarian political systems to these means.

Dr. Paul Seabury, Professor of Political Science at the University of California at Berkeley, and Dr. Richard Bissell, Managing Editor of *ORBIS*, concur with Professor Bozeman that the postwar American study of politics and international relations, basically has not facilitated the practitioners' understanding of foreign cultures and statecraft. Professor Seabury, however, suggests that there may be other reasons why policymakers have been unable to adequately understand and affect foreign societies. Dr. Bissell argues that in spite of various deficiencies Americans do possess the skills to affect foreign societies through covert means.

Chapters Three and Four begin to examine conditions in various parts of the world that lend themselves to covert action in the 1980's. In Chapter Three, General Vernon Walters, former Deputy Director of Central Intelligence and now Special Advisor to the Secretary of State, suggests that all major societies, including the US itself, are vulnerable and that, with careful analysis and proper recruitment and training, the US can identify and take advantage of political conditions abroad where covert action might prudently be used as a US policy tool. Dr. Ray Cline, a former Deputy Director for Intelligence in the CIA, and former Director of the Bureau of Intelligence and Research at the Department of State, stresses that we should not regard covert political action as an instrument of last resort, but instead we should seek to influence, through both overt and covert means, as a natural part of our strategic design. Dr. Abram Shulsky, now Minority Staff Director of the Senate Select Committee on Intelligence, basically agrees with Walters and Cline and seeks to identify further kinds of political activities which might be effective against the Soviet Union in the 1980's.

In Chapter Four, Theodore Shackley, who spent almost thirty years in CIA and held a range of senior intelligence posts before retiring in 1979, maintains that the US in the 1980's will be confronted by situations in the world that will require paramilitary action. The most serious and the most prevalent, he states, will be communist-directed or supported insurgencies and he puts forward a number of measures that have to be taken to deal with them. Daniel Arnold, who joined the CIA's clandestine service in 1952 and became the Agency's senior representative in a number of Asian countries, agrees with Shackley that the US must maintain covert paramilitary capabilities to deal with insurgencies in the 1980's. He stresses also that the US must be able and willing to support foreigners in coups and countercoups, when this is consistent with our interests. Dr. Frank N. Trager, Professor of International Affairs and Director of the National Security Program at New York University, maintains that in the 1980's we also must develop the means to take the initiative rather than merely to react, to "punch" as well as to "counter-punch."

Chapter Five is devoted to major trends in Soviet covert action. Donald Jameson, a former covert action specialist in the Soviet Division of the CIA's clandestine service focuses on the political and propaganda activities of the Soviet government. Barring major up-heaval, or major Western reaction, Jameson maintains that Soviet covert action will continue unabated, and on a grandiose scale. Fur-ther, it will be well-coordinated with other instruments of policy, and run by cynical men more interested in power than Marxism-Leninism.

Jameson's thesis is fully supported both by data currently in the public domain and by an even larger body of data which eventually may become public, maintains John Barron, author of a number of important articles and books on Soviet intelligence, and a senior editor with *Reader's Digest*. Barron also believes that contemporary KGB officials have become cynical. They also have demonstrated a willingness to work with foreigners not under their control, even with anti-Communists who are also anti-American. As a result, they have become more effective than ever. Herbert Romerstein, a professional staff member of the House Intelligence Committee, agrees with Jameson's overall thesis but believes the paper devotes insufficient attention to covert Soviet involvement in violence, terrorism and paramilitary activities in the non-Communist world. While conceding it is difficult, based on public sources, to document Soviet involve-ment in these activities, Romerstein seeks to provide examples of Soviet-supported violence, even in the US.

Strengths and weaknesses of past US covert action are analyzed in Chapter Six. Hugh Tovar, a veteran of the OSS, whose CIA service spanned thirty years, including Chief of the Covert Action Staff, seeks to identify factors in the US government as well as in American society as a whole which explain US successes and fail-ures. Tovar believes most of our weaknesses are correctable and suggests how this could be done.

Dr. Samuel Huntington, Professor of Government and Director of the Center for International Affairs at Harvard University, who also served during 1977-1978 as coordinator of security planning for the National Security Council, believes US covert action on the whole has been effective. However, he stresses that at the same time, the US has suffered from a crippling weakness, namely that covert action is perceived by many Americans to be an illegitimate instrument of policy. Huntington suggests that an attempt be made to bridge the way in which we must act in foreign affairs and the way important elites believe we ought to act. It is very difficult if not impossible to determine publicly US strengths and weaknesses, according to Philippe Thyraud de Vosjoli, because we know only of the US activities which have become public, and, because they have become public, these activities must be considered failures. Mr. de Vosjoli, who had been involved in French intelligence since joining the Underground in 1941, served as a senior official in the postwar S.D.E.C.E. until 1963. He stresses, however, that the US has enjoyed many successes and he suggests several measures that should be taken to ensure that the US can do so again.

The final chapter, on the necessary means for future covert action, brings together many of the themes raised throughout. Donald Purcell maintains that by the late 1970's, US covert action capabilities had eroded to the point where they were almost incapable of responding effectively to the missions assigned by the President. Mr. Purcell, a 21-year veteran of the CIA's Directorate of Operations, who served as Chief of the Covert Action Staff from 1976 until he retired in 1978, presents a brief summary of past US covert action programs and then explores long-term organizational, intellectual, human, and material requirements that he believes will be necessary to rebuild and revitalize US covert action in the 1980's.

Three leading Congressional specialists on intelligence, basically concur with Mr. Purcell, but from varying perspectives. Senator Malcolm Wallop and Congressman Les Aspin, who were prevented at the last moment from attending the Colloquium, contributed prepared remarks. Senator Wallop, Chairman of the Budget Authorization, Collection, Production, and Quality Subcommittee of the Senate Intelligence Committee, stresses that the Executive, and particularly the CIA itself, had been primarily responsible for the decline in US capabilities. (Congress, he agrees, took a hand, but a smaller one than is often generally assumed.) Senator Wallop states that reversing course will not be easy, but given the challenges and opportunities in the 1980's, the task has to be undertaken.

Congressman Aspin, Chairman of the Oversight Subcommittee of the House Intelligence Committee, maintains that proposed US covert action should not be approached on a simple yes or no basis and that each proposal must be considered on its merits. The Congressman then lists a number of operational questions that he believes the President must answer before he approves a given proposal.

Congressman C. W. Bill Young, a member of the House Intelligence Committee, who has made many visits to intelligence personnel in the field, maintains that current morale and performance are lower than necessary because of the perception of many "in the trenches" that they are not receiving adequate support from Washington. He believes that the negative drift of recent years has been reversed, but that both the administration and the Congress must do more to ensure effective performance.

While a broad consensus was reached on many issues in the course of the Colloquium, the views expressed in the papers and the comments of the discussants are those of the individuals alone. This is particularly true of current US government employees, whether in the Executive or Legislative branches, whose views in no way should be taken to represent those of the individual agency, department, or committee. Nevertheless, it is hoped that the papers and discussion summarized here, necessarily greatly compressed, will add to public understanding of covert action and its relationship with other components of intelligence and foreign policy, as well as to greater understanding of major challenges facing the US and how they can be met by American statecraft.

CHAPTER TWO

Covert Action and Foreign Policy

Paper:

I. Adda B. Bozeman
II. Angelo Codevilla

Discussants:

Dr. Paul Seabury
Dr. Richard Bissell

I. Adda B. Bozeman

Introduction

Is our understanding of the relation between covert action and foreign policy internationally valid?

How relevant to policymaking in the present world environment are our distinctions between different elements of intelligence and our definitions of each of these elements, specifically of covert action?

This paper assumes that US intelligence systems and operations are essentially aspects or functions of the nation's foreign policy. Policies may thus be faulted by ineffective intelligence. However, and conversely, sound intelligence theories and practices may be misused or come to naught by poor policymaking. Any assessment of intelligence therefore requires an assessment also of foreign policy and strategic thought, and any evaluation of the latter must include a close analysis of intelligence.

A second underlying assumption is to the effect that statecraft in its entirety is everywhere the reflection of a given society's sustaining culture and value system. This means that the whole of a culture needs to be mapped reliably before one of its aspects, in this case statecraft, is to be adequately understood. It suggests, further, that foreign policies as well as intelligence projects and actions are apt to fall short of success if this infrastructure of beliefs and dispositions remains unknown.

Understandings of this kind are not congenial to the US. Condi-

15

tioned by its own values to believe that people everywhere are basically alike, and that the world's different governments should therefore be expected to comply with the norms so eloquently set forth in the American Declaration of Independence, the nation has been led throughout its history to trust its own favored image of a unified mankind and to overlook the plurality of culturally diverse images, worldviews, and patterns of behavior. These dispositions were accentuated and sanctioned as it were by the Charter of the United Nations which borrowed heavily from American constitutionalism, and by the swift creation, after 1945, of new states in Africa and Asia whose original laws and constitutions were also modelled on Euro-American precedents.

The successful diffusion of this political language and of related means of technical communication helps explain why most Americans continued to believe that their own, now internationalized, vocabulary, was actually carrying trans-nationally shared values and commitments and why the nation's policymakers were slow in realizing that the rhetoric of communication masked profound discords on matters of substance. But by the late 1950's it had become clear that our language of law and democracy had come to cover lawless despotisms of the authoritarian and the totalitarian kind; that all aspects of statecraft, specifically diplomacy and intelligence, were being conceptualized quite differently in the world's numerous non-western provinces; in short that the real identities of foreign states and other international actors were being misperceived.

It is the main thesis of the present paper that most recent US policy and intelligence failures have ensued from these defects in strategic thought and vision. The responsibility here rests primarily with the academic community, not with the Intelligence Community and not with the Department of State; for it is after all the former which is traditionally charged with providing educational and professional guidance to the latter. It is therefore urgently necessary today to analyze the causes of our policy and intelligence failures, discover ways for avoiding them in the future and come up with improved methods of teaching intelligence and its relation to foreign policy and national security—the major purpose of the Consortium for the Study of Intelligence (See Appendix I for the Statement of Purpose).

Significant improvements have been made in the last decades when it comes to understanding the Soviet Union and other Marxist-Leninist societies. However, little has changed in our common perception of non-communist non-western peoples. Some of their deviations from what we view as trans-nationally valid standards of reasoning and behavior are simply dismissed as "irrational" or "mindless" actions. However, in general it continues to be customary to ascribe all their shortcomings to the lack of economic development, a purely temporary condition, so the teaching goes, that will be overcome given material aid and modernization over time. This paper assumes, by contrast, that we are dealing in most instances with very ancient societies and thus with firmly imbedded cultural patterns which prescribe or proscribe thought and action, whether in regard to economics or to statecraft.

The paper should ideally consist of case studies of Japan, South Korea and Taiwan; South Asia, notably India; the ASEAN states of Southeast Asia; Latin America; Black Africa and the Islamic Middle East. However, limitations of time for the oral presentation of findings, and of space for the printed version of the Colloquium's proceedings determined me to focus this set of comparative studies on the Middle East in the hope that there will be other opportunities to complete the panorama of culturally diverse approaches to intelligence. Furthermore, and as this text is designed to illustrate, comparative studies of statecraft in general and of the relation between foreign policy and covert action in particular are tedious because they require multi-disciplinary approaches.

Part I of the paper consists of a restatement of current US definitions of the different components of intelligence; a critical review of US norms of covert action and foreign policy, and a commentary on the decay of the moral, legal and political language that carries our vital norms, values and interests.

Part II addresses the need for comparative studies. Its core is a draft inventory of propositions or questions that require answers before we devise foreign policies and intelligence projects in regard to a non-western society.

Part III, together with the preceding four pages, addresses the need for a revision of the parameters within which our intelligence and foreign affairs specialists think about the different societies of the Middle East. Since all of the region's peoples are deeply conscious of their histories, and since the craft of intelligence in particular was first perfected between the 6th and 4th centuries BC by Achaemenid Persia, in order then to be copied diligently by several Arab/Islamic caliphates, the Seljuq and the Ottoman (Turkish) empires, a variety of Mongol rulers and the Mogul empire in NW India, my analysis follows suit. I choose to include a case study of classical Hindu India because it brings the most refined and systematized Oriental intelligence set-up (it too was modelled on the Persian). By contrast, the section closes with the Republic of Venice. This European state endured for a millennium by dint of an intelligence system which I view as just about the best the Occident has produced.

I. Definitions and US Policy

A. The Language of US Intelligence

The Consortium for the Study of Intelligence and the Colloquia organized under its auspices are joint ventures linking intelligence professionals and academic scholars with a special interest in foreign policy and intelligence. I am not an expert in intelligence operations. Everything I know about them I learned here from past and present members of the American intelligence community, and I intend to continue that learning process. Before writing this paper I therefore carefully reread the records of the colloquia that relate directly to the present topics, noting in particular the following definitions and descriptions:

> Clandestine operations are activities conducted in secret by an intelligence service. They encompass collection of intelligence, counterintelligence, and covert action. Here the term *covert* though synonymous with *clandestine* describes an activity or event which generally occurs in the public domain, observable by those who happen to be at hand. It has an identifiable instigator or sponsor, and its covertness lies in the relationship between the latter and some hidden, unacknowledged authority or source of assistance.
>
> Covert action for present purposes thus entails activity in which the US government's involvement is deliberately concealed. Its aim is to get something done in ways which are compatible with US interests. . . . We are taking sides in a local issue, i.e. intervening in a manner which infringes on the host country's sovereignty.
>
> Covert mechanisms are used to supplement diplomatic and other open channels.
>
> The U.S. has restricted itself to clandestine collection of intelligence. Covert action no longer figures significantly in the operational posture of the CIA. Covert action in the late 1970's shows all the earmarks of a dying art form. This is regrettable. The US has engaged in various types of covert action since its earliest days and the time for recovering the art is "now."[1]
>
> Counterintelligence, defined as the national effort to prevent foreign intelligence services from infiltrating our institutions and establishing the potential to engage in espionage, subversion, terrorism and sabotage, is the base for a healthy intelligence system.[2]

It has become apparent in the last years that several components of American intelligence—clandestine collection, counterintelligence, covert action, and analysis—are not functioning well. No nation's intelligence can do well, if *any* of these components malfunction.

The CIA's original core, its primary unilateral responsibility, was the clandestine collection of foreign intelligence and covert action in support of US policy.[3]

The term "clandestine collection" is another way of saying "espionage," entailing the use of human sources and technical devices. In other words, it is old-fashioned spying involving the manipulation of people. The use of clandestine collection is costly in terms of time and manpower, unlike covert action which usually requires a larger expenditure of money as well. Clandestine collection requires a long lead time to identify and recruit those human sources who might have access to the required information. It is a slow and laborious process which is used only as a last resort.[4]

The operations that must be kept secure are of two kinds, clandestine and covert. Clandestine operations consist of two types: espionage and counterintelligence.

Espionage is conducted largely through human (i.e. spies) and technical agents. At the heart of the undertaking and crucial to its success is secrecy.

Counterespionage consists of catching spies and either neutralizing them or compelling them to serve the captor's ends.

Non-clandestine functions as assigned to the CIA since the 1950's are covert action, paramilitary operations, counter-guerrilla activity, countering the traffic in drugs and the rest of it.

Covert action does not strive for invisibility and by its nature it cannot be secret. Its raison d'être is to identify the common ground or areas of agreement between the US and other countries, and to further activity which will support and expand these shared interests. Covert action *programs*, by contrast, need to be kept secret.

Paramilitary operations cannot be kept secret, i.e. they are not clandestine.[5]

These American or Western understandings of particularized intelligence functions provide one set of measures for the comparisons and analyses developed in this text. They are important in my general scheme because they help assure the kind of common thought and discourse between the professionals and those of us who are primarily academic scholars upon which the work of the Consortium depends. Other standards of comparison derive from my own studies of foreign affairs in the world society and in international history, and some of them diverge from what may well be orthodox political science in America today. For example, since I am persuaded that there are few if any universally accepted norms and beliefs, I cannot assume that our definitions and understandings of phenomena in international relations and statecraft are *ipso facto* reliable renditions of reality also in non-American or non-western societies. Further, and in contrast to many of my colleagues, I believe that all comparative studies, whether of art and religion or of diplomacy, intelligence and the relation between covert action and foreign policy, can yield tenable conclusions only after one has explored the whole of a given society or culture.

Such approaches are obviously not congenial to the American mind because they conflict with long-established preferred images of one world, one type of man and therefore one kind of truth, whether in government, public law or ethics (differences in art, religion, social customs and private law are readily acknowledged). "The men of system" in our universities thus continue to imagine that they can arrange the different members of the world society with as much ease as the hand arranges the different pieces on a chess board. But as Adam Smith observed 200 years ago, they do not consider that the pieces upon the chess board have no other principle of motion beside that which the hand impresses upon them, whereas in the great chess board of human society every single piece has a principle of motion of its own. This truth is not doubted by students of art, architecture, music, religion, philosophy and even history, but it is definitely being bypassed by scholars working in the social sciences including the sociology of law, international law and ethics. At any rate, no evidence of diversity in human thought, behavior and experience has so far effectively discouraged the dominant trend, namely, that of maintaining the universal validity of American-made models and theories of the rational man, democratic government and human rights as well as of the function of diplomacy, the nature of revolution, or the relation of war to peace and law.

"The men of action," meanwhile, notably those in charge of government and foreign policy, continue to trust these academic models rather than their own powers of observing other men and other models in other places. Failures in policy and intelligence thus continue to be commonplace. Senior officers in the Carter Administration and in intelligence are thus reported to have agreed that the recent war between Iran and Iraq exposed serious deficiencies in US intelligence-gathering abilities. They are said to have noted in particular that the US was poorly informed about specific events in the Persian Gulf Area, that it knew next to nothing about political, cultural and economic trends in the region, and that it was therefore unable to make accurate predictions about the future course of the war. "We are weak in the bazaars, on the campuses, in the streets where the life of a nation takes place," was one comment. Another admitted: "Frankly, we're in the Dark Ages when it comes to knowing what makes these nations tick."[6]

The causes of this intelligence lapse as of all other policy and intelligence failures are no doubt numerous and complex. However, and in light of the fact that "the men of action" have been tutored by "the men of system," I tend to think that the nation's recent and ongoing troubles in international relations are in the final analysis failures of scholarship and learning in our institutions of higher education.

Some of these basic issues in intercultural relations have been addressed succinctly by Dr. Robert Livingston, a well-known neurophysiologist, who points out that we act as if there existed a universal common logic of thinking shared by all thinking people; as if there is one metaphysical pool of universal human thought upon which all can draw, and as if we can count on some elementary objective spirit. Such predispositions, Livingston explains, make for the simplistic belief that the persistence of disparities or the failure of communication can be ascribed to the absence of objectivity. Even more important, they totally screen the irrefutable fact that perception is guided by culture, and in culture, especially by language. This is so, he writes, because the logical processes of thinking are everywhere relative to the language learned. If all of us would better understand the biological, psychological, linguistic and cultural mechanisms affecting perception, judgment, motivation and action, Livingston concludes, we would be more willing to be tentative rather than hasty in our responses and better able to sort out ambiguous situations correctly.[7]

This strikes me as a fair diagnosis of the blindspot in our national vision. It is also good advice for all Americans in an age in which people in Africa, Asia, Oceania, Latin America and parts of Europe continue to divest themselves of Western norms of law, government, ethics, education, diplomacy and other forms of international behavior which they had accepted in an earlier era when Western civilization was deemed prestigious and attractive and when Western power was not as readily challenged as it is today. Yet—and this is the main point here—we in this country do not seem capable or willing to adjust our vision to these radically changed circumstances. Dimsighted in our view of other actors in the world environment, reluctant to distinguish between our domestic and our foreign affairs,

or between the concerns of the US and those espoused by other
nations, our government has for quite some time now been unable to
fathom a strategic design for long-range foreign policies. Improvi-
sation has therefore been the order of the day in policymaking circles,
and rhetoric has come to fill the void left by departed thought.

These developments have had stultifying effects upon our intelligence community. Cut off from Intelligence Writ Large, deprived of
concise guidelines for the implementation of coherent policy decisions and left to administer reams of usually contradictory declarations, explanations, retractions, apologias and strictures emanating
from up high, officers have not been able, by and large, to anticipate
or frustrate threatening moves by adversaries or to give advance
warning of impending events. In such circumstances it is not surprising that coups, revolutions, armed invasions, wars and shifts in
ideological commitment, political orientation or the distribution of
power usually take us by surprise: after all, the forces shaping such
events have long been effectively camouflaged by our own rigidly
ethnocentric perceptions and commitments.

The foreign policy crisis implicit in such haphazard approaches to
the relationship between perception of reality, thought and language
is aggravated by the circumstance first, that the meaning content of
our basic vocabulary has long ceased to be internationally valid; and
second, that the distance between words—notably those having a
universal ring in *our* ears—and the substantive realities they purport
to cover, has widened immeasurably.

Studies of non-Western and communist societies should thus have
persuaded us long ago that *our* conceptions of war and peace, *our*
ideas of the state and sovereignty, *our* notion of the function of
diplomacy, and *our* values of good faith and contractual ethics in the
conduct of international relations are not shared by them. What is
being shared throughout the world is the vocabulary of words which
has been fashioned in the West to carry these, and only these, ideas
but which has been conscripted in this century to serve also as
protective cover for rival causes advanced by alien and adversary
political systems. Keen awareness of the semantic aspects of revolutionary tactics, more particularly of the need for verbal dissimulation, thus explains the stipulation in Lenin's operational code,
namely that psychological and diplomatic attack campaigns against
the capitalist West must be launched in the value language of the
West if they are to reach, confound, and eventually conquer the
minds of people targeted for takeover.[8]

These policies and techniques of communication were barely rec-

ognized, certainly not seriously contested in America. Mole-like in
inception and operation, they could therefore be effective as "double
agents" in debasing our language, perverting the meanings of some
of our strategically most important words and thus in dis-ordering
our thought processes. In short, they could penetrate, in Sun Tzu's
phrase "encircle" our intelligence which simply does not accommodate the communist formula that covert thought must spearhead
covert as well as overt action.

B. US Foreign Policy and the Norms of Covert Action

A few brief references to recent policy and intelligence failures
will illustrate the rigidities of our general approaches to foreign societies, and therewith also, by implication, the awesome ambiguities
with which the minds of individual intelligence officers must wrestle
daily, never more so than when pondering covert operations and
their implications.

Mr. Colby's account of his life in the CIA[9] is most instructive in
these respects. Openly critical of the new breed of systems analysts,
Colby came to wonder during his Indochina mission whether their
opinions had not become too firmly fixed and whether their objectivity had not come to reflect academia's bias that our programs in
Vietnam just could not succeed.[10] Yet, at the same time he himself
failed to realize that the Vietnam program was bound to fail if it had
to be carried out in strict compliance only with American moral and
legal standards. The Colby (1969) directive on assassination and
"other repugnant activities" which related to project Phoenix, thus
makes strange reading when it states that American personnel are
specifically not authorized to engage in assassinations or other violations of the rules of land warfare, but that they *are* entitled to use
such reasonable military force as is necessary to obtain the goals of
rallying, capturing or eliminating the VCI in the Republic of Vietnam.
Since the rules of land warfare had not been drafted for the context
of combat with irregular guerrilla forces that are bent on terrorizing
villages and towns of an allied Asian state, and since assassination
was then and continues to be today, an integral part of communist
ways of war and administration, it was obviously impossible to comply with both requirements of the directive: on the one hand to oust
the enemy, on the other to meet American standards of reasonableness in the use of military force.

Throughout this last tragic phase of our involvement in Vietnam
it appears that "decision making" in the matter of norms and stan-

dards, whether of reasonableness, rationality, law or ethics, proceeded exclusively from the vantage point of America's own more
recent experiences and expectations. There is no hint in Mr. Colby's
volume that our decisions, judgments and commitments had been
made in full awareness of Vietnam's own social and moral infrastructure and historical traditions which had sustained the cultural integrity of this nation for many centuries. In fact and as Mr. Colby's
further comment shows, this infrastructure was deliberately under-
mined so that "Phoenix ends and our (American) means" would be
"well within moral limits":

> When one of my officers reported that a district chief had shot out of
> hand a woman prisoner and I took the case up with the Prime Minister
> and had the district chief sacked and punished, the same province officer
> complained that the district chief was one of the best in the province and
> should be excused for his action because the woman had been engaged in
> a terrorist attack on one of the chief's own family.[11]

This episode in our relations with a major, critically embattled
Asian ally is particularly significant for purposes of the present in-
quiry because it shows that we had in no way corrected our earlier
misperceptions of reality in Vietnam, namely those that determined
us to sanction the elimination of Ngo Dinh Diem and his authentically
Vietnamese government on the ground that they represented authoritarian, and thus un-American, principles of rule. The result of
this fateful decision, which had ensued from grave errors in thought
and understanding, was our own military involvement in the area, its
eventual ignominious collapse, the destruction of independent Vietnam, and the establishment of communist rule over the entire region,
including Laos and Cambodia.

The disposition to chip away and thus gradually dissemble the very
identities of non-Western nations whose independence we had vowed
to preserve has now hardened into a policy line, perhaps even a
doctrine. This is borne out by the records of our diplomatic relations
with, among others, South Korea, the Philippines, Nicaragua, El
Salvador, Chile, South Africa and pre-revolutionary Iran. Radically
different from each other as these societies surely are, *our* objective
has been the same everywhere. Mechanistically conceived, pro-
fessed and administered, it is the establishment of democracy, the
rule of law, and more specifically insistence on respect for human
rights. Meaningful definitions of either of these references are missing
altogether. Dropped from consciousness is the fact, so elaborately
explicated in readily available accounts of Asian, Latin American,
and African culture history, that "democracy" with its Western

connotations of parliamentary or congressional institutions, a multi-party system, elections, constitutional law and bills of rights is basically alien to each of the non-Western realms. Indeed, this knowledge seems to have left the minds not only of policymakers but also of politically concerned academic specialists and representatives of the media, and that precisely at a time in history when this kind of knowledge should have controlled perception and commitment in strategic thought.

With the nation's general intelligence thus anesthetized, it is small wonder that the KGB and other enemy agencies were successful in executing their strategic deception, covert action and disinformation programs; that our own intelligence community was often unable to analyze the adversary's mind set, anticipate and detect his operations and sift factual truth from disinformation; and that reformist congressional legislation such as S. 2525 and its successor bills did not require the intelligence community to have a capability for covertly influencing events abroad.

The bills here in issue thus prohibit any employee of any intelligence agency from killing any official of a nation or faction thereof, and that even if that official happens to be threatening American lives. They also ban any covert action project which might work against a "democratic" government abroad, leaving totally undefined the term "democratic." In fact, and as Michael M. Uhlmann notes in his critical commentary on these legislative efforts,[12] our governing authorities go on assuming that other nations in the world are prepared to play the intelligence "game" in accordance with rules laid down by the US (see sect. 114 (j) of S. 2525), and that legal terms of art customary in our political culture cover the universe of human experience. Sec. 137 S. 2525 thus explicitly prohibits the US intelligence community from directly or indirectly encouraging or assisting individuals, organizations or foreign governments to do anything that the American intelligence community itself is prohibited from doing. As Uhlmann writes: "Whatever may be its intention, that language certainly sounds like an attempt to make the rest of the world conform to American law."[13] Indeed, "that language" may even be a faithful expression of the widely current assumption that "law" *is* the same everywhere, if only because all human experience is essentially the same. Since this persuasion has been cultivated in our academic institutions in the last decades under the covering titles of "empiricism" and a "value-free social science" it is not surprising that it has also come to mark the outlook of the national intelligence community. As Angelo Codevilla explains the matter in an earlier paper:[14]

> In intelligence, empiricism's practical tenet is to define what one is looking for in terms of quantifiable units, then to count those units and to monitor their rate of change. Whatever cannot be counted is deemed not to exist. . . . Moreover, unless something can be counted it cannot be used as currency in bureaucratic controversies . . .

With regard to evaluating Soviet strategic forces the rule thus seems to have been: "What we've not seen doesn't exist." And since mental calculations of purposes and designs of strategic doctrine cannot be "seen," tabulated and quantified, they have been seriously neglected by our analysts, with the result that the Soviet's strategic build-up between 1975-78 could proceed virtually without detection.[15]

The same type of malfunction in processes of analysis also explains our misjudgments of the character and intentions of terrorist organizations, "liberation" fronts and guerrilla forces which have long been active in the Middle East, Latin America (notably Central America), and Africa. As Codevilla remarks in respect of the PLO, our specialists refrained from examining the organizations, behavioral records and ideological sources, choosing rather to perceive the PLO as the sum total of its public statements which could be read, heard and tabulated. When the most recent of these declarations were found to be relatively restrained, the conclusion was drawn that the organization was becoming moderate. The fact that rhetoric is often used in radical groups for purposes of camouflaging "real" intentions and operations does not seem to have made much of an impact upon the evaluations.

These new aspects of the American mindset have been re-enforced by other intellectual rigidities also bred in our universities, among them an unquestioning reliance upon models.[16] It has thus become an article of faith that only "socialist" governments can stand in the way of communist ones.[17] No one seems to mind that the term "socialist" is as undefined in our trade literature as the term "democracy." Further, no allowance is commonly made for the incontrovertible fact that "socialism" stands for communism in Marxist-Leninist usage. Here, too, one finds that American diplomats and intelligence officers have all too often followed suit. In the early 60's they thus supported a left-wing government in Italy even though it was clear from the outset that our communist adversaries would be busy manipulating the Trojan Horse they had introduced for the purpose of concretizing the transition from a "socialist" to a communist regime.

In later years, our policymakers demonstrated the same Pavlovian reflex reaction to their favorite verbal stereotypes—"socialism," "democracy" and "human rights"—when they treated terrorist guerrillas intent on building communist-type despotisms in southern Africa, Central America and the Islamic Middle East as if they were freedom fighters intent on building American-type democracies. Deluded by our own theories and models, we thus hardly noticed that the Soviet-Cuban apparatus of subversion was in the process of succeeding to ready the Central American Isthmus and the Caribbean island space for communist takeovers, and thus for transformation into a staging area for further and more direct aggressively anti-American designs; and also to radicalize and satellitize several strategically crucial states in eastern and southern Africa, among them Ethiopia, Angola, Mozambique and, in all likelihood, Zimbabwe. Nor were we mentally, politically or militarily prepared to checkmate the Soviet Union in either of its several but interdependent moves to gain control over the Persian Gulf area, the Near East and the Middle East. As Paul Nitze explains the Soviet program in a masterful essay on "Strategy for the '80's,"[18] the penetration of South Yemen and Iran led directly to the thrust into Afghanistan. This move, again, advanced the Soviet base structure by 500 miles so as to outflank Iran and bear directly on the Arabian Sea, and thus greatly increased the immediacy of a military threat to our now isolated ally Pakistan.

Only one of the societies targeted for takeover or penetration—namely Afghanistan—was openly invaded and occupied by Soviet military forces. Each of the others could be effectively enfeebled and destabilized by reliance first on the type of covert warfare judged appropriate to the society's culture and social structure; second, on the continuous deployment of threat-centered forms of diplomacy and psychological encirclement known in post-war Europe as Finlandization; and third, in my view chiefly, on the incapacity of the US to deal effectively with both, the offensive political processes issuing from the communist mindset and the thought world of the non-Western societies with whose viability as independent states we have associated our vital interests since 1945.

II. The Need for Comparative Studies in Statecraft

Comparative studies in statecraft may help us to clear up the intellectual and political disarray in which we find ourselves today, provided that we ask "the right questions" of the numerous culturally separate societies with which we coexist in the world society. We have done that, by and large, when it comes to the Soviet Union, modern Western Europe and Israel. However, it has been rightly observed that the US has not asked the right questions of what for want of a better term is still called the Third World, for we obviously do not know well enough "how these nations tick." Unless and until we know more about that, we cannot speculate profitably about the meaning of foreign policy and intelligence, and the place of what we distinguish as covert action in such societies as Uganda, Zimbabwe, Iraq, Iran, Turkey, Brazil, Korea or India. This means that we are not in a position to devise long-term foreign policies and diplomatic methods or develop intelligence projects that fit the needs in each case.

Further, since we deal everywhere in the Third World with societies that are older than our own and more attached to the past than we are, explorations of history are essential. And in that context again, it is important in each instance to distinguish between substratal indigenous characteristics on one hand, and recent imports from Western and Marxist-Leninist sources on the other. It goes without saying that all such endeavors would proceed best with the aid of linguistically qualified authorities.

Next, a reliable inventory of foreign policy related propositions presupposes familiarity with the domestic order of the society in question. The linkage here is organic, for as we know from our own experience, dispositions toward foreign affairs issue from thought-ways, norms and institutions developed *within* society. Moreover, and with special regard to covert and other intelligence operations, most decisive actions take place in the domestic field of a foreign nation. It thus follows that the latter's inner normative order must be understood on its own terms if we are to recruit the right agents, direct them effectively in desired ways and evaluate them properly, or if we are to cope successfully with other peoples' spies and, in general, if we are to know how to estimate the intentions and capabilities of "host" countries, be they allies or adversaries.[19]

Psychology is thus in theory a key discipline. However, it cannot be said that modern texts in this academic discipline shed much light on the problems here under consideration. Not only do they bypass the concerns of statecraft but more importantly, they proceed from the assumption that human beings everywhere conform to norms encapsuling the life styles of Americans and Europeans. Patterns of individual and social life, or configurations of "ideal" or "normal" types as these emerge from the records of African and Asian experiences have so far not found explicit recognition. And similar com-plaints are justified in regard to disciplines treating of ethics, law, government and economics.[20]

The following, then, is a draft questionnaire that transcends or crosses academic divisions in order to elicit information on the levels first, of domestic, and second, of foreign affairs.

A. Domestic Affairs

Which fundamental beliefs, ideas and values seem to sustain the society in time?

Which purposes and meanings are assigned to life?

How do people think about power, wealth, authority, order, justice?

What are the sources of the basic beliefs, norms and commitments? religion? ethnic or national customs? ideology? pragmatism? economic acquisitiveness?

How free and self-directed is the individual?

Which personality types are trusted and respected? which, by contrast, are distrusted or feared? which are favored for leadership roles?

What is the general core of fellowship? Which hierarchical pecking orders are freely accepted?

How limited or extensive are such feelings as affection, sympathy, and friendship? how common and accepted are hatred and vindictiveness?

What is the value content of intrigue and conflict?

In which circumstances is violence condoned? what is the ceiling for tolerance of violence within society?

How open or secretive is the society in general, such groupings as clans, families, brotherhoods, guilds, or fellowships of friends in particular?

Which dispositions toward oaths and promises or contracts are prevalent?

Are communications between likeminded men direct or indirect and round-about? in which conditions is duplicity allowed? when can one count on sincerity and good faith?

Do members of special groups communicate through the use of special, politically or socially significant metaphors and symbols?

Which precepts make up the moral order of society?

What do men regard as "law"?

Is law distinct from religion? from the political authority of the day?

In which ways does "law" recognize and protect the individual?

Is citizenship a developed concept?

How is political authority rendered?

Which elements make for stability in society? which, by contrast, induce disorder?

B. Foreign Affairs

Which political units or organisms should be recognized for purposes of foreign policy and intelligence assessments?

Is our perception too narrowly focused on "the modern state" or "nation state"?

Has the time come to admit that this modern European form of political organization has ceased being a universally valid norm in international relations, or that it is today effectively de-Europeanized?

What is the actual *locus* of political decisionmaking in foreign affairs today?

Which non-state units merit acknowledgment?

Is territoriality a chief factor in definitions of the non-state bodies?

Is there an underlying ethic that requires attention when one deals with these non-Western associational schemes, and if so what is it?

What is the prevalent world view?

How are relations with other independent societies conceptualized?

Do presumptions stress enmity and conflict, or friendship and cooperation?

Is war considered "bad" by definition?

Is war accepted as a norm or way of life, and if so, what do people fight for? When is war activated? which forms does it take? and how is it ended?

How do people think about peace?
Is it a definable condition?
What is its relation to war?

What distinguishes statecraft in general and foreign policy making in particular?

Are there regionally or culturally accepted rules for the conduct of foreign relations in war and/or in peace?

What is subsumed under the term "diplomacy"?

What is the relation of diplomacy to espionage?

In which ways are existing codes of international or inter-group behavior analogous to, or different from those accepted by a) Occidental democracies; b) communist societies?

What typifies the society's negotiating style?

What is the place of deception in the society's conduct of foreign relations? Is it generally accepted in war and peace or is it commonly reserved for specific conditions, if so which?

What is the place of "intelligence" in the society's system of foreign operations?

How valid or pertinent are our distinctions and definitions of the elements that make up "intelligence"?[21]

The questions raised in the foregoing draft inventory of propositions may not be relevant for the Soviet Union, and that for the simple reason that the entire Soviet government is marked by the KGB mentality. This judgment also holds for satellite and surrogate states of Soviet Russia; the new communist Vietnamese imperium in southeast Asia, and communist China where Marxist-Leninist doctrine as reenforced by traditional Legalist principles insists that all organization, whether of the village or the world, is war organization. Superior and inferior units in each of these contexts are therefore garrison states in which the craft of intelligence is the core of both, domestic and foreign policies, and in which all moves and operations are mapped in accordance with carefully crafted strategic designs. Although the latter consist of premises and programs to which we do not subscribe, they yet seem to accommodate the particular definitions with which we identify the different elements of intelligence.

The situation in non-Western states that are not penetrated decisively by communism is, in my view, very different. Many of them, specifically those in the Middle East and Black Africa, continue to be ruled by men who do not need, or cannot afford, to conceptualize long-range programs of action of any kind. In all of these cases we may therefore have to answer questions such as the ones raised earlier before we know which if any elements of intelligence are developed and whether our policies and intelligence operations are properly conceived, defined and implemented. For example:

- If a society is traditionally rent by internecine conflicts between contending personalities, ethnically different units or rival religious groupings which require ongoing conspiratorial activities and dissimulation, its foreign relations are apt to be cast in analogous terms.

- If warfare is a socially, morally and politically accepted course of action, or if hostility to outsiders is a normal disposition, diplomacy is likely to be an adjunct rather of war than of peace.

- If the normal grounds for war are strong feelings such as hatred, religious zeal, insistence to settle old scores or redress past humiliations, rather than precise calculations of national advantage, references to law or UN Charter provisions are irrelevant.

- If statehood rests upon strong political traditions that do not include the principle of territorially fixed frontiers, as it does in the Arabic/Islamic domain and in Black Africa, lines of demarcation between what in established international law is understood as international war (i.e. war between states) and internal war, as well as between war and peace cease to carry compelling meanings. Indeed, and as suggested earlier, in these conditions the state itself forfeits credibility as both, idea and reality. This conclusion extends itself *mutatis mutandis* to the classical law of nations, standing assumptions about foreign policy making, diplomatic methods and institutions, and to all aspects and phases of the intelligence process as we understand them today.

These propositions are well illustrated by recent developments in the Arab-Islamic regions of the Middle East where the identities of some states are continuously shifting while those of others are slowly being erased by war.

Lebanon—admittedly a state with shallow roots in history—is thus a no-man's land today, its capital an open city in which anyone can do whatever he can get away with, and in which more than 20 private armies and unknown numbers of militias are found to operate freely, each financed by outside sponsors and each complete with its own military intelligence service.[22] Jordan, also a fragile creation, continues to exist precariously, its population divided in its basic loyalties, its contours forever questioned alike by Israelis and by Arabs. Syria and Iraq, meanwhile, two other successor states of the Ottoman Empire, continue to alternate between friendship and enmity in their mutual relations, and to shift positions in inter-Arab affairs, especially when it comes to plans for merging states so as to come closer to the ancient goal of creating one great Arab nation. This traditional dream was preempted as recently as 1980 by the radical rulers of Libya and Iraq when they announced a fusion of their states.

In short, the state is near-irrelevant in this culture area today. This means, in my opinion, that the American intelligence community too will have to transcend the context "state" if it is to do its work effectively in this part of the world.

The case for a such reassessment is hardened by Middle Eastern developments in diplomatic practice. These are exemplified by Colonel Qaddafi's decision to replace Libya's embassies (those in Bern, Bonn, Vienna, Ankara, London and Washington were prominently mentioned as early as in September 1979) by the same "People's Committees for the Liquidation of Enemies of the Revolution" that are empowered to govern Libya itself in accordance with the doctrines of Qaddafi's "Green Book." All of the "Bureaus" are instruments of the regime's secret service, a body that rules supreme, answering only to Qaddafi and the other surviving officers who overthrew King Idris about ten years ago. The business of the secret service and the people's committees is to clear the land of elements considered undersirable by the chief of state. Arrests and executions are thus the mandate. Indeed the government openly announced that death lists were on file, and that hit teams would be sent abroad to hunt down and kill all expatriates, dissidents and traitors who could be regarded as guilty of corruption and/or opposition to the regime. Numerous assassinations are thus on record, mostly in the capitals of the West, and for many of them the cover has been Libyan embassies, now transformed into arsenals well stocked with explosives, false passports and other necessary tools of the terrorist trade.[23]

It is important to note that Qaddafi rationalizes these revolutionary moves by arguing that "traditional diplomacy" was the invention of imperialist powers in the heyday of colonialism, and that its norms can therefore in no way be expected to bind Third World countries. Foreign embassies in Libya are thus not considered inviolate, and diplomats like other foreign residents are routinely subjected to harassment, even arrest, the latter usually on charges of espionage. Other Arab nations, among them Iraq and Iran, seem to be in full accord with these policies and dispositions. At any rate, they too appear determined to stamp out the form and substance of customary international diplomacy and erase frontiers between sovereign states so as to accommodate terrorism and war.

Lastly, then, and with further reference to the need for a revision of the parameters within which our intelligence community operates today in the Middle East, it is imperative to review the relationship between covert action and war. The war between Iran and Iraq is a case in point.

Iran's theocratic Islamic regime had alarmed neighboring Iraq's secular Islamic government by calling on all Shi'ite communities in the region, in particular that of Iraq, to form a united country without frontiers. It had also invited the faithful to wage a Holy War against the "Satan Puppet" in Baghdad (and therewith, by implication, against the "Master Satan" in Washington). Iraq, in turn, was determined to avenge diplomatic and military defeats which "racist Persian tyrants" had inflicted upon its soil as well as upon its national dignity. These are identified in our times with the Pahlavi monarchs, in past centuries and millennia with the non-Islamic dynasties of the Achaemenids and Sassanians whose imperial rule had extended over numerous Arab provinces, including some now encompassed by Iraq.

To the astonishment of most observers, this war became almost instantly a total war, with both sides willing and able to attack vital strategic targets, particularly oil and nuclear power facilities, knock out cities quite without regard for civilian life and bring ruination upon their respective economies, heedless of future national and regional needs. Such actions struck a White House national security official as "completely irrational" and convinced a State Department specialist that if either or both of the contending states had possessed nuclear weapons, they probably would have been used. Other analysts have concluded that we now have a preview of what future wars between well-armed but otherwise less-developed nations would be like. Pointing to Yehezkel Dror's book *Crazy States*, they cite its warning that conflicts between Third World nations which are ruled by radical governments and equipped with modern military hardware, are likely to degenerate into all-out wars and thus into grave threats to international stability.[24] Whether one finds merit in this general prediction or not, the Iran-Iraq war indicates that covert actions and clandestine operations are neither wanted nor needed here since it is only open war that satisfies.

III. Case Studies

The following comparative studies of non-American and non-communist dispositions toward the relation between foreign policy, covert action and other aspects of intelligence begin with a profile of Iran, and that for the following reasons.

Iran has been, and continues to be a central concern for the United States. Our policies were severely tested and found wanting here. The record of these policies is the subject of numerous published analyses and this makes possible further exploratory discourse in our midst.

Next, Persia/Iran has occupied a pivotal position in world affairs from the 6th century BC onward. Perceived by European scholars as the watershed separating Occident and Orient and as the major counterplayer to classical Greece then representing Europe, and viewed with awe as the "prestige nation" in the Orient, Persia qualifies as a seed-bed civilization (Talcot Parson's category) in the sense that its impact on other societies has been pervasive and indelible, in no field more so than in statecraft.

This was the case in ancient India (once a satrapy of the Persian Empire), the Arab/Islamic caliphates, the Ottoman Empire and the Mogul Empire which held sway over much of what is India today as well as over adjacent regions including Pakistan. The case study of Iran is thus intended as an introduction to much of Oriental statecraft, all the more so as the present format does not allow for full presentations of the other societies just mentioned.[25]

The last study introduces the Republic of Venice, an essentially European but now defunct state.[26] The main reason for this selection is the recognition that Venice can teach us much about statecraft and survival that is particularly relevant to the challenges facing the US today.

A. Persia/Iran

Post-mortem commentaries on our recent and ongoing policy debacle in Iran illustrate the tenacity with which we continue to hold to our pre-fabricated models and our pre-conceived, entirely untested truths about this geopolitically, economically and historically most important state. Everyone was aware, Daniel O. Graham notes,[27] that, as the Shah was falling, a score of highly paid CIA analysts was writing that Iran was not in a revolutionary, or even a pre-revolutionary situation. The base assumption here is obviously that a certain model of "revolution," constructed by Western sociologists and historians with data culled from the records mainly of the 18th century French revolution, is an accurate measure, and thus also a reliable forecasting device, for the kind of upheaval which has been convulsing Iran in the last years.

Developments, most of them entirely unforeseen by us, have not borne out this assumption. In fact, they also displace several related suppositions that crowd contemporary political science as well as intelligence estimates and analyses. The Department of State, congressional committees and representatives of the intelligence community thus seem to be in broad agreement with Iranian revolutionaries, be they Islamic radicals, Marxist economists or members of the Tudeh party, that "the Shah" was personally responsible for everything that has befallen Iran and that has gone wrong in US policy. In many commentaries the reasoning is as simplistic as this: "Shah" stands for "king," and "king" stands for "reaction"; "revolution," and therewith "opposition," by contrast, stand for "progress"; and "progress" denotes "democracy" and respect for "human rights."

Such thought-killing stereotypes have at times also interfered with the task of reliably evaluating other kingdoms and sheikhdoms in the Middle East, notably the monarchies of Iraq, Saudi Arabia, Jordan, Libya and Morocco. However, it is interesting that they usually do not obsess our thinking about non-royal dictators in the Middle East, most of them successors to the kings they overthrew or killed. If we had overcome our traditional reluctance to think historically, we would have remembered that modern monarchical regimes in the Middle East have by and large been more moderate, innovative and progressive in their social policies, and more reliable in the conduct of their foreign relations, notably with Occidental states, than the dictators who followed them. And most importantly, if we had read a little bit more ambitiously in the records of the past, we would have realized that authoritarian rule is the absolute norm in this entire culture realm. Further, if we had studied Iran in particular, we might have come to know that the two 20th century Pahlavi shahs had a complex dual commitment on the one hand as Muslims of the Shi'ite persuasion, on the other as culture conscious representatives of the much older pre-Islamic traditions bequeathed by Persia's classical dynasties and by the Zoroastrian belief system.[28]

It is this second set of references which everyone interested in the relation between foreign policy and intelligence, specifically covert action, should study, for it tells of the principles and institutions of statecraft that sustained the multi-national Persian Empire throughout antiquity as the "prestige nation" in the Eurasian world. The services that elicited the greatest admiration and emulation in the Orient, related to diplomacy, policing methods, espionage and other clandestine operations for which a group of renowned Achaemenid overseers—the "eyes and ears" of the King of Kings—was responsible. No single document attests to this Persian legacy more faithfully than the Indian *Arthasastra*, a manual on the science of government composed in the fourth century BC by a Brahman adviser for the Maurya king Chandragupta, who founded, in Northwestern India, the first vast centralized Indian state.[29]

In light of Persia's history it is not surprising that it was the Achaemenid tradition which provided the Pahlavi regimes with a model for a secular, territorially conceived state; allowed for secular law and secular education, tolerance of ethnic and religious minorities and the emancipation of women, and which stood for the principle of progress and continuity in time, thus inviting future-directed social reforms. These ideas are commonplace in the intellectual history of the West, and Europeans, beginning with the ancient Greeks, have therefore always been aware of their affinities with the Persians, even when their mutual relations were rent by war. But none of this holds for the Islamic Near East, for here each of the clusters of concepts just mentioned is absolutely anathema to the Shi'ite mind and fundamentally uncongenial also to the orthodox Sunni faith. As the Ayatollah Khomeini reminded the Iranians shortly after his ascendancy to power: "There are only two groups: Islam and Non-Islam. We are all Muslims, and therefore Iranians have to choose between the Koran and the *Book of Kings*." (The last reference is an evocation of Persia's non-Islamic heritage of secular rule).

The religious establishment which represents, after all, the primary cause in behalf of which the Arabs made war on Persia[30] was thus by definition committed to hatred for the Pahlavi shahs. Each reform, including of course the extensive expropriations of land held by the

leadership of the religious establishment, was therefore bitterly re-
sented as a betrayal of Islam and an usurpation of the Shi'ite mission
in government and society at large. The Pahlavi elites thus had the
strenuous task of administering the coexistence in their realm of
near-incompatible principles if they were to keep Iran from slipping
into the kind of political formlessness typical of neighboring Arab
nations,[31] and if they were to succeed, instead, in maintaining Iran
as an independent state capable of being effective in domestic and
foreign affairs.

By and large the dynasty was able to meet this ongoing challenge.
This was so partly because the complexity of Iran's internal and
external situation was well understood in Western Europe as well as
in the United States. From the 1970's onward, however, amnesia
gripped America; and the void left by failing memory or ignorance
was swiftly filled with such utopian policy projects as installing "democracy" and "human rights."

It has since been suggested by several analyses of our debacle in
Iran that our policy had miscarried because those responsible for its
formulation and implementation in State, Defense and CIA had not
asked the right questions. The main critical data that we missed, it
is being argued today, were knowledge of the Shah's medical history
(i.e. the fact that he had suffered from cancer longer than we had
presumed), and knowledge of "the opposition." The real failing of
field work by CIA and State is thus said to have been neglect in
collecting information about the opposition and therefore failure to
communicate with anti-government elements. An evaluation of US
intelligence performance in Iran by the House Intelligence Subcommittee's Staff thus concludes[32] that close identification with the Shah
limited the opportunities for US officials to hear from Iranians who
opposed him, thereby causing Iran to resemble a closed society from
the US perspective, with even clandestine collection of Iran's politics
discouraged.

These judgments and the reasoning that led to them must be re-
butted on the ground that they bear no relation to reality. And the
same goes for the implicit assumption in this and other papers on the
subject that there existed in Iran the equivalent of the Republican
Party USA or of Her Majesty's Loyal Opposition in England with
which our representatives could have communicated at will if the
Shah's regime had not frustrated their attempts to do so. The heart
of the matter—and it could have been identified readily—is that Iran
is simply not cast in the mold of an "open" society on the order of
Western Democracies. Neither here nor elsewhere in the Islamic

Middle East can we therefore expect to get to know the society's inner social order and its patterns of conflict by discoursing at ease with representatives of an openly organized opposition party. Rather, and as pointed out in the preceding pages of this paper, the main opposition to the Shah's or any other secular government (the Communist Tudeh party is not considered here) is deeply entrenched, all-pervasive, permanent and institutionalized in ways that make communication of the kind we anticipate hardly possible.

In short, the "failings" that emerge from all of these post mortem notices were and continue to be, failings of scholarship and education that could have been avoided or corrected by collecting information in our libraries. No "assets" and secret contacts were required for that.

Scholarly work of this kind would also have equipped policy makers and their agents with the knowledge that "the opposition" would be at least as authoritarian in the discharge of the functions of government as the Pahlavi monarchy was, even as it would in all likelihood be less capable of maintaining the state. This had already proved to be true of the short-lived essentially secular Mossadegh regime which dismissed parliament and ruled without any regard for law, and it should have been forecast also in the years during which the Ayatollah Khomeini and his Shi'ite divines were preparing the overthrow of the Shah. Subsequent developments leave no doubt, unfortunately, that we knew very little, probably nothing, about the nature of Iranian alternatives to Pahlavi rule; for while our governmental agents and representatives of the media fell all over themselves in kowtows before the Ayatollah (widely viewed as another George Washington and, by Andrew Young, as "a kind of saint"), the latter's kangaroo courts and execution squads simply proceeded in a matter of fact way with their grisly work of killing Iranians.

The basic American supposition that the ouster of the Shah's "lawless regime" would somehow lead Iran back to the norms of its Western-type constitution of 1906 and thus by implication also to concordance with American commitments to "human rights," simply disintegrated as yet another illusion as Shi'ite Iran returned resolutely to its roots. One is thus entitled to be surprised that the Carter Administration had not been forewarned by its legal advisers and area specialists about the likely consequences which revolutionary Iran's thrust back into the past would have on constitutional, penal and international law. As it was, we merely registered consternation when we learned that Iranian citizens pronounced guilty of sundry crimes such as selling alcohol and committing adultery were programatically buried up to their chests and stoned to death, all to the sound of ceremonial prayers and exuberant acclamations by attending masses. No one in the ranks of our policymakers seems to have been given access to the rich literature (in English) on precisely the issues here in contention which has long been available to every literate person. At any rate it was obviously not expected that the complex of norms which we call "law" and which westernizing Iranian governments had grafted rather carefully upon the substratum of Islamic precepts and values, would be dismantled speedily. This was so, it is here suggested, because no one in authority knew that the term "law" relates to "religion" in the context of orthodox Islam, and that this religious "law" *(shari'a)* is a comprehensive order of precepts which encompasses not only what we call "law" but also what we distinguish as philosophy, ethics, jurisprudence, economics, government and foreign relations. Lastly, it seems strange to me that our "eyes and ears" abroad—be they journalists or diplomats—had not alerted our policy-making elites to the open comeback of this entire complex of religion throughout the Islamic world.

"Their" law, then, has nothing to do with "our" law, and President Carter's instruction to the intelligence community that its members may not violate the laws of a foreign government would have needed considerable amplification in the case of Iran if they were intended to be meaningful and wise.[33]

The conclusion that comparative studies of law, religion, ethics and politics had not been conducted by our government when critical decisions in our foreign policy had to be made is particularly relevant in the context of international law and diplomatic method. As noted earlier, the territorially delimited state had not been a fundamental norm in Arab/Islamic politics before Westernization (Egypt, Turkey and Iran do not belong into this category for reasons cited earlier.) History thus tells us in great detail that Islam mandates expansion and the creation of an all-Islamic state, not an international order of multiple sovereignties, and that it does not stipulate the kind of polarization between war and peace which today consider normative in the conduct of international relations. As most everywhere, cultures in the Middle East accept, even value, conflict, conspiracy and war. Societies here were thus routinely convulsed by intrigues and bloody power struggles between contesting men or factions and by well-organized religious uprisings that aimed at punishing immorality and at purifying life on earth by resort to war. The Wahabi movement in Arabia is one such illustration. Another is the Order of the Assassins in Iran, an offspring of the Shi'ite sect of the Ismailites which terrorized the land during the 11th-13th centuries AD by meticulously planned assassinations.[34]

Traditions such as these have been reinforced, rechannelled and in some respects of course deformed by 20th century Eurasian theories and practices of terrorism and guerrilla warfare. Neither of the two ideological commitments that are thus joined today makes allowance for the basic norms of international law and diplomacy which we in the US continue to regard as universally accepted and therefore as universally binding. The quasi-religious pledge to kill the Shah,[35] his children and his extended family, indeed the entire ''opposition'' to Khomeini's regime, was thus conceived and openly advertised as a trans-territorial mandate, to be carried out without any regard whatsoever for the territorial integrity and the laws of other states with which Iran was—from the Occidental viewpoint—at ''peace.''

This blueprint for murder could be concretized effectively because agents in charge of such covert operations—the reference here is mainly to episodes in the United States, France and England—can rely on interlocking nets of collaborators in the ranks of Iranian and other Mohammedan radicals who are resident in the host country; on the succour of selected sympathetic Islamic embassies, and on the generosity or weakness of the democratic legal systems within which such actions occur. And the same combination of factors naturally facilitates such related operations as the unleashing of Iranian student mobs in American cities and the dispensing by the Khomeini regime of covert aid for the general purpose of inciting violence in the US.

These developments have severely tried the institution of diplomacy and its attendant system of norms. Indeed, as so-called students are allowed to storm and occupy embassies in Tehran; as foreign diplomats are being held hostage; as people's committees are replacing Iranian embassies, and as covert action operatives are taking the place of diplomats, the conclusion is not far-fetched that diplomacy as we have known it in the last two centuries has been fatally struck. Furthermore and in the same extended context, the thought is justified that government-sponsored terrorism of the kind made evident here has had the effect of levelling existing distinctions between war and peace. Iran's present foreign policy—and allowance must be made for the fact that it emanates from power centers that are chronically feuding in secret—is thus essentially a covert war policy. Conceived in unmitigated hatred of the West, in particular the US, it aims solely at humiliating this foe and at exorcising his ''satanic,''

"corrupting" influences from all domains of Iranian life and thought.
"We are a superpower," Khomeini declared not long ago: "we are
not Americans; we do not belong to pragmatism." "Final victory"
is therefore officially identified here not with economic development
and wealth, nor with nationally secure frontiers, but with the expulsion of the Americans who symbolize the Occident as did the Shah.

It would in my view be a mistake to think of the frenzy of Iran's
xenophobia and of the relentless scapegoating in which its spokesmen
engage as temporary aberrations of the national psyche, or as expressions of a passing malaise on the part of a hard-pressed, confused
revolutionary leadership. After all, Iranians in all age groups and
walks of life, whether living in Iran or the US, whether home-bred
ayatollahs and ulemas, or American-educated economists and political scientists, consistently reveal themselves as enthusiastically active participants in these foreign policy orgies.[36]

What needs to be faced in the area of psychology is what has been
suggested earlier in this paper in regard to religion, law, history,
philosophy and government, namely that there are very few—if
any—transnationally valid norms and values.

Hugh Tovar addressed this matter at the Consortium's 1979 Colloquium when he noted that:

> It is hard for Americans to fathom the turbulent well of Islamic radicalism
> and its seemingly mindless violence. We are stunned when friendly gov-
> ernments are suddenly engulfed and overthrown in explosive outbreaks
> that seem beyond our ability to influence, much less to modulate.[37]

My own response to this American malaise is somewhat sterner: why
do we not realize in the 1980's what the preceding decades of this
century have made manifest in no uncertain terms namely, that what
is "irrational" in our universe of experience may well be perfectly
rational in that of other, culturally different peoples. In the case of
modern Islam and Iran in particular we should have been well prepared for the likelihood of the kind of outbursts we are witnessing
now. It is thus odd to have to recognize that those concerned with
the Middle East in matters of foreign policy have not read Gustave
von Grunebaum's analyses of the Islamic self-view in history and
international relations, *Modern Islam: The Search for Cultural Identity,*
or H.A.R. Gibb's critique of Islamic modernism in *Modern Trends in
Islam,* and J. J. Saunders' exploration of the factors that have made
for the freezing of Islamic culture. These are just three exquisite
texts among many others that deal precisely with the psychological
motifs, so prominently displayed today. Likewise, it does not seem
plausible that those in charge of the State Department's Iran desk

have missed out on William S. Haas' analysis in *Iran* of the Persian mind as moulded by Persia's tortured history.

Haas points out that the strong Persian commitment to the dissident Shi'ite persuasion and to Sufism evolved from an admirable, but inevitably only partially successful attempt to separate the Persian mind from the Sunni faith of the old empire's Arab conquerors. Conceived in terms of mental and psychological self-protection and defense, the effort soon found expression in a peculiar custom—one distinctly relevant to comparative studies of clandestine and covert operations—namely the dissimulation of faith by mental reservation *(ketman)*. Under the protective cover of what eventually became a theological doctrine, a Shi'ite was allowed to pretend that he was a Sunni, or even a Christian or a Jew, whenever he felt he was in danger because of the fact that he actually was a Shi'ite and a believer in the eventual appearance of the Hidden Imam. This fundamentally religious practice communicated itself gradually to other life contexts. In that of statecraft as this had developed before the 20th century reforms, *ketman* gave rise in Persia to a technique of cunning, simulation, and ruse that Persians in many walks of life learned to master with rare perfection, nowhere more effectively, Haas notes, than in diplomacy and in government circles in which "inferiors" evolved a strategy of self-defense against superiors that allowed them to slip through the meshes of any net thrown around them.[38]

B. The Islamic Empires

The great Islamic empires from which numerous nation states have disengaged themselves in recent times, share several characteristics that are relevant for modern comparative studies of statecraft, intelligence and covert action. A substantiation of this conclusion needs the following preliminary information.

The Arab and Arabized caliphates, the Seljuq and Ottoman empires, the Mogul empire and the Islamized Persian empire were despotisms in which the twin ideas of citizenship and a common public secular law never developed. Each was born of war and organized for conquests; each was a tax-taking, not a legislating polity on the order of the classical Roman and the modern European empires, and each relied heavily on institutionalized slavery. Further, neither empire, excepting that of the Persians, had fathomed or could concretize the concept of the secular state since Islamic religious law had consigned this notion to the realm of illegitimacy, along

with that of legislation—the latter on the ground that God, acting
through Mohammed, had legislated once and for all.

Next, West Asia's Islamic empires were plural societies, composed of multiple, ethnically and culturally diverse tribes, villages,
provinces and religious sects. Heavily taxed and viewed as conglom-
erates of subject or inferior peoples, these communities were yet
allowed a considerable measure of autonomy in matters of belief and
social customs. Totally missing in the Islamic context was a unifying
framework for the secular governance of a vast, culturally frag-
mented international society that would assure stabilization of all
that arms and ideology had won.

This standing challenge explains why the Islamic victors borrowed
so heavily from the records of statecraft left by the defeated, notably
Persia and Byzantium. After all, the latter, too, had been universal
empires as well as culturally heterogeneous societies in which religion—Zoroastrianism in one case, Christianity in another—was
taken very seriously. But contrary to the upstart empires of the
nomadic peoples from the deserts of Arabia and the steppes of Central Asia, Persia (7th century BC—7th AD) and Byzantium (5th
century AD—15th AD) had known how to allow for legitimate interaction between institutionalized religion and political organization.
This they accomplished by relying on solid bodies of public secular
law, stressing the idea of the state as the superior all-encompassing
reality, cultivating statecraft through the medium of refined intelligence and communication, and creating specialized bureaucratic services for overseeing affairs of state at home and abroad.[39]

It was the latter aspect of the Persian and Byzantine designs that
most intrigued first the Arab dynasties of the Umayyads (7th century
AD) and the Abbasids (8th century AD) and later the Turks and
Mongols—if only because Islam could not accommodate the other
organizational aspects. However, it should be noted that the conquering bands of Turks and Mongols—in contrast to the Arabs—had
also been vitally influenced by the Chinese and the Tatars of the
steppes, and that they had brought with them their own well-tested
ideas of how to govern men and nations. After 1258 (the sack of
Baghdad) Mongol sovereigns thus relied heavily on their own customary laws, despite their conversion to Islam. This factor explains,
authorities note, why their despotisms were never as closely related
to the *Shari'a* as that of say Suleiman's (the Magnificent) administration in Istanbul, (16th century AD) and why the slave system in
Akbar's Indian Mogul empire (16th century) was not nearly as harsh
and elaborate as that imposed by Turkish rulers upon Christian

communities. Yet, and after full allowance is made for the diversity of cultural borrowing processes, the fact is indisputable that it was Persia in each of its multiple incarnations that exerted the paramount influence upon the new Islamic polities. This was so, an Abbasid caliph is said to have explained, because the Persians had ruled for a thousand years and had not needed "us Arabs" even for a day; but we (Arabs) have been ruling for one or two centuries and cannot do without them for an hour.

An inheritance which the Abbasids valued particularly was Persia's elaborate system of trunk roads and postal communications—the indispensable framework for all intelligence related services. In the Abbasid context the postmaster-general was also, indeed primarily, the chief of the espionage system. In this dual capacity he acted as the confidential agent of the central government: all provincial postmasters reported to him or directly to the caliph on the conduct of government officials as well as on the activities of adversaries and foreign enemies. Scores of merchants, pedlars and travellers were employed as agents in the caliphal espionage network. The records of Al-Ma'mum's rule also show that his particular service included some 1700 aged women, and that spies of both sexes, intricately disguised as traders, journeymen or physicians, were nowhere more active that in conquered Byzantine territory.

Among the different "Persias" in history it was the one ruled by the Sassanians (3rd to 7th century AD) which recommended itself as the chief organizational model because it had known how to evolve and maintain an elaborate bureaucratic establishment, a highly efficient military system and an intricate network of diplomacy and espionage—three services that together had assured the security, stability and glory of the realm. All records of statecraft relating to these Iranian "kings of kings" were thus diligently studied, among them in particular the 10th century *Book of Kings* and Firdausi's great epic *shāhnāma* as well as the famous "Mirrors for Princes" which had been composed by men of affairs and letters for the instruction of rulers and their ministers. All of them emphasized the need for gathering intelligence, with some of the later manuals advising that networks of spies should cover the entire realm since a sovereign must know the people's secrets if he is to enjoy a long and successful reign.

Under the impact of this Iranian tradition of "rational statecraft," the Dar al-Islām was early set in the mould of the "Power State."[40] This political phenomenon was expounded and analysed by Nizām al-Mulk (d. 1092 AD) in *The Book of Government* (Seyāsat-nāmeh)[41]—

a remarkable text of timeless significance about which an early scribe wrote that "no king or emperor can afford not to possess and know this book, especially in these days." Anchored firmly in reflections on history and political expedience, the work owes nothing to Islamic theory and religion, even as it aimed openly at protecting the cause of orthodox Islam.

Nizām al-Mulk ("Regulator of the Kingdom") was born into the highly cultured Persian administrating class, became vizir to Alp Arslan when the latter was supreme overlord of the new Seljuq rulers and advanced to the top post of Grand Vizir ("burden bearer" for the Sultan) when his Seljuq master became sultan over an empire that stretched from the Oxus in the East to Khwarezm and the southern Caucasus and westward into central Anatolia. During thirty years of stewardship Nizām al-Mulk established an unchallenged reputation as the quintessential vizir. Wise, prudent, resourceful and successful, Nizām al-Mulk was consistently praised by successive generations as an outstanding statesman and administrator, and above all as the main architect of an exemplary empire in which prosperity and security were firmly established.

Nizām al-Mulk seems to have stood steadfastly by the following propositions while he recorded these accomplishments. He was determined to upgrade Turkish rule by relating it firmly to Iran's superior traditions of statecraft. He believed that the ruler was chosen by God for the task of preserving stability in the kingdom; that his power had to be absolute; that all administration should be centralized in his person, and that having ultimate ownership of all land, the sultan must be presumed to own the kingship. Furthermore, deep religious convictions combined with considerations of "reason of state" convinced Nizām al-Mulk that it was necessary to maintain the Sunni faith. He was therefore determined to combat all heterodox sects, among them mainly the Shi'ites and the Order of the Assassins they had spawned. (Numerous training schools were thus founded by him for the purpose of countering Shi'ite propaganda.)

Nizām al-Mulk's "Power State" could not have realized either of these or any other policy objectives if it had not concentrated its attention upon two particular instruments of rule: a powerful fighting army that could be expected to be always in place and ready to support the momentum of expansion; and a tightly organized, totally reliable network of intelligence (*bārid*) whose officers kept watch over and reported on events taking place in various parts of the empire, thus assuring the speedy transmission of messages between government agents in the provinces and central controls in the capital. The importance attached to this system of communication is well conveyed by the following excerpts from *The Book of Government*.[42]

> It is the king's duty to enquire into the condition of his peasantry and army, both far and near, and to know more or less how things are. If he does not do this he is at fault and people will charge him with negligence, laziness and tyranny, saying, 'Either the king knows about the oppression and extortion going on in the country, or he does not know. If he knows and does nothing to prevent it and remedy it, that is because he is an oppressor like the rest and acquiesces in their oppression; and if he does not know then he is negligent and ignorant.' Neither of these imputations is desirable. Inevitably therefore he must have postmasters; and in every age in the time of ignorance and of Islam, kings have had postmasters, through whom they have learnt everything that goes on, good and bad. For instance, if anybody wrongly took so much as a chicken or a bag of straw from another (and that five hundred farsangs away) the king would know about it and have the offender punished, so that others knew that the king was vigilant. In every place they appointed informers and so far checked the activities of oppressors that men enjoyed security and justice for the pursuit of trade and cultivation. But this is a delicate business involving some unpleasantness; it must be entrusted to the hands and tongues and pens of men who are completely above suspicion and without self-interest, for the weal or woe of the country depends on them. They must be directly responsible to the king and not to anyone else; and they must receive their monthly salaries regularly from the treasury so that they may do their work without any worries. In this way the king will know of every event that takes place and will be able to give his orders as appropriate, meting out unexpected reward, punishment or commendation to the persons concerned. When a king is like this, men are always eager to be obedient, fearing the king's displeasure, and nobody can possibly have the audacity to disobey the king or plot any mischief. Thus the employment of intelligence agents and reporters contributes to the justice, vigilance and prudence of the king, and to the prosperity of the country.
>
> Spies must constantly go out to the limits of the kingdom in the guise of merchants, travellers, sufis, pedlars (of medicines), and mendicants, and bring back reports of everything they hear, so that no matters of any kind remain concealed, and if anything (untoward) happens it can in due course be remedied. In the past it has often happened that governors, assignees, officers, and army-commanders have planned rebellion and resistance, and plotted mischief against the king, but spies forestalled them and informed the king, who was thus enabled to set out immediately with all speed and, coming upon them unawares, to strike them down and frustrate their plans; and if any foreign king or army was preparing to attack the country, the spies informed the king, and he took action and repelled them. Likewise they brought news, whether good or bad, about the condition of the peasants, and the king gave the matter his attention, as did Adud ad Daula on one occasion.

After a lengthy section on the king's need for "boon companions" (these must not be government officials but may serve as body guards), Nizām al-Mulk turns to foreign affairs and diplomacy:

> When ambassadors come from foreign countries, nobody is aware of their movements until they actually arrive at the city gates; nobody gives any information (that they are coming) and nobody makes any preparation for them; and they will surely attribute this to our negligence and indifference. So officers at the frontiers must be told that whenever anyone approaches their stations, they should at once despatch a rider and find out who it is who is coming, how many men there are with him, mounted and unmounted, how much baggage and equipment he has, and what is his business. A trustworthy person must be appointed to accompany them and conduct them to the nearest big city; there he will hand them over to another agent who will likewise go with them to the next city (and district), and so on until they reach the court. Whenever they arrive at a place where there is cultivation, it must be a standing order that officers, tax-collectors and assignees should give them hospitality and entertain them well so that they depart satisfied. When they return, the same procedure is to be followed. Whatever treatment is given to an ambassador, whether good or bad, it is as if it were done to the very king who sent them, and kings have always shewn the greatest respect to one another and treated envoys well, for by this their own dignity has been enhanced. And if at any time there has been disagreement or enmity between kings, and if ambassadors have still come and gone as occasion requires, and discharged their missions according to their instructions, never have they been molested or treated with less than usual courtesy. Such a thing would be disgraceful, as God (to Him be power and glory) says (in the Quran 24.53), 'The messenger has only to convey the message plainly.'

> It should also be realized that when kings send ambassadors to one another their purpose is not merely the message or the letter which they communicate openly, but secretly they have a hundred other points and objects in view. In fact they want to know about the state of roads, mountain passes, rivers and grazing grounds, to see whether an army can pass or not; where fodder is available and where not; who are the officers in every place; what is the size of that king's army and how well it is armed and equipped; what is the standard of his table and his company; what is the organization and etiquette of his court and audience hall; does he play polo and hunt; what are his qualities and manners, his designs and intentions, his appearance and bearing; is he cruel or just, old or young, is his country flourishing or decaying; are his troops contented or not; are the peasants rich or poor; is he avaricious or generous; is he alert or negligent in affairs; is his vazir competent or the reverse, of good faith and high principles or of impure faith and bad principles; are his generals experienced and battle-tried or not; are his boon-companions polite and worthy; what are his likes and dislikes; in his cups is he jovial and good-natured or not; is he strict in religious matters and does he shew magnanimity and mercy, or is he careless; does he incline more to jesting or to gravity; and does he prefer boys or women. So that, if at any time they want to win over that king, or oppose his designs or criticize his faults,

being informed of all his affairs they can think out their plan of campaign, and being aware of all the circumstances, they can take effective action, as happened to your humble servant in the time of The Martyr Sultan Alp Arslan (may Allah sanctify his soul).

Nizām al-Mulk wrote the book shortly before he was assassinated. The murder was probably committed by an Ismá'ili from the castle of the Assassins with the complicity of a court rival, of the queen and possibly even of Malik-Shāh himself. Within a month the sultan too was dead, and the disintegration of the great empire was proceeding ineluctably.

The imminence of this development had been predicted by Nizām al-Mulk who had expressed great anxiety about the sultan's careless disregard for protocol, the decline in prestige of important officials, and, above all, about the neglect of the intelligence service. For contrary to his advice, the sultan had ended up abolishing the *bārid* on the ground that it engendered an atmosphere of mistrust and suspicion amongst friends and foes alike. This meant that effective checks and controls were missing and that the ruler could not be secured against rebellion, injustice, or extortion by his officials. It was anxiety about this state of affairs the led Nizām al-Mulk to emphasize the need for an efficient system of espionage to be backed by an armed forced strong enough to overpower all opposition. The sultan, he advised, now had to have informers and spies throughout the empire and among all classes of the population, including that of the *qādis*.

The pattern of rise, expansion, contraction and decay, so dramatically illustrated by the Seljuq Empire, continued to mark the histories of Islamic despotisms in West Asia, and foreign relations between established Muslim polities continued to be cast in terms of war relations, with ambitious princes and the dynasties they spawned for ever determined to seek new glory and dominion by besting actual or potential rivals.[43] The model of the Perso-Turkish power state which presumed the ruler's omnipotence and required a powerful army as main instrument of statecraft, had become firmly established and was therefore reenacted time and time again between the 11th and the end of the 18th centuries, most impressively in the 16th century Ottoman Empire of Suleiman the Magnificent where government had been deeply influenced by Byzantine traditions from the taking of Constantinople onward (1453). In accordance with established pattern this empire, too, declined after Suleiman's death, and the main cause here, as in the earlier Seljuq, Persian and Mongol empires, was the degeneration of the ruling establishment, not any deleterious impact wrought by continuous war.

This was so, it appears, because the sultan's complex court was not just an ordinary government. Rather, it was a direct projection or representation of his identity and biography; of his personality, power and vitality. And since the sultan personified the state, it was therefore in the final analysis his security and survival that constituted the prime concern in domestic as well as in foreign affairs. Indeed, these two dimensions of statecraft can hardly be disentangled in the Islamic context. Thus, when something goes wrong with the ruler and his court, something goes very wrong also with the state. The ruling institution itself, then, was the hub and core of all statecraft, the battleground between contending men and nations, and the uncontested center radiating vitality as well as decay.

The success or failure of a given Islamic despotism at home and abroad was thus being determined then as it is now—one thinks of Tripolis, Baghdad, Damascus, Teheran or Algiers—by events unfolding in the immediate entourage of the leading man. This therefore was and continues to be the theatre of most intelligence operations, including covert actions.

The dynamics that determined the deployment of clandestine and covert methods were strong and complex feelings on the part of all governing elites, foremost among them fear of treachery, distrust and vindictiveness. These could be activated at will because enmity, jealousy and the propensity to engage in conspiracy were generally accepted human traits, and because codes of law and ethics were missing when it came to affairs of state. Sultanates, caliphates and emirates were thus normally rent by open civil war, rebellion, secession and above all by internecine strife. More particularly, they were usually prey to one or the other kind of forceable seizure, most of them involving murder.

In the absence of reliable rules of succession, regicide, fratricide and other forms of assassination were common as were wars between fathers and sons or between elder and younger brothers. For example, Shah Abbas the Great of Persia (17th century AD) had two sons blinded and indulged in intricate plots to murder his eldest son because he had become popular. Shah Jehan in the Mogul Empire (17th Century AD) had to contend with four rebellious sons who also fought against each other until the last was able to encompass the death of the others and keep his father imprisoned during the last seven years of his life. Each new sultan in the Ottoman Empire had his surviving brothers strangled usually with a silken bowstring so as not to shed blood. In fact, to avoid the dangers implicit in a disputed succession, the Ottomans adopted a "Law of Fratricide" which provided that to whichever son the sultanate may be vouchsafed, it is proper for him to put his brothers to death, so as to preserve the order of the world. Further, and perhaps by way of mitigating the harshness of such destinies, it became customary to keep all princes in the harem. Here they lived a life of gilded imprisonment in the company of their mothers, slaves and eunuchs until they emerged in order to die or reign.[44] As a contemporary chronicler reports, to be born a prince was misfortune of the worst and most embarrassing kind: he must die by clemency, or wade through the blood of his family to safety and empire.

How to induce loyalty and how to locate reliable agents while avoiding security risks were the standing challenges in all Oriental despotisms. The sovereigns in each of the different empires found different ways of recruiting and maintaining appropriate categories of "despotic agents." Yet all, including ancient Persia and China, (at times also Rome and Byzantium), relied heavily on eunuchs. The shared natural expectation here was that, having no family ambitions of their own, eunuchs could be made to serve the monarch exclusively, mainly by preventing or uncovering murderous plots and subversive activities. This category of councillors was especially well developed in the Islamic Middle East, more particularly in the Ottoman Empire, where "black" eunuchs, "white" eunuchs and other sub-groups were in charge of all essential offices, among them the sultan's harem.[45]

The other major human resource for recruitment was slavery. In the Ottoman Empire, slaves were the backbone of the army, the bureaucracy and the courtly household. Most were Christians, and they were acquired either as prisoners or—until at least the 17th century—through the medium of regular levies upon Christian villages. Here too the rationale was that the despot needed men without roots, and Christian youths were therefore detached from their families early in life so as to be trained in special palace schools for slaves where their evolution into loyal servants was closely supervised by trusted eunuchs.

Variously defined as a power state and a slave state, the Islamic empire was also a closed society in which clandestine operations and covert actions were called for if the ruling institution was to rule successfully. However, as remarked earlier, it was also a layered society, composed of numerous essentially self-sufficient corporations, guilds, bazaars, sects and religious brotherhoods. These too were closed societies in the sense that each was beholden to its own codes and customs, spurning cooperation with others. But contrary to the state, each could count on the loyalty of its constituency if only because the individual member derived his essential status and identity from the grouping he belonged to. And since most corporate associations were as hostile to the state as the general population, they often did act in concert to resist or defy state authority, sometimes in open rebellion, but usually by engaging in what we today call clandestine and covert operations. These, it is important to point out, were routinely deployed also in relations between rival factions and movements.

In such a context of dispositions, flights into subversive associations were commonplace and "the secret society" became the normative organizational model for religious and political activism, especially in Persia and the Arab lands. The Order of the Assassins to which reference has already been made, is a case in point. As Brockelmann explains, it was built up in various degrees:

> While the narrowest circle of initiates professed a libertinism which negated any limitations by morality or religion, their agents were trained in the severest fanaticism. The murder of an enemy of the true faith designated by their master was presented to them as a work well pleasing to God, the execution of which would assure them of the joys of Paradise. Such murderers were called *Fidá'is*, "the Self-Sacrificers," or *Hashishis* (whence Assassins), those intoxicated by hashish . . .[46]

To destroy in the name of purity was the motivating force also of the Arab *Ikhwan* ("Sincere Brethren") and the Wahhabites. The latter group which had been initiated by an Arab tribesman (Muhammad ibn-'Abd-al Wahhab) in revulsion against the abuses that had penetrated Islam, notably as practiced by the Turks, swiftly evolved into a great national revival after it had rallied most Beduin tribes of the Najd. This revolt which climaxed in an attack on Mecca in 1803, may be said to have launched the complex and protracted "awakening" process during which the entire Middle Eastern region became honeycombed with secret societies working underground in revolt against Turkish rule.[47]

One of the earliest and most important of these clandestine organisms was the Bairut Secret Society which began toward the end of the 19th century as "a whispered conspiracy" of like-minded opponents to the Turkish regime (all original founders were Christians) until it was emboldened to launch violent exhortations to rebellion, mainly through the medium of placards. These could remain anonymous because their creators had refined the art of disguising handwritings, literary styles and standards to such an extent that ruling authorities were simply incapable of conjecturing the identities of these subversive elements. Operations were nonetheless endangered by the government's secret agents, and the Society dissolved itself voluntarily after a few years' existence, leaving no account of its activities. Its scanty records were deliberately destroyed, and its members emigrated, mostly to Egypt. In short, the secret was well kept to the end, and, as George Antonius concludes from his own exploration of this long episode, the identities of the conspirators never became known either to the government or to the public. What was left was the society's device representing a drawn sword below which there was this line: "By the sword may distant aims be attained: seek with it if you mean to succeed."

This remained the general motto for all societies in the 20th century that aimed at Arab independence. Most of them unified their membership by common passwords, signals for identification, a clandestine press, a common treasury and, above all, a total commitment to loyalty and secrecy. *Al-Fatāt*, the most effective of these Arab societies, was remarkable alike for its objects and methods as for the admirable discipline of its members. A long period of probation preceded admission. Each recruit was introduced by one of the sworn members but was kept in ignorance of the identity of all the other members until he had been tried and proved, when he would be invited to take an oath to serve the ends of the society, to the point of forfeiting his life, if need be, in its service. The society's membership gradually rose to 200, the majority being Moslems. The secret of its existence was guarded to the end, Antonius reports. Indeed, the Arab countries had gained their liberation from Turkish rule before it was disclosed. During the war, when the Turks were prosecuting Arab nationlists for treason, one member of *Al-Fatāt* was driven by physical torture to attempt suicide, and another went to the gallows rather than betray the society's secret.[48] *Al-Qahtaniya* was similarly organized and equally renowned for discipline. It chose only those whose patriotism was beyond question and who could be trusted to guard a secret. When suspicion of betrayal in their midst arose, members found it impossible to continue work, and the society was allowed to die of wilful neglect.

The preceding assessments of Islamic societies as they existed between the 7th-20th centuries AD relate directly to most of the issues raised in the questionnaire.[49] Reflections on present and historical records thus suggest that secrecy, dissimulation and covert activities are part of the general life style; that social and political relations are marked by intrigue, deception and conflict; that the

image of "the enemy" is highly developed; that fighting is viewed
positively as a noble undertaking and that people tolerate high levels
of violence. Trust, loyalty and peace are valued positively within
small fellowships of like-minded men who know each other well.
Power and success are respected as attributes of biography; they are
distrusted in the arena of government. In fact, government is always
suspect, unless it is viewed as irredeemably illegitimate, and it is
expected to be harsh.

Most if not all of these norms, values and dispositions are sanctioned by religious texts, foremost among them the Old Testament
and the Koran, and by authoritative interpreters of the *Shāri'a*. Such
questions as "Can Covert Action be Just?" would thus simply not
suggest themselves in the context of Mohammedan law and ethics.

The foreign policies emanating from these societies relay the
norms, values and traditions that are dominant within society. Since
neither the state nor the notion of a long-term national interest is
fully developed in Arab/Islamic thought and actuality, foreign policy
is apt to be as personalized as is the state itself.

The long record of inter-Arab, inter-Islamic and general international relations shows that war has been and continues to be endemic
in this culture realm—a reality explicitly confirmed and approved by
theory and religion. As Majid Khadduri explains,[50] the conduct of
foreign relations has therefore traditionally been dealt with under the
heading of *jihād*. This doctrine of a permanent state of holy war
between "believers" and "unbelievers"—and the latter often included Mohammedans as preceding discussions have illustrated—
was affirmed and explicated in the 14th century by Ibn Khaldūn, the
most esteemed Islamic theoretician. It instructed the faithful that
defeated Muslims were entitled to hope and plan for a resumption of
battle, however long the wait for such a second round, and that the
idea of the *jihād* could be rendered in terms of a *guerra fria* or a
psychological war of nerves, rather than in those of continuous
physical fighting.[51] In this design, then, peace becomes a state of
dormant war and diplomacy an auxiliary or substitute for war. Envoys were therefore naturally suspect as spies, and peace treaties
had to be viewed as diplomatic expedients only.

The advent of lively relations between the Ottoman, Mogul and
Persian empires on one hand, and Western European states on the
other, brought the realization that these traditional Islamic orientations were inadequate and that adjustments to the Occidental law of
war and peace would have to be made. And this revisionist approach

was intensified when Westernization became the watch-word in the 19th and 20th centuries. However, and as preceding sections of this paper have suggested, a near total reversal of orientations set in as soon as Islamic governments discovered toward the end of this century that the West had ceased to press its case effectively.

The clandestine life of the Middle East has obviously always been suffused with "intelligence" and appropriate communication networks. Assassination and related ways of checking enemy lives and activities were common practices. Espionage, being a prerequisite for diplomacy and war, was highly developed in pre-Islamic and Islamic times, among Persians, Turks and Mongols as among Arabs. And the same holds for military intelligence as the dense records of the great transcontinental invasions, campaigns, battles and sieges show. For example, the twin causes of war and espionage have been consistently well served in the Orient by "tunnelling" the enemy's spatial and psychological terrain. This particular art which seems to have originated with the Mongols, was copied and perfected by the Turks, the Chinese and adjacent Asian peoples. In our times it is being exemplified by relentless North Korean attempts to undermine Seoul and take over South Korea by employing this tunnelling tactic. In mid-15th century it was dramatically deployed by the Ottoman Turks during the last phase of their determined yet protracted siege of Constantinople, the Byzantine Empire's prize. In fact, and as described by the Venetian ambassador Nicolò Barbaro in his diary of this historic siege, tunnelling may well have been the decisive Turkish stratagem; for neither bombardments nor pitched battles on ship were as demoralizing to the spirited defenders of the Christian city as the daily discovery of yet another tunnel undermining the foundations of their walls, and therewith also of their willpower and identity.

These and other psychological aspects of intelligence and warfare were developed throughout Asia, most systematically in Achaemenid Persia's statecraft, India's *Arthasastra* world (authoritatively defined as early as the 4th century BC) and the records of China's Legalist statesmen (those who succeeded in the 3rd century BC in unifying China), among them in particular Sun Tzu's *Art of War* (probable date between 400-320 BC) in which the stress in strategy is squarely placed on the need to "encircle" the enemy's mind. The striking convergence of these greatly different Oriental cultures upon affirmation of the need to cancel, neutralize or subvert the human mind is a function of the fact that all Asian despotisms were, and continue to be, conceived as conflict systems in which human nature is feared and distrusted and in which considerations of war have traditionally eclipsed considerations of peace.

The traditional relation of foreign policy to intelligence including covert action can thus not be covered by our distinctions and definitions which derive from premises altogether contrary to those accepted in the East. Further, developments strongly indicate that Westernization has not displaced the basic norms of statecraft which have conditioned thought and behavior for more than a millennium and which are widely (and naturally) associated by present generations with the Orient's superiority, in some cases victory, over the Occidental enemy. The American CIA may have been considered worthy of imitation by Westernized ruling elites in Egypt, South Korea and other states as long as they had reason to associate it with US influence and power. No such reason is perceivable today. The US has forfeited too much of its power, and the American "model" CIA is discredited, having been knocked out deliberately by the government and nation that it was designed to serve.

In this situation which is aggravated by the tutorial presence of Soviet, Cuban and East German intelligence advisors in such nearby countries as Ethiopia, Libya and Syria, non-Western non-communist governments should be allowed, if not encouraged, to trust their own modes of perceiving the enemy and of assessing threats.

C. *Classical India*

A comparative historical review of political systems justifies the view that the one brought forth by Hindu India is philosophically the most impressive, even as it may well have been politically the most ruinous. My main reason for presenting this Indian creation in brief outline is twofold: no other system has addressed problems of intelligence, specifically covert action, as comprehensively and methodically, and none stands in greater contrast to American statecraft than this one.

It should be noted by way of preface that the *artha* world of warring kingdoms vanished in the wake of Arab, Turkish and Mongol conquests, and that the *artha* philosophy of success was officially either subsumed or superseded by non-Hindu strands of thought, among them, after the 18th century, English common law and equity. However, many learned and patriotic members of the anglicized Indian elite continue to maintain that if modern Indian administration is analysed to its bases, *artha* doctrines and practices as elucidated by Kautilya, the Brahmin counsellor of Chandragupta Maurya (probable dates for the Maurya dynasty: 322-185 BC), will be found to be still in force; in fact, that Indian society as described in the *Mahabharata* (not later than the 4th century AD) is not essentially different from what holds its sway in India today.[52]

This perspective had already been projected in 1880 by Sir Henry Maine in his comparative studies of Eastern and Western village communities where he remarks that Mohammedan influences on Indian institutions and customs had been so slight as to be hardly worth taking into account. And the same theme has been stressed recently by the Bengali writer Nirad Chaudhuri as when he notes in a commentary on Mrs. Gandhi's determined policy to weaken Pakistan that all Muslim conquests had driven the Hindu mind back to its roots, leaving nothing but a residue of bitter hatred for these conquerors. Believing that the anglicized Hindus are the recessive not the dominant minority in India today, Chaudhuri concludes, regretfully, that a similar "return to roots" is in full swing today and that the effects of Westernization will not last.

The only decisive foreign influence that has been consistently acknowledged in India, usually in terms of praise and particularly eloquently by Jawaharlal Nehru in *The Discovery of India*, is that which Achaemenid Persia exerted on the Maurya state in NW India. The case for this special Indo-Persian relationship is strongly confirmed by historians, among them E. J. Rapson:

> If we must seek for any foreign influence in Maurya times, we should think (rather) of the Achaemenids, whose domination extended to the Indus. As is well known, the architecture of the period, and also the style of Acoka's edicts, show definite traces of Persian influence, and the expressions "the King's eye" and "the King's ears," occurring in the Arthasastra (p. 175 and p. 328) seem to furnish literary indications pointing in the same direction.[53]

It is further strengthened by the fact first, that Persian influences continued to reach India during the Afghan and Mogul periods when the Islamic courts were strictly Persianized, and second, that Persian remained the language of courtlife and diplomacy right up to the British period.

The principles of statecraft with which Hinduism is identified, are set out clearly, precisely and usually poetically in India's classical literature, more particularly in the *Arthasastras* (of which Kautilya's is the most renowned), the *Dharmasastras*, the Laws of Manu, the *Mahabharata* (India's great national epic), the *Ramayana* and several collections of didactic beastfables—texts that Indians have been reading, reciting or memorizing throughout time. All converge on the message that in the domain of *artha*—which comprises the science of politics, economics, diplomacy and war—only winning counts. What needs to be borne in mind though is that *artha* norms for thought and conduct are carefully set apart in Hindu logic and metaphysics from three codes that are equally mandatory in the pursuit of three other major ends of life: namely, *kama* (pleasure), *dharma* (duty, especially as it relates to caste regulations), and *moksa* (the quest for release from life and its illusions, including *artha* aims).

In marked contrast to biographical patterns common in Europe and America which express the aspiration to develop an all-encompassing philosophy of life, Hindus have been directed for millennia to live by a plurality of philosophies. And the complexity of these separate commitments grows when one remembers that guidelines for proper behavior also differ for each of the four castes and each of the four stages of life.

The *artha* polity was conceived and administered from Maurya times onward as a bureaucratic police state. Its keystone was the monarch who belonged to the warrior caste. This meant that each king—and the subcontinent was dotted with *artha* principalities—had the sacred duty (not a political option) to be at war if he was to gain spiritual merit. Likewise, he was instructed by his *dharma* to keep his subjects in their respective caste places and enforce his rule upon them by wielding *danda*, the rod of punishment, "lest the strong torment the weak as fish are fried on a pike or as in water they devour each other." It is in accordance with this law of the fishes that Kautilya sets out in minutest detail "four kinds of torture, six punishments, seven kinds of whipping, two kinds of suspension from above and the water tube."

All texts are pervaded by the assumption that no human being can ever be trusted, that enemies lurk everywhere, and that the king must know how to distinguish and deal with different battles of intrigues and different groups of troubles, molestations and obstructions. On the authority of the *Mahabharata* each kingdom must therefore have its roots in spies and secret agents; for "as the wind moves everywhere and penetrates all created beings, so should the king penetrate everywhere by sending his spies to report disloyalty among subjects, ministers and heirs."

The Maurya palace as described by the Greek ambassador Megasthenes and by Kautilya remained the model for future kings. Everything here bespeaks caution, we read. The structure of the palace itself includes mazes, secret and underground passages, hollow pillars, hidden staircases, collapsible floors. Everyone has his own apartments here, none of the interior officials are allowed to

communicate with the outside, and the king must change his living
quarter daily. The kitchen too is in a secret place, and a multitude of
tasters are at work. The signs of poison in the viands and in the
demeanor of persons are carefully noted, and the instruments of the
shampooer and others must be handled by the body guard. The royal
executive's daily agenda was about as follows:

> Aroused by music at the end of the sixth nocturnal hour, he receives the
> salutations of his counsellors, and interviews the doctors and kitchen
> officials; then he reflects upon the principles of polity and forms his plans,
> after which he sends out his secret emissaries, and hears reports of his
> military and financial advisers. Next comes the hour for appearing in the
> Audience Hall or in the Law Courts, and considering the affairs of the
> public. . . . After this the King retires for his bath and repast; receives
> those who bear gifts, interviews his inspectors, corresponds by letters
> with his ministers, and makes plans of espionage. This sixth hour having
> now arrived, he takes his ease and reconsiders his policy. In the seventh
> and eighth hours, the cool of the day, he inspects his horses, elephants
> and arsenal, and consults with the commander-in-chief; at sunset he per-
> forms the usual religious ceremony. The first hour of night brings in the
> reports of spies. Then come the second bath and meal, followed by
> religious meditation. To the sound of music His Majesty retires for rest.[54]

It is the considered judgment of Indian and foreign authorities that
the Indian genius for systematic exposition finds its culmination in
foreign policy and that the doctrine of the *mandala* is the most remarkable of many original ideas in this domain. The theory holds
that a kingdom is an ally or an enemy according to its geographical
position with respect to the intending conqueror. The *mandala* or
circle of states usually consists of twelve kings, although the system
could be enlarged to include many more.[55] Each king (note that "the
state" is not the unit here) is expected to chart the course of aggression upon which he must be engaged scientifically and realistically,
viewing his own domain as the center or target of the *mandalas* or
rings of states. In this context his natural enemies are his next door
neighbors, his natural friends are in the adjoining circle. The third
ring is composed of his enemies' friends, the fourth of friends of his
allies, and so forth. The king is admonished to be particularly careful
in measuring his distance from the dominant power, that is to say
from that king in the galaxy of kings who has the capacity to fight
without allies and is therefore known as the "neutral" king.

The workings of this principle can be seen throughout the history
of Hindu India in the temporary alliances of two kingdoms to accomplish the encirclement and destruction of the kingdoms between
them—at which time of course the former "friend" becomes automatically enemy number one, i.e. the immediate subject of the next

attack. However, theory and reality also converge on the proposition that none of the positions or relations indicated by this model of political geometry should be absolutely trusted. Rather, Indian inter-kingdom relations were conceived as an endless game of chess, a ritual as it were, in which each player was expected to improve his status by every possible means at his disposal, for as the *Mahabharata* has it, "both kinds of wisdom, straight and crooked, should be within call of the king."

Six major instruments of policy (*Arthasastra*, Book VII) are available to the king so that he may advance from deterioration via stagnation to progress, and each of these has its subdivisions and didactically important illustrations in which the need for covert operations is invariably stressed. Whoever knows the interdependence of the six kinds of policy, we read, plays at his pleasure with kings. The paramount policy is war in the name of *danda*. Its opposite is peace, but the syndrome of peace, negotiation and conciliation is here understood as appeasement in the way of the snake charmer, by deceit and trickery, or by casting illusions. In short, peace is a tactic of war in Hindu statecraft as shown by the following excerpts from the major texts:

> The whole world stands in awe of the king ready to strike.
> If you have no power, you are a conquered king.
> Only rulers who have no other remedy should seek peace.
> Only weakness calls for conciliation and alliances.
> Like a snake devouring a mouse, the Earth devours a king who is inclined to peace.

However, the advantages of a "double policy" are also pressed (*Arthasastra* Books 6-14):

> As a fowler, carefully uttering cries similar to those of the birds he wishes to seize or kill, captures and brings them under his power, even so should a king bring his foes under subjection and then slay them if he likes.
>
> Without trusting one's foe in reality, one should behave as if one trusted him completely.
>
> Speak soft words before you smite and while you smite the foe . . . by a sudden pitched battle, by poison, by corrupting his allies, by gift of wealth, by any means you should destroy your foe.
>
> The enemy should be broken into fragments like an earthen jar on a rock.

The interpenetration of domestic and foreign statecraft to which reference was made earlier, is well illustrated by these political maxims which point to the concept of "the enemy" and to the consequent need for intrigue and espionage as main unifying factors. Kautilya thus instructs the king that as between power and skill for intrigue, intrigue is more reliable, for:

> He who has the eye of knowledge, and is acquainted with the science of polity, can with little effort make use of his skills for intrigue, and can succeed by means of conciliation, and other strategic means and by spies and chemical appliances in overreaching even those kings who are possessed of enthusiam and power.[56]

The key to successful intrigue is good espionage. This wisdom reaches back to the *Rg Veda* where the spies of the god Varuna are pictured seated around him in prominent positions while he holds court. This was the case also at the Maurya court where Megasthenes found spies numerous enough to be considered a special class of society. Of them he writes:

> The sixth class consists of the overseers, to whom is assigned the duty of watching all that goes on and making reports secretly to the king. Some are entrusted with the inspection of the city, and others with that of the army. The former employ as their co-adjutors the courtesans of the city, and the latter the courtesans of the camp. The ablest and most trustworthy men are appointed to fill these offices.[57]

Assisted by their ministers, who had themselves been tested under espionage, Hindu kings thus proceeded to create spies for every fathomable contingency—spies under the guise of a fraudulent disciple, a recluse, a householder, a merchant, an ascetic practicing austerities, a classmate or a colleague, a fire-brand, a prisoner, a mendicant woman and near countless other categories of recruits. In fact, no subject in the *Arthasastra* receives as devoted and detailed attention as this one. Under such headings as "Government based on Deceit" and "Battle of Intrigues" we learn how spies under the guise of physicians or saucemakers may make a seditious minister believe that he is suffering from a fatal disease in order then to contrive to poison him by prescribing a medication; how suspects may learn through the device of fortune-telling of an impending disaster in their lives—a forecast that is then promptly carried out; and how prostitute spies in the guise of chaste women may cause themselves to be enamored of persons who are seditious and thus "entrap" them. Spies trained to pose as hunchbacks, mendicants or saints might have the task of luring a prince to kill the king his father, deal secret death to disloyal royal servants or sow seeds of dissensions in an enemy camp. No method of trickery was out of bounds here. Yet the very same type of agent was also sent wandering in the realm so as to report on adulteration of food or on injustice and corruption in the courts.

External spying proceeded in analogous ways. The text advises that foreign spies must be found out by spies of like profession and that one must always conceal one's emotions before the spies of one's enemy. We also read that foreign spies are dealt with best when they are seduced by female spies and then murdered. The main object of sending spies into another kingdom is to sow dissension, seek information, and "seduce wild tribes with rewards of wealth and honor so that they may be incited to devastate the enemy land." Extra credit is given for killing a king, "slaying the enemy's commander-in-chief and inciting a circle of states." These activities fall under the heading of "fiery spies"—Asia's earliest guerrillas. Spies with weapons, fire and poison, are thus dispatched to destroy supply stores and granaries, and in the guise of nightwalkers or firekeepers, to set fires and generally demoralize the population. "Taking advantage of peace and friendship with the enemy,"[58] they penetrate his fort disguised as ascetics, merchants, members of caravans or of processions leading a bride, for the purpose of killing the king, destroying his cattle or his merchandise, and of poisoning his food supplies. All such operations are meticulously prepared as the following passage from Kautilya illustrates:

> The conqueror's spies who are residing as traders in the enemy's forts, and those who are living as cultivators in the enemy's villages, as well as those who are living as cowherds or ascetics in the district borders of the enemy's country, may send through merchants information to another neighboring enemy, or a wild chief, or a scion of the enemy's family, or an imprisoned prince, that the enemy's country is to be captured. When their secret emissaries come as invited, they are to be pleased with rewards of wealth and honour and shown the enemy's weak points; and with the help of the emissaries, the spies should strike the enemy at his weak points.[59]

The most favored and talked about category of operatives in this conspiratorial system is that comprising the "shaven heads," monks and holy men who have licence to conspire and kill in holy places which the enemy, under the influence of faith, frequents on occasions of worshipping gods or of pilgrimage.[60] And lastly, there were the official diplomats. Numerous categories of envoys are distinguished in the texts, but all seem to have been well integrated in the "system." In fact, an ambassador is described as "but an open spy," and it is expected that he live with his spies in whatever disguises these are required to function. However, according to the Laws of Manu it is "he alone who makes and breaks the allies of the king."[61]

All types of agents were directed by a regular department of espionage which was in charge of checking incoming information through three separate channels; correlating the reports it received from the agents, and above all seeing to it that there were spies to spy on spies. Discipline was harsh, of course: whoever divulged a secret as by talking in his sleep "was to be torn to pieces."

Not much would be gained—in fact the comparative method might be strained to the breaking point—if we were to compare American and Indian approaches to intelligence, or to juxtapose the CIA and the ancient Indian institutes of espionage. From our point of view the entire *artha* order is as irrational as it is pointless. It may even impress some as utterly immoral, since there is nothing here that could be brought in line with what we call law and ethics, or with what we read in the Declaration of Independence about universal human rights. And yet, while Indian kingdoms rose and fell in seemingly endless "times of trouble," Indian civilization soared. And this—it is here suggested—is by no means freakish or coincidental; for the very same ways of thought and perception that made for the *Arthasastra* and the life in which only winning counted, also made for sculptured works of art and for the *Upanishads,* which few minds in the West would not judge to be sublime. As Heinrich Zimmer observed in connection with this seeming paradox,[62] the ruthless philosophy of politics and the super-human achievements in metaphysics represent the two sides of a single experience in life.

D. *Venice and the United States*

The preceding sections have indicated that Persian, Indian, Arab and Turkish predispositions to politics in general and the relation between foreign policy and intelligence in particular converge on numerous conceptual and organizational points, and that there are a few elements in each of these Asian systems which have suggestive or didactic value also for us. By and large, however, these records are culturally too alien and historically too distant to be considered relevant in our nation's present quest for better security through better intelligence, even though they do help to explain why we have significantly failed in recent times to locate and assess crucial intelligence-related data in the societies now administering these non-Western traditions.

This kind of judgment does not hold for the old republic of Venice which provides the last case study of statecraft for this paper. In fact, the analogies between Venice and the United States are quite numerous. Each took off from Christian Western Europe's law-centered civilization, yet each soon deviated from its heritage and succeeded in fashioning its own destiny as a culturally and politically unique society. The story of the American emancipation is well known. In respect of Venice one must note that it began its political existence as a small settler nation on the very edge of Italy's northeastern coast, but that it was almost immediately drawn into close relations with the Greek Orthodox Byzantine Empire (then in official control of the region) and with the Islamic nations of the Levant, even as it was briefly part also of Charlemagne's realm. The territorial home base of the island city state was thus slight and precarious, whereas that of the US was an immense landmass flanked by oceans. Yet both were cast by geography into the mold of outward looking maritime nations, and both were determined from the start to defy all foreign pressures that might compromise the political independence and cultural uniqueness they had won.

At this juncture in time, only 200 years away from its creation, we cannot predict America's future. Of independent Venice we know that it endured from the 7th century to 1797 when its statehood was extinguished by Napoleon. Not unlike Byzantium, (its mentor nation in many significant ways), which had also preserved its identity for one thousand years (from circa the 5th century to 1453 when Constantinople was taken by the Turks), but quite contrary to the US, Venice had always been fully conscious of the fact that it had to maintain its liberty and statehood in a multicultural world environment and that it was encircled by alien, usually hostile peoples. Also like the Byzantines, Venetians knew that they could not rely exclusively on defence through warfare which would have exhausted available energies and resources, and that they had to perfect systems of diplomacy and intelligence if survival and advance to greatness were to be assured.

The prerequisite for this type of statecraft was a well developed sense of national identity and knowledge of just what it was that had to be defended and perfected at all cost. The basic dispositions, values and institutions which sustained this existential mode were distinctly European, having been refined in Italy during the centuries of the Renaissance. They were thus the birthright as it were of all city states, but it was the Venetian imprimatur they received which stamped them with timeless significance in international history.

For example, the concept of the secular state was taken seriously throughout Italy, but it was in Venice only that the idea rallied all citizens in a spirit of fierce loyalty and patriotism. This was so, Bouwsma explains,[63] because Venice represented to generations of Venetians a realm of unique and abiding values which it was their particular obligation to conserve and to transmit to subsequent generations. Further, this sense of continuity was cultivated deliberately. From the early 16th century onward Venice thus relied on an official historian who was charged to guard the state's traditions; for as explicitly noted in a decree, history solidifies the reputation of states even as it instructs rulers in the management of their daily business and assists them "to foresee with greater prudence things to come." Historical analysis was thus generally accepted here as an instrument of statecraft—a fact noted with admiration by the 16th century Florentine historian Guicciardini in his *History of Italy* as when he comments on the conviction shared by "certain of the oldest and most reputable members of the Venetian Senate that Venice enjoyed a particular advantage in her ability to wait for the opportunity of times and the maturity of occasions."

These ongoing civic commitments explain why Venetian institutions of government, being the organic growth of centuries, aroused pride and loyalty, why Venice was not plagued by the kind of chronic internal dissensions that marred the art of government elsewhere, and why Venetian policies were steadier than those of rival states.

Venice, then, was essentially unified when it had to cope with problems in its farflung foreign relations—and these were legion in each century.[64] Moreover, it could count on a cosmopolitan citizenry which understood the problems and ever changing realities in the conduct of foreign affairs. Being primarily a nation of merchants, seafarers, and travellers, Venetians had thus been conditioned from early times onward to view the world as a complex of ascertainable facts. This meant that they were always keenly aware of the need to sharpen their faculties of observation, appraise their risks and opportunities realistically and perfect their methods of evaluating the intelligence they got so as to be able to enter their gains and losses on the proper side of the business ledgers they kept.

Realism and objectivity were inbred Venetian qualities and diplomacy was rightly viewed as a natural calling for Venetians. It was thus expected that any citizen abroad was likely to think of himself as the nation's agent or asset, eager to collect and forward information that might be useful to the national cause. The records tell us, for example, that Venetian physicians whose services were loaned to foreign sovereigns felt morally free to send their home government detailed reports whenever important political and commercial matters would come to their attention. Likewise, it was well known among contemporaries in Italy that a Venetian cardinal was first and foremost a nationalist who could be persuaded easily to transmit to his government confidential intelligence to which he had had access in his capacity as servant of the Catholic Church at Rome.

However, the fame of Venetian statecraft does not rest on the unofficial *ad hoc* functions of Venetian citizens abroad, or on the *sub rosa* activities of the kind of secret agents and native informers that were used increasingly as the fortunes of the state were declining. Rather, it rests on the official operations of a specially qualified diplomatic intelligence service and on the systematic supervision of all foreign missions by the home government.

In respect of training and endowment it was generally understood in Renaissance Italy that diplomacy demands "the whole man." A Venetian ambassador was thus expected to live up to this model and know "how to do things well." And indeed, the typical envoy who emerges from biographical and other contemporary records is at once a statesman, a soldier, a man of business, a linguist and a scholar who spends his leisure hours in literary and scientific studies or in correspondence with artists and authors from many lands. However, all of these gifts and accomplishments were conceived primarily as resources of the state for it was the envoy's primary function to uphold Venetian interests against the rest of the world by carrying out the government's policies and orders, no matter what they might be. Further, and as carefully set out by Ermaleo Barbaro, a renowned Venetian authority on diplomatic method, ambassadors were supposed to listen, observe, and cultivate the confidence of heads of state and other influential personages. They were admonished not to behave like spies,[65] nor were they to associate diplomacy with conspiracy, assassination, or corruption.

Clandestine operations of all kinds, including hard espionage and counter-espionage, gradually accrued to all European intelligence systems from the 16th century onward. Two principal factors accounted for this development: the increasingly aggressive policies emanating from France and Spain (the Spanish intelligence apparatus as administered at the English Court by Chapuys and Gondomar appears to have been the most diversified in the 16th century) and the spread of resident embassies. Odd as it may seem to us, the latter were generally distrusted.[66] A special, that is a non-resident envoy could afford to be an honorable Christian gentleman, we learn, but a resident had to be viewed as at best a kind of licensed spy. At any rate, resident embassies became the norm throughout Europe—with Venice maintaining most of them—and by 1600 under-cover agents were employed by just about all of them.

Yet, and after full allowance is made for aspects of intelligence

work that contemporaries found unsavoury, the fact remains that the
resident ambassadors in 15th century Italy—and among them particularly those representing Venice—succeeded time and time again in
averting war, preserving or restoring the peninsular system of the
balance of power, and thus in assuring four crucially important decades of relative peace during which the civilization of Renaissance
Italy could reach its full maturity.

This accomplishment is of course a function of the talents, training
and discipline of agents who knew how to detect each shift in power
relations and facilitate realignments and who knew how to communicate swiftly with their home governments. In fact, it is this latter
aspect of statecraft, namely the relation between diplomats and the
supervising central administration, which accounts for the renown
of the Venetian intelligence system.

The sovereignty of Venice resided in the Great Council. At the
next level of decision-making was the Senate which supervised all
affairs of state, administered foreign policy, waged war, concluded
peace and appointed ambassadors. Standing somewhat apart from
the official hierarchy of governing bodies was the Council of Ten.
Established early in the 14th century to deal with a particular crisis,
it nonetheless became an alternative to the Senate and was regularly
asked to deal with extraordinary problems, no doubt because—being
small—it could act with speed and secrecy. Its position was strengthened in the 16th century by the addition to it of a group of leading
senators known as the *Giunta*.[67] Lest one forgets, at the very top of
the Venetian administration was the Doge who was important mainly
as the corporeal symbol of the idea of liberty.

All envoys and agents had to report to the Senate that had given
them their appointments and instructions in the first place, and they
did so regularly by dispatches—often sent daily—which informed the
government of the course of events within the envoy's range of
observation. But at the end of their term of duty they were obligated,
in accordance with a decree of the Grand Council (1268), to deliver
a full *viva voce* report of their mission; and a later decree (1425)
ordered that these "relations" (*relazioni*) be committed to writing.
Not all of the *Relations of the Ambassadors* survive, but as Mattingly
concludes from his readings of the records,[68] a formal relation was
experienced as an intellectual treat by the senators. And the same
was true of contemporaries in Italy and the rest of Europe—whether
allies or adversaries—who consulted a Venetian report as we would
an authoritative text on current international affairs. Manuscript

copies therefore caught high prices as early as two years after the report had actually been presented.

The very conception of this mode of collecting intelligence elicited admiration, and it is not surprising therefore that the Venetian precedent was soon emulated first by Spain and later by most other European nations. However, it is of course the content of these unequalled archives that has earned them time-transcendent significance. What readers found in the *relazioni* were carefully prepared statements of the political situation at the ambassador's post that addressed a wide range of topics. Apart from summarizing recent events and prevalent trends and projecting likely future developments, they drew the government's attention to the area's topography, geography and economy, and they assessed trade possibilities, local laws, and governmental institutions. Further and above all perhaps, they noted the historical antecedents of all phenomena to which they attached particular importance, and they dwelt in considerable depth upon the biographies and character traits of all leading men, Barbaro's diary of the siege of Constantinople (*supra*) exemplifies the sensitivity and precision of such assessments in conditions of extraordinary stress. And the same holds for the remarkable series of *relazioni* that mirrored the lifestyle, ruling institutions and policy making processes of the Ottoman regime—documents without which important chapters in the history of the entire region could not possibly have been written,[69] as well as for the multitude of accounts that analysed the turbulence in the Papal establishment, the policies and plots of Spain, the complex English scenario in which Henry VIII and his successors forged the destiny of their nation, and so on.

One of the tentative conclusions which a comparison of Venetian and American intelligence systems suggests, is to the effect that diplomatic representation and intelligence work were much more closely linked in Venice than they are in the US. And in the specific context of intelligence it appears that the integral Venetian approach did not favor the kind of categorization of several distinct elements of intelligence that is institutionalized here. Venetian ambassadors had their public declared functions as do ours, but contrary to the latter, they were also supposed to be undercover agents specifically commissioned to shape the thought patterns of men and thus the policies of foreign governments.

In the discharge of this latter task they were given wide leeway as well as reliable protection. One reason for this official disposition was of course the absence of international accords on the legal status of diplomats (notably residents) and their embassies abroad. And in this respect, the Venetians may be said to have anticipated Grotius who was to argue that although justice and equity required equal penalties for equal crimes, the law of nations made an exception of ambassadors because their security as a class was more important to the public welfare than their punishment as individuals. Their security would rest on a slippery foundation, he concluded, if they were accountable to anyone but their own sovereign. But the main explanation for the comprehensive nature of the entire Venetian foreign policy establishment is found in the broad national consensus on the nature of foreign affairs and the purposes of intelligence operations upon which the government and its foreign agents were able to count for several centuries.

Something approaching this kind of moral unity has also marked American intelligence operations after the end of the Second World War. The covert action program linking the CIA with the NSA is a case in point, all the more so as I think that the Venetians would have viewed it as a normal diplomatic enterprise. In reflecting on this 15 year-long relationship Cord Meyer explains[70] that this cooperative venture was anchored in a broad agreement as to what the course of American foreign policy should be and in a shared commitment to support democratic organizations and oppose communist attempts to dominate the international student community. But the consensus gradually eroded under the pressure of student opposition to the Vietnam war until it was extinguished by the *Ramparts* revelation, an episode that had altogether nefarious consequences for the nation as a whole. Meyer believes that if the Agency had assessed more realistically and promptly the shift in student opinion, it could have moved in time to arrange for an amicable severance of relations with the NSA. However, it is not likely that such a dénouement would have had the effect also of arresting the drift toward demoralization to which the entire intelligence community was more or less deliberately consigned by its own presiding officers when they chose to elevate their personal moral scruples of the day into guiding principles for long range national policies and operations.

Venice never produced the equivalent of the Schlesinger memorandum (dated May 9, 1973)[71] which directed every employee and ex-employee to report on past and present Agency activities which might be construed to be outside the legislative charter of the Agency. Yet in the 16th century—a period closely similar to the era in which we find ourselves—it too was buffetted by profound crises of self-confidence and they too were symbolized by leaks and other violations of the norms of confidentiality. The particular developments in foreign relations that induced the widespread consciousness of the nation's faltering destiny were connected with the League of Cambrai (1509)—a massive conspiracy on the part of France and Spain to knock out Venice. Constrained by these continuous threats in the Christian West to come to terms with the Islamic East, the government (in this case the Council of Ten) directed its plenipotentiary at Constantinople to try and procure a settlement on the basis of an exchange of prisoners and territory equivalent to the arrangement of a *status quo ante bellum.* However, the envoy had in reserve the power of concluding peace on any terms. Knowledge of the latter terms was communicated to the Porte by treachery and the Republic was therefore forced to surrender several places in the Morea.

The shock of this experience (1538-39) and the discovery that the informers, among them the secretary to the Ten, had been in the pay of France, led in 1539 to the formal establishment[72] of three *Inquisitors into Revelation of State Secrets* whose powers were practically unlimited provided that the three functionaries agreed.

The Inquisitors in concert with the Decimvirs sometimes committed serious mistakes, but scholarly authorities on their recorded operations (1411 to 1793) agree that a weakened Venice was strongly sustained by this institution, if only because diplomacy was the only shield of the Republic in the ensuing centuries.

Conclusion

The challenges confronting US statecraft today require many kinds of responses, among them the following.

On the level of strategic thought in general we should remember that sound foreign policies and definitions of the national interest depend upon self-knowledge as well as upon accurate perceptions of other nations. We should therefore recognize that the US is a culturally unique society with a heritage not shared by other peoples. This means that we should drop or seriously modify the traditional assumption that our primary norms and values are in theory at least valid everywhere. It also means that we should abandon the single-minded search for international systems and such allegedly universally acceptable principles as civil liberties or human rights—a policy course which has preoccupied us in the last troubled decades, but one which has brought us perilously close to losing our national identity and therewith our bearings in the world environment. The urgent need today is rather to find out just what *our* truly inalienable sustaining ideas and interests really are so that we may proceed to structure our relations with other states and systems in a realistic way.

This task presupposes a careful stock-taking of all other societies, be they friendly or hostile. It is in my view best accomplished by employing the comparative method, perhaps by reliance on the type of propositional inventory included in this paper. Intelligence gathering of the kind there suggested seems indispensable if we wish to devise and deploy modes of statecraft that are appropriate to each of the greatly various systems, states and peoples that we are dealing with today, nowhere more so than in contexts bearing on the relation between foreign policy and covert action.

The foregoing case studies of South Asian, West Asian and North African societies address most of the themes listed in the questionnaire, and a comparison of those findings shows a consensus on the following: Traditional and modern patterns of political organization do not accommodate either the Western norm of the territorially delimited nation state or constitutional democracy. Rather, they converge on expansionism and personalized authoritarian rule. Neither of these polities and ruling establishments is legitimized in terms of local codes of law or ethics. All—be they empires, kingdoms or modern despotisms disguised as republics—are therefore absolutely dependent upon military force and statecraft, more particularly espionage and covert action.

In the absence of orderly provisions for succession, changes in government are thus routinely induced today as they were formerly by coups d'état and assassinations. Further, in the absence of fixed state borders, pretenders to power simply strike out from established bases so as to acquire dominion over other lands and nations. What is noteworthy here is this: the tactics in such extended power plays are the same as those employed in conspiratorial operations at the home base, for both situations routinely call for the kind of intelligence and policing work that will assure the ouster of an incumbent or rival claimant. In other words, and as exemplified in history by the see-saw campaigns of Mongol, Afghan and Persian armies in central and southwest Asia, and in our times by the military moves of Libyan and Algerian imperialisms into the vast Saharan and sub-Saharan reaches of Africa, domestic and foreign affairs interpenetrate here in ways not common in the West. This means, *mutatis mutandis*, that domestic and foreign espionage interpenetrate also, and that our careful distinctions between the functions of the FBI and the CIA have no equivalents there. In short, intelligence actions dominate the government as well as all transactions in foreign relations, thus corroborating the wisdom of India's sacred literature which is to the effect that a kingdom is totally dependent on spies and secret agents.

Further, but in the same integral context of oriental statecraft, we should not forget that "peace" and "war" are not the opposites we perceive them to be. After all, not only is peace traditionally viewed in Asian and African cultures as stagnation or as a tactic of war, but fighting is esteemed everywhere as a natural and noble activity. Also, the conviction rules that there is always an enemy somewhere. The world views prevalent in the non-western non-communist societies surveyed for purposes of this paper allow for "world unity" through conquest or, as in Islam in particular, through conversion to the faith. However, they exclude hopes for "A World Without War" or for a world of culturally disparate nations, all unified by visions of peace. It is this constellation of values and traditions which explains why diplomacy is related more closely to war than to peace and why it is commonly assumed that diplomats are meant to be spies. Contrary to the US, then, these two categories of personnel are not held to radically different jurisdictional and behavioral norms. Nor is either hamstrung in its operations by legislative or moral inhibitions.

The traditions of statecraft here discussed could not have settled in such enduring ways had society itself not continued to be a proving ground for their deployment. As suggested in different sections of this paper, generation after generation was tutored in such arts of intelligence as verbal dissimulation, indirect allusive communication, conspiracy and above all confidentiality. Covert thought and covert action are thus rational and normal here where men have come to value the closed, not the open society.

The point that our modes of perception, thought, organization and communication are significantly different from those here analysed, needs not to be labored in this conclusion. Nor is it reasonable to indulge in the expectation that these non-western societies will slowly but surely adapt their orientations to ours. In fact, and as developments in criminal law, government and diplomacy have incontrovertibly shown in the last decades, "progress" and security are being identified with a return to trusted models of their own past, not with our visions of the future. And since it cannot be denied that some aspects of non-western statecraft are congruous—albeit superficially—with Marxist-Leninist thought and practice, it should be in our interest to focus on these traditions rather than on our preferred visions.

In further elaboration of the need to modify our approaches to these culturally alien societies, it is here suggested that we must relax our commitments to certain theories, systems and definitions if we wish our intelligence services to do their work successfully.

Our guidelines for conceptualizing and actualizing intelligence include numerous definitions which distinguish carefully between covert action, clandestine collection or espionage, counterintelligence, paramilitary operations, and other aspects, and which indicate unequivocally what can and what cannot be done lawfully, and which are or are not secret operations. All definitions issue from records of shared experience, and these are no exception to the norm. They therefore belong to our administrative system. However, they are not meaningful in the societies surveyed in this paper, and they may therefore greatly inhibit our intelligence operations in these foreign fields. Here where secrecy is the *sine qua non* of success, the domain of what we call covert action is all encompassing. Yet it is precisely this element of intelligence which is critically embattled in the US today.

It is no doubt difficult to revive the dying art of covert action in the present climate of opinion, but it should be possible to loosen the hold of law upon this art and to tighten the rules assuring confidentiality. In reexamining the relationship between foreign policy and covert action we would in general be well advised to return to Dean Acheson's counsel which was to the effect that the vocabulary of morals and ethics is inadequate to discuss or test the foreign politics of states.[73]

Notes

1. Hugh Tovar, "Covert Action" in Roy Godson ed., *Intelligence Requirements for the 1980's: Elements of Intelligence*, (National Strategy Information Center, Inc., Washington, D.C. 1979), pp. 65-79.

2. Newton S. Miler, "Counterintelligence," in Godson ed., *op. cit.*, pp. 49-60.

3. Daniel O. Graham, "Analysis and Estimates" in Godson, ed., *op. cit.*, pp. 23-29.

4. Samel Halpern. "Clandestine Collection," in Godson, ed., *op. cit.*, pp. 37-43.

5. Donovan Pratt, "Operational Security: What Ought to be the relationship between Counterintelligence, Collection and Covert Action?", Colloquium April 1980. See Godson, ed., *Intelligence Requirements for the 1980's: Counterintelligence*, National Strategy Information Center, Inc. (Washington, D.C. 1980), pp. 228-245.

6. *The New York Times*, September 27, 1980.

7. "Perception and Commitment," *Bulletin of the Atomic Scientists*, vol. XIX, No. 1, February 1963, pp. 14 ff.

8. For an elaboration of this theme see Adda B. Bozeman, "The Roots of the American Commitment to the Rights of Man" in *Rights and Responsibilities; International, Social and Individual Dimensions*, Proceedings of a Conference at the Center for Study of the American Experience, Annenberg School of Communications, University of Southern California, November 1978, pp. 51-102 (University of Southern California Press, 1980); "Interference or Legitimate International Concerns: The Human Factor in US-Soviet Relations" Proceedings of the *National Security Affairs Conference*, July 1977, National Defense University, pp. 167-183 (Washington, D.C., August 1977); reprinted as *How to Think About Human Rights* by the National Strategy Information Center, New York, 1978;"Law and Diplomacy in the Quest for Peace," in *The Virginia Quarterly Review*, vol. 55, Winter 1979, No. 1, pp. 1-21; and *The Future of Law in a Multicultural World*, (Princeton University Press, 1971).

9. William Colby and Peter Forbath, *Honorable Men, My Life in the CIA* (New York, 1978).

10. *Op. cit.*, p. 298 in connection with comments on the CIA's Third Culture Analysis.

11. *Ibid.* p. 275.

12. "Approaches to Reform of the Intelligence Community" in Godson ed., *Intelligence Requirements for the 1980's: Elements of Intelligence*, National Strategy Information Center, Inc. (Washington, DC 1979), pp. 13, 14.

13. See *loc. cit.* and Arnold Beichman and Roy Godson, "Legal Constraints and Incentives" in Godson ed., *Intelligence Requirements for the 1980's: Counterintelligence*, National Strategy Information Center, Inc. (Washington, DC 1980).

14. "Comparative Historical Experience of Doctrine and Organization," in Godson ed., *Intelligence Requirements for the 1980's: Analysis and Estimates*, National Strategy Information Center, Inc. (Washington, DC 1980), p. 32 ff.

15. Cp. Daniel Graham, "Analysis and Estimates" in Godson ed., *op. cit.* (1979), p. 23, to the effect that the malfunction of analysis is potentially the most serious drawback which any nation's intelligence can experience.

16. See *supra* this paper.

17. Daniel Graham, *loc. cit.* p. 24.

18. Presented at the Civilian-Military Institute, Denver, Colorado, May 5, 1980, published in *Foreign Affairs* (Fall 1980).

19. Compare Tovar, *loc. cit.*, pp. 68-69.

20. I have dealt with these and other academic aspects of the Consortium's work in a "Memorandum of Suggestions for the Consortium's Program of Studies" (November, 1979).

21. See *supra* this paper.

22. *New York Times*, June 17, 1980.

23. See *Neue Zürcher Zeitung*, May 14, 1980, for a comprehensive analysis of this set of issues.

24. For these accounts see Richard Burt, *New York Times*, October 7, 1980.

25. Being an admirer of traditional China's international system, which I view as the only rival of the Grotian or Modern European States System, I greatly regret not being able to discuss it here. But see Adda B. Bozeman, "War and the Clash of Ideas," ORBIS, vol. 20, no. 1, Spring 1976, pp. 61-102, for references especially to the period of "The Warring States" in which political philosophy and statecraft were impressively well integrated; *The Future of Law in a Multicultural World*, pp. 140-160, and "On the Relevance of Hugo Grotius and *De Jure Belli Ac Pacis* for Our Times" in *Grotiana*, vol. 1, no. 1, Winter 1980.

26. I had planned to include analyses of statecraft in the Byzantine Empire (5th to 15th c.AD) and in the history of the Papacy, particularly as this trans-national

government had functioned in the multicultural world society of the 15th century. However, the scope of the paper simply did not allow for this extension.

27. "Analysis and Estimates" in Godson ed., *op. cit.*

28. For commentaries on Achaemenian Persia see Adda B. Bozeman, *Politics and Culture in International History*, (Princeton University Press, 1960) pp. 43-56; "Iran: U.S. Foreign Policy and the Tradition of Persian Statecraft," ORBIS, vol. 23, no. 2, Summer 1979, pp. 387-402; also "Civilizations Under Stress: Reflections on Cultural Borrowing and Survival," *The Virginia Quarterly Review*, vol. 51, Winter 1975, no. 1, pp. 1-18.

    For particularly interesting reports see James Morier, *A Journey Through Persia, Armenia, and Asia Minor to Constantinople, in the Years 1808 and 1809* . . . (Philadelphia 1816):

    "The history of Persia from the death of Nadir Shah to the accession of the present king, comprehending a period of fifty-one years, presents little else than a catalogue of the names of tyrants, usurpers, and a succession of murders, treacheries, and scenes of misery." (p. ix)

    Of Kerim Khan, who ruled from 1755-1779, Morier remarks the following:

    "On the 13th of March, 1779, Kerim Khan died a natural death, an extraordinary occurrence in the modern history of Persia, having reigned (according to the different dates assigned to his accession, from the deaths of different competitors) from nineteen to thirty years. From the fall of Mohamed Hassan Khan, the better epoch, his conqueror lived nineteen years, with almost undisputed authority. After his death all was again confusion; and the kingdom presented a renewal of blood and usurpation. . . ." (p. xi)

29. See *infra* this paper.

30. Today, Iraq's main enemy is Iran, and it is interesting that the latter is now referred to by Iraq's press as "Persia."

    "The Problem of Islamic Decadence," *Journal of World History*, vol. vii, no. 3, 1963, pp. 701-702.

31. Egypt and Turkey, like Iran, represent a different cultural heritage.

32. US Congress, House. *Iran: Evaluation of US Intelligence Performance Prior to November 1978*, (1979) (US House Intelligence Subcommittee Report). For commentaries on this Report see Richard H. Giza, "The Problem of the Intelligence Consumer" in Godson ed., *Intelligence Requirements for the 1980's: Analysis and Estimates*, (1980), 189-206, and Michael Handel, "Avoiding Political and Technological Surprise in the 1980's," in *op. cit.*, 85-111.

33. Cp. *supra* this paper for Mr. Colby's misperception of Vietnamese values and norms.

34. Iran was doctrinally unified by the Shi'ite faith in the 17th century, but it is pertinent to note that the 17th century cities of Safavid Persia were scenes of mass persecutions of large Sunni elements.

35. It is interesting that anti-Shah groups in the Administration, the universities and the media have made little if anything of the fact that the Shah's government had neither murdered, nor had plotted to murder, either Khomeini or Mossadegh.

36. For the varied backgrounds of some of present-day Iran's political leaders see a report by R. W. Apple, Jr. in *NYT* November 11, 1979, Section 4.

37. "Covert Action" in Roy Godson ed., *Intelligence Requirements for the 1980's: Elements of Intelligence*, 1979, p. 72.

38. See also Ann K. S. Lambton, "The Spiritual Influence of Islam in Persia" in A. J. Arberry and Rom Landau, *Islam Today*, (London, 1943), pp. 163-177 on the doctrine of *taqiya*, a dispensation from the requirements of religion under compulsion or threat of injury.

39. See Adda B. Bozeman, *Politics and Culture in International History*, (Princeton 1960), pp. 324 ff on Byzantine diplomacy and *supra* this paper for authorities on pre-Islamic, mainly Achaemenid Persian methods of diplomacy. Also Richard N. Frye, *The Heritage of Persia*, (New York, 1966), ch. 6 on Sassanian Persia.

40. See H. A. R. Gibb, "Constitutional Organization" in *Law in the Middle East*, vol. I, *Origin and Development of Islamic Law*, ed. Majid Khadduri and Herbert J. Liebesny. (Washington, 1955), p. 21.

For the Ottoman Empire, see Albert Howe Lybyer, *The Government of the Ottoman Empire in the Time of Suleiman the Magnificent*, (Cambridge, Mass. 1913), p. 227 on the influence of Chinese traditions of rule upon the Turks; Appendix IV on "The Government of the Mogul Empire in India." Bernard Lewis, *Istanbul and the Civilization of the Ottoman Empire*, (Norman, Oklahoma, 1963). H. A. R. Gibb and Harold Bowen, *Islamic Society and the West*, vol. I, parts 1 and 2. (London and New York, 1950-57).

41. Reuben Levy, *An Introduction to Persian Literature*, (Columbia University Press, New York, 1969), pp. 53 ff; 64 ff. "Nizām al-Mulk," *Encyclopaedia Britannica*, (Macropaedia), vol. 13, pp. 135-36.

J. A. Boyle, ed., *The Cambridge History of Iran*, vol. 5, *The Seljuq and Mongol Periods* (Cambridge, at the University Press, 1968), pp. 76, 80 ff, 206 ff.

James Kritzek, *Anthology of Islamic Literature*, (Holt, Rinehart & Winston, New York, 1964), pp. 153 ff for excerpts from *The Book of Government*.

For a full English translation of the work, see Hubert Darke, *The Book of Government; or, Rules for Kings*, (1960).

42. From Kritzek, *op. cit.*, pp. 154-157.

43. See Carl Brockelmann, *History of the Islamic Peoples* (translated by Joel Carmichael and Moshe Perlmann), (New York, 1949), pp. 240-255, on the aggressive incursions of Turks and Mongols into Persia and adjacent Eastern regions during the 12th-14th centuries.

44. See Lewis, *op. cit.* 47 ff; also authorities on the principle of "The Emirate by Seizure," and *The Book of Counsel for Vezirs and Governors of Sari Mehmed Pasha, The Defterdār*, introd., transl. and notes by Walter Livingston Wright, Jr. (Glenwood Press, Westport, Conn. 1971; originally publ. by Princeton University Press, 1935).

45. See Lewis, *op. cit.*, p. 57; Lybyer, *op. cit.*, appendix I, pp. 244 ff for Venetian reports on the role of eunuchs, and Sari Mehmed Pasha's *Book of Counsel . . .*, *op. cit.*, 21-60.

46. See *op. cit.*, p. 179; also pp. 250 ff. On the authority of Marco Polo who had passed through the territory of the Assassins in the late 13th century, Brockelmann notes that *fida's*, while intoxicated by hashish, were placed in a section of the Alamut gardens fitted out as Paradise, with young women as huris, in order to make the assassins amenable to the orders of the leader by giving them a foretaste of the pleasures awaiting them in the hereafter. See Bernard Lewis, *The Assassins: A Radical Sect in Islam*, (New York, 1968), for a full account. Freya Stark, *The Valleys of the Assassins*, and other Persian Travels, London, John John Murray, 1937.

47. The Sanusi fraternity in Cyrenaica (Libya) which was founded in the middle of the 19th century, subscribed to tenets greatly similar to those espoused by the Wahhabi movement. See Duncan Black MacDonald, *Development of Muslim Theology, Jurisprudence and Constitutional Theory*, (London and New York, 1903; reprinted, New York, 1965) for several chapters dealing with the Ikhwan, the Order of the Assassins, and the Wahhabites; T. E. Lawrence, *Seven Pillars of Wisdom*, (New York, 1935), pp. 46 ff on the *Fetah*; Gibb and Bowen, *op. cit.*, p. 285 on religious guilds, and above all, George Antonius, *The Arab Awakening*, (London, 1939; 1945), pp. 79, 110, 121.

48. Antonius, *op. cit.*, p. 111.

49. See *supra* pp. 16-19.

50. *War and Peace in the Law of Islam*, 61, 64 f, 136 ff; and *The Islamic Law of Nations; Shaybani's Siyar*, (transl. with Introduction, Notes, and Appendices by Majid Khadduri), Baltimore, Maryland, 1966).

Religion and theory confirmed existing life styles in the Near and Middle East which converged on the principle that war was the major external purpose of any organized society (government being the internal purpose). Among contemporary complimentary comments upon the Turks there is one which says: Turks come together for war as though they had been invited to a wedding. See Lybyer, *op. cit.*, 108.

51. Compare Bozeman, *The Future of Law in a Multicultural World*, pp. 50-85, and "War and the Clash of Ideas," *loc. cit.*, pp. 83 ff.

52. On the classical Indian *arthasastra* system and the historical context in which it evolved see B. Shamasastry, ed., *Kautilya's Arthasastra*, (Mysore, 1951); John W. Spellman, *Political Theory of Ancient India*, (Oxford, 1964); Upendra N. Ghoshal, *A History of Indian Political Ideas; The Ancient Period and the Period of Transition to the Middle Ages*, (London, 1966); K. M. Panikkar, *A Survey of Indian History*, (Bombay, 1954) and authorities listed in Bozeman, *Politics and Culture in International History*, and *The Future of Law*, pp. 121 ff "India and Indianized Asia."

53. E. J. Rapson, ed., *The Cambridge History of India*, vol. I, *Ancient India* (First Indian reprint, Delhi, 1955), p. 455.

54. See Rapson, *op. cit.*, 444 f.

55. See Spellman, *op. cit.*, p: 157 for a graph of such a *mandala*; see also *Kautilya's Arthasastra*.

56. Kautilya's *Arthasastra*, Bk. IX, ch. 1.

57. J. W. McCrindle, *Ancient India as Described by Megathenes and Arrian*, (Bombay, 1877), pp. 85 f.

58. Kautilya's *Arthasastra*, Bk. XIII, ch. III.

59. *op. cit.*, Bk. XII, ch. IV.

60. Almost two millennia separate us from Ancient India's political order which was implanted also in Indianized Southeast Asia, notably Cambodia, Java, and parts of what later became Vietnam. Yet readings in Indian political philosophy, as for example in the *Arthasastra*, inevitably remind one that "shaven heads" and "pagodas" also combined to create "contrivances" during the Vietnam war, and that our "eyes" and "ears" had not been adequately trained to perceive them in the perspective proper to this Asian culture.

61. See Spellman, *op. cit.*, 141 ff.

62. See Heinrich Zimmer, *The Philosophies of India*. Edited by Joseph Campbell, (Bollingen Series xxvi, New York, 1951) p. 83.

63. William J. Bouwsma, *Venice and the Defense of Republican Liberty; Renaissance Values in the Age of the Counter Reformation*, (Berkeley and Los Angeles, 1968), p. 65.

64. For comments on these aspects see Bozeman, *Politics and Culture in International History*, pp. 457-489, and authorities there cited; also Frederic Lane, *Venice and History*, pp. 36-55).

65. See W. Carew Hazlitt, *The Venetian Republic*, 2 vls., (London, 1915) vol. II, pp. 498 ff for a full account of Venetian practices; also Garrett Mattingly, *Renaissance Diplomacy*, (Boston, 1955), pp. 112 ff; and 241 ff.

66. Even Grotius expressed sceptical concern about this institution because he could not find a legal way to rationalize the civil immunities which resident embassies required except by resorting to the fiction of extraterritoriality.

67. See Bouwsma, *op. cit.*, pp. 61 ff.
68. *Op. cit.*, 113.
69. See Lybyer, *op. cit.*, for a listing of the *relations* upon which his work is based.
70. Cord Meyer, *Facing Reality: From World Federalism to the CIA*, (New York, 1980), pp. 103 ff.
71. See Meyer, *op. cit.*, Appendix, pp. 410 f. and pp. 158 ff in the text.
72. The Inquisitors of State had been temporary officials since 1411. The origin of this office is classical Rome.
73. See Dean Acheson, "Ethics in International Relations Today," *Amherst Alumni News*, (Winter, 1965).

II. Angelo Codevilla

Introduction

Secret actions in foreign affairs have been controversial in the United States since Woodrow Wilson's time. During the interwar period, "secrecy and dispatch," the characteristic tools of foreign policy so emphasized in *The Federalist Papers,* came to be seen as anomalies. Foreign affairs were studied in an almost exclusively legalistic way. The Second World War and its aftermath forced Americans to undertake a broad range of activities to influence foreign governments and factions. But Americans nevertheless have continued to look upon secret means of bringing influence to bear as somehow beyond the pale of ordinary foreign policy. The very terms "covert action" and "special activity" have tended to signify that although the secret things for which they stand may serve foreign policy, they are made of different stuff than is the substance of foreign policy.

The first part of this paper, however, argues that secret means of exerting influence are part and parcel of foreign affairs, intrinsically no more and no less appropriate than other means. One can imagine few policies which can be pursued wholly openly, just as one can imagine few which a sensible statesman would (or could) pursue wholly in secret. Most policies, in most circumstances, are best pursued by some mixture of openness and secrecy. The activities we have come to label "covert action" or "special activities" usually make sense as parts of broader campaigns to achieve foreign policy objectives. They are not ends in themselves any more than are diplomatic pleasantries. All are logically under the broader category, "political action." In fact, the aura which surrounds secret political activity is probably due not to secrecy but to the fact that nations have found secret acts peculiarly useful for interfering in other nations' internal affairs.

The second part describes the kinds of secret means by which nations have taken part in each others' political process, either (1) to influence each others' decisions, or (2) to change or affect each others' leaders, as well as political or social structures. Friends cultivated in another nation's councils may help to influence that nation's decisions. Such people are usually termed "agents of influence." If they are subject to one's control, and are highly placed, common parlance terms them "puppets." If one nation manages puppets in another, it can do more than affect this or that decision. Simply by having acquired them it has changed the other nation's body politic. Nations may also affect decisions abroad by secretly aiding, hindering, encouraging or discouraging individuals or factions (which they do not control) within the target regime. Alliances with foreign individuals or factions can also be intended to topple an official or government or to aid the rise of another. But even if there is no intention of bringing about fundamental changes, if a nation repeatedly does this sort of thing in another, it will eventually build up or tear down the influence of certain parts of the other's government or society. Similarly, a nation may affect decisions in other states by providing information which appears to come from a source other than the actual one. If a nation does so successfully, consistently, and on a large scale, it may indeed change the shape of political discourse in another. Finally, violence or the threat thereof, whether overt or covert, has ever been known to affect the decisions of officials and the shape of governments.

The third part examines how the covert aspects of political action can affect the different kinds of regimes in the world today. Different types of government have different vulnerabilities. Political action is most efficiently targeted on the ruling element in a regime. A palace coup, for example, would make little sense where the "palace" is of small importance. Efforts to affect public opinion may bear no immediate fruit where the shape of the government or its decisions do not depend on public opinion. Similarly, it makes little sense to expend effort, overt or covert, to affect a regime's ruling element unless that element is accessible. Less crucial, but more accessible targets may make more sense. Moreover, because each kind of regime is peculiarly fit to conduct a certain kind of foreign policy, each is better fit to conduct certain kinds of political action. Democracies, for example, must be particularly careful that even the most covert details of their activities be justifiable in terms which domestic public opinion could accept.

In sum, the paper concludes that the conduct of American foreign policy would benefit were we to concentrate on the opportunities which present themselves for advancing this country's interests, and pay less attention than we have heretofore to whether some of the activities necessary to advance those interests fit more or less snugly into the highly artificial American category of "covert action."

Covert Political Action Is One Among Many Tools of Foreign Policy

Political acts naturally aim to effect change. Covert action is a modern American term under which is grouped a variety of activities by which a government can promote changes in the policies, the leadership or the environment of foreign governments or factions without those governments or factions knowing who is promoting those changes.* Moreover, there is no general agreement on how secret an action which otherwise fits in the category must be in order to be considered a covert action. The term covert action does not denote a category of human activity distinct from foreign policy and its execution, nor even a distinct category of means. Rather, the term covers certain means used by governments (not private parties) in a peculiar way, that is, secretly, for political purposes.

Present-day America is unique in classifying these means under a single label. Although history is full of examples of nations carrying out what contemporary Americans call covert action, none but American statesmen and writers have ever set these actions apart for separate consideration. That is because, apart from a greater degree of secrecy, the means of covert action do not appear to be different from those of overt political activity. Usually, neither international law nor political theory treats the political acts in question differently when they are done with a greater degree of secrecy than when they are done with a lesser degree of secrecy. Military action is violent, regardless of whether its source is acknowledged. In political theory, acknowledgment of the source of a military act by itself does not justify an unjust one, nor does the opposite condemn a just one. As regards military activity, contemporary international law

---

*In current usage the term also covers means by which governments secretly affect political groups within its borders. But, by general agreement, the term "domestic covert action" does not cover these very same means when these are used secretly to disrupt non-political groups, such as organized crime. Nor, of course, does the term cover these very same means when they are not used secretly.

does not require war to be declared before the duties and immunities of belligerency apply. International law, however, still requires combatants to wear insignias in order to enjoy belligerent status. A politician who acts at the behest of foreigners doeș so regardless of how many people notice. Political theory is more concerned with the motives and the results of both the leader and the led than it is with whether they avow their relationship. International law is silent on the entire matter. The laws of various countries differ. A state can try to influence public opinion in another overtly, as well as covertly, and may use both overt and covert means to build up or tear down the influence of certain individuals and factions in another state. Neither the efficacy nor the moral worth of such actions depends primarily on the degree of secrecy with which they are undertaken.

It is often argued that covert action is not properly part of the function of intelligence services. Of course, the primary reason why covert activities are undertaken by intelligence services is that these are best equipped to maintain secrecy. More important, they are alone among public or private agencies in maintaining networks of clandestine contacts. Part of the argument is that intelligence works best when the subject of interest never finds out that information has been collected; however, it is almost always impossible to prevent the target of covert action from realizing that a change has taken place. Even very secret operations are usually part of a broader scheme of overt ones. In short, overtness is a constituent part of covert political action. Whether any given secret activity should be conducted by an intelligence service or by another department of government, whether the risk inherent in the activity would more seriously jeopardize the intelligence service or any other department assigned to carry it out, of course depends on the circumstances. In short, none but variable prudential considerations indicate that covert actions ought to be undertaken by intelligence services.

However, secrecy and deception, in some measure, appear to be constituent parts of overt political activity. What overt political activity—foreign or domestic—does not at one time or another include the judgment "I think it would be better if they heard this from you rather than from us?" (or vice-versa). It seems then, that the appropriateness of political action, direct or indirect, violent or nonviolent, more or less covert, is to be judged by a single standard: How well does it serve policy, bearing in mind that no policy is well served if pursued by means not proportionate to the good the policy seeks to achieve.

Before examining the ways in which covert activities may serve the ends of foreign policy let us look at what many consider their most troublesome aspect, that is, the *use* to which secret activities are best suited, interference in other nations' internal affairs. Upon examination, arguments that covert activities are extraneous to foreign policy will appear to be objections to interfering in other states' internal affairs. Such arguments, though not without basis, are invalid.

It must be reemphasized that interference in other nations' affairs can be quite overt. OPEC's overt raising of oil prices has changed much in the world. In 1979, Iran put itself in a position to affect the outcome of the American presidential election of 1980 by taking 52 American hostages. These overt acts were not without covert aspects. In some well-known matters the mixture of overtness and covertness is more nearly even. The Soviet Union, in the past, has told American businessmen that growth in trade, something in which the businessmen are quite interested, would depend upon the US Government renouncing the principle of the Jackson-Vanik Amendment. The Soviets clearly expect these businessmen to influence debates inside the US in ways favorable to Soviet interests but not to trumpet the fact that they stand to gain by their alignment with Soviet policy. Therefore if the objective of foreign policy is to change decisions which foreign states would otherwise make, then it makes no sense to disapprove of some methods precisely on the ground that they interfere in other states' internal affairs. Let us look further.

Historically, there has existed a proportional relationship between the ends which states have sought to achieve and the means by which they have pursued them. Simple negotiations with regard to commercial matters of marginal interest do not normally call forth attempts to bypass the other side's official negotiators, much less to alter the political system which the negotiators represent. On the other hand, when states believe that either their highest interests, their most cherished beliefs, or both, are at stake, it would be surprising if they limited themselves to official contacts and eschewed attempts to take part in the other side's political process. But, since states normally allow only their own citizens to take part in their own political process, foreigners, especially adversaries, can best take part in other nations' affairs covertly.

The proximate purposes of foreign policy, whether pursued covertly or not, are the same: to affect the other side's decisions. But, *whereas overt acts speak to the other side's body politic, as it were, from the outside, covert ones are meant to exercise influence from within the other side's body politic—to exercise prerogatives which that body politic*

normally reserves for its own members. Of course, if one nation allowed
another to take part in its political process it would not be a question
of subversion. Indeed, from time to time nations do invite foreigners
briefly to take part in their political process. But no wholly "open"
political process could exist, at least not for long.

A very brief review of Western history serves to put the present
status of covert action into perspective. Prior to the Peloponnesian
War, Greek cities often allowed foreign ambassadors to argue their
case directly in their assemblies. These ambassadors would lodge
with local friends and, presumably, would seek to drum up support
for their proposals unofficially outside the assembly, as well as officially within it. Yet, both Thucydides and Aristotle note that seldom
did cities seek to promote their ends by disturbing other regimes.
Especially did they eschew making alliances with the other cities'
serfs. Their disputes did not warrant taking such risks of self-destruc-
tion. Yet during the decades of the Peloponnesian war, the secret
cultivation of factions in other cities became a substantial part of
Greek diplomacy.

Consider also the difference between diplomacy in Europe—except for the Italian cities—before and after the Reformation. During
the Middle Ages all of Christendom was theoretically one polity. The
ambassadors of the various Christian potentates were technically
lawyers, who would normally argue their client's case with the other
party, and could then theoretically argue the same case before either
the Papal or Imperial court. Medieval ambassadors did not hesitate
to try to build support within the other side's court for their claims.
But their attempts to interfere in the other side's politics were pale
compared to the efforts of their successors in the sixteenth century.
In Europe, at least, the notion that ambassadors are to be presumed
subversives dates from those turbulent times of religious war when
emissaries did little *but* interfere in other courts' affairs. The Treaty
of Westphalia, which established the present state system, ratified
the belief that foreign policy is essentially subversive activity. Consequently, it circumscribed the role of foreigners in host countries
and of foreign policy itself. The rule, "Whose the Kingdom, His is
the religion," was the prototype of the principle that states would
not interfere in each others' internal affairs.

Not surprisingly, the rule that foreign policies should not involve
attempts to go "over the head" of governments has been respected
when the stakes have been perceived as relatively low, e.g., the
years 1648-1775 and 1815 to 1914. However, as Karl Marx wrote,
even during the latter period the Russian Czars believed they had a

very high stake in maintaining the monarchic and clerical character of West European regimes. Therefore, especially prior to 1848, the Czars used a variety of secret means to suppress revolutionary movements in Europe.

But one cannot begin to understand international relations during the American and French revolutions, and since 1914, without taking note of wholesale interference by the major nations in each others' internal affairs. In the twentieth century, supporters of universalist ideologies have deprived the central principle of the Treaty of Westphalia of much of its validity by pressing their claims with scant regard for borders. However, in the past century, mutual interference in internal affairs has increased for an entirely unrelated set of reasons: The growth of trade, the ease and speed of travel and communications have made it difficult for citizens of one nation *not* to affect the political climate in other nations. Governments can choose whether and how to direct their citizens' interference in the internal affairs of other nations, but today they can hardly stop it.

The argument has sometimes been made that such interference is inappropriate for democracies. But simply because a nation is a democracy, it may not disregard with impunity the requirements for survival which the environment may impose. Democracies which fail to use the means required to prevail over those who intend their destruction simply perish. Yet democracy as a system neither necessarily deprives a government of executive powers capable of engaging in subversion abroad nor does it doom a people to being subverted by those it has engaged to subvert others. The competence of fighting forces and the exercise of control over them are tasks incumbent on any form of government.

Yet the argument has valid aspects: it is inappropriate for democracies, especially in our times, to try to subvert *other democracies* because in such governments power resides in popular opinion, and because modern liberal democracies do not restrict what citizens can hear. If the political leaders of one democracy wish to interfere in another's politics, they have but to do abroad what they do at home. It may be objected that because a nation's electorate would not take kindly to foreign advice, a foreigner seeking to interfere would do so most effectively by supporting local agents whom their fellow citizens would falsely believe were acting on their own. Of course, when such acts occur, they are subversive. It must be recognized that to undertake such acts is to place higher value on the results expected than on the democratic process in a target country. Such a choice might well be justified if the subversive act is intended to bolster a democratic process, which is already being subverted from another quarter. However, in a democracy, the best means of countering subversion should be overt exposure. Where public opinion is the heart of the regime, and access to it is unhindered, why direct political action anywhere else? Finally, if a democracy actually chose to subvert another country's healthy, functioning democracy, it would thereby make its own environment more alien.

Influencing Decisions and Political and Social Structures

What political operator from the precinct level to the international level does not dream of having a friend strategically located in the opposition's camp? That friend does not have to engage in espionage in order to be useful. His influence can help lead the opposition away from effective tactics, can oppose the rise of effective leaders, can occupy the opposition with wasteful pursuits, or sow division in its ranks. Of course, any such "friend" or agent must hide the true purpose of his actions in order to function, or even to survive. The difference between such an "agent of influence" and a person in the opposition's camp who is merely well-disposed toward a foreign nation is that the "agent" coordinates his actions with those of the foreign nation.

The amount of coordination can vary greatly. Examples of the least coordination are professors or journalists so taken with certain foreign countries, or factions thereof, that they frequently meet with officials of those countries and discuss ways in which their common cause can be furthered. A simple expedient is for a government, a political party, or its agents, to invite a professor, journalist or official for a series of visits. If all goes well, that person will soon be regarded as an expert and will spread his host's view abroad. The foreign country need never order the expert to advance a line of discussion favorable to them. But most of the time, in all probability he will.

An example of closer coordination might be that of a high political official, or a relative of a high official, who takes bribes or receives other assistance from a foreign country in exchange for arranging special access for its emissaries or for influencing occasional decisions. Or they might be people who, because they support a foreign government's policies, try to take leading roles in their own country, and coordinate their actions with the country whose success they seek.

Close coordination is typified by the conscious agent who can subordinate personal and professional goals to the interests of the foreign power. Such agents are as difficult to manage as they are to recruit. Aside from the problems of maintaining the clandestinity of the relationship, there is always the temptation to use the really good ones so much that their sympathies become well know, or to use them for espionage or to bring them into contact with spies. Association with espionage, of course, was the beginning of the end for Alger Hiss' role as a Soviet agent.

Finally, we should not give the impression that conscious agents are necessarily highly placed, ideologically committed, or that they dedicate their lives to their work. In short, agents of influence are not necessarily "moles." They may be private citizens who can be induced by a variety of motives to perform politically significant activities from time to time. Money can play a role in the agent's relationship with the country on whose behalf he acts. But, it is less important as a source of motivation than it is as support for the agent's activities. In free countries, however, the most successful agents of influence have the means to finance their own activities. It is a serious misunderstanding to think of covert agents as anything but allies. They always have their own objectives, and in most cases, it is futile to try to substitute others. The art of managing them, and the groups they may infiltrate, consists of accentuating and facilitating the achievement of the common goals of both parties.

Because the distinguishing feature of covert action is that the identity or motives of those promoting political changes be dissimulated, covert action depends primarily upon the availability of human beings who are well-enough placed to act, who are willing and able to act, and who maintain wholly or partly clandestine relations with the country on whose behalf they act

The most obvious use of well-placed covert agents is to take direct part in the target country's decision-making process. The implications of this require little elaboration. Agents who are government officials, of course, can make some decisions themselves and contribute to others. Agents who are businessmen or other persons of substance—editors, prominent professionals, entertainers, etc., can bring the weight of their position to bear on those who make decisions. But more often, agents can only bring *indirect* pressure to bear upon decisions. The most common means is to spread and give credit to facts, lies, or opinions while hiding the fact that these come from a foreign power or, at any rate, are intended to serve its purposes.

The Soviet Union's various campaigns—for a cessation of nuclear tests in the late 1950's and early 1960's; against the United States' role in Indochina in the 1960's and early 1970's; and against the modernization of NATO's nuclear arsenal in the late 1970's—are examples of occasions on which agents introduced or helped to spread certain lines of thought in the Western public, e.g., that nuclear war would be the end of mankind. This is not to say that any given expression of such views is the result of Soviet covert action but rather, to point out that had it not been for Soviet initiatives these views would not have been expressed either in the quantity or with the concentration in which they were. *Of course, the Soviet Union openly proclaimed that it intended to spread these "lines." But, these "lines" would not have had the success they did had their targets been able to identify a significant proportion of those who spread them as Soviet agents.*

Information from a dissimulated source can have even more direct effects by conveying information to a political leader that another leader, faction, or state is about to do something, or by providing an explanation for why the other party did something. By supplying such information, one can either trigger the leader's reaction, or confirm him in his plans, or induce him to alter them. For example, in 1965, the Indonesian Communist Party is said to have launched its ill-timed attempt at a coup d'état in response to false information that President Sukharno was dying. This move resulted in a disaster from which the Indonesian Communist Party has never recovered. The truth or falsity of the information does not necessarily affect its usefulness. Whether true or false, information can calm or inflame factional disputes, raise or lower confidence, and raise or lower the stock of an official. The key question regarding any item is "How will it affect the recipient?" Information *may* achieve the very same effects when conveyed openly. Open propaganda is indeed useful. But, if someone knows the real source of the information, and can determine how the source would want him to respond to the information, he is quite likely to restrain his natural impulses. Thus, it may be worth the effort to try to have the information conveyed by an agent whom the recipient believes to be friendly or disinterested.

Covert agents are also useful for mobilizing the support or opposition of factions within the target regime. Perhaps the most elementary operation of this kind involves attempting to raise or lower the political stock of a member of the target regime. Leaders can be discredited most easily by passing information which suggests either corruption, disloyalty, or both. Such information can be developed by involving the targeted official in compromising activities. It is more difficult, however, to strengthen the credit of a friendly foreign official without tipping one's hand. For example, arranging successes at the negotiating table is easy, but transparent. If there is in place a network of supporters to bolster the targeted official in this or that controversy, a great deal can be achieved. But first one must have the network and then know how to use it.

The art of mobilizing factions in other countries to influence a given decision, such as deployment of the neutron weapon, first requires agents sufficiently well-placed to affect the behavior of factions. But, above all, it requires the ability to coordinate the actions of each agent so as to keep the target groups moving in the desired direction. The nature of the task can be seen by examining the Soviet Union's role in the ''peace'' movements of Western countries. In its efforts to split Europe from North America over the past generation, the Soviets have stimulated labor unions to organize propaganda campaigns, to threaten and sometimes to carry out violence. They have caused intellectuals to write appeals. These acts are often focused on individual issues, such as country X's decision to join NATO. Shall it keep its commitment to the alliance by raising the necessary forces? What shall the country's position be regarding new weapons or the wars in Korea, Vietnam, the Middle East, Africa? Each issue has required a campaign with its own peculiar motivations and its own list of supporters. The individual groups which have consistently supported the Soviet line have identified themselves rather well. Successful mobilization of foreign factions over a long period of time ceases to be covert. Therefore there is a constant scramble for new forms of cover. Nevertheless, persistence often prevails because, although even a whole generation may be aware that an individual or group is compromised by a pattern of activities, the succeeding generation may not know.

Of course, groups cannot be mobilized if they are not already infiltrated, or unless agents have some leverage over them. Achieving such penetrations or acquiring such leverage seldom results from anything but long years of effort involving contact both overt and clandestine with the groups which one hopes one day to press into service. Moreover, successful infiltrations of groups will not be useful unless those who seek to use those groups know them well enough to be sure how they can be moved. For example, a group persuaded of the rightness of bringing a certain kind of pressure on its own government may not be willing to cease that pressure even after the instigators' purposes have ben fulfilled. A group moved by deception may discover this and become an enemy. Finally, those who have been bought are susceptible to alternative offers.

Each method has inherent advantages and disadvantages. A decision over which risks should be taken belongs to those who are responsible for the whole covert action. One should not leave to agents decision about whether the group's leaders are best moved by conviction, bribery, or deception, any more than one would leave to agents the choice of strategic objectives. Most important, mobilizing the support or opposition of factions within the target regime requires meticulous but flexible plans executed with precise timing so that the influence of several groups is applied in just the right amount and in ways that are not self-cancelling. Too much pressure for a change of policy might stiffen resistance. Soviet efforts to control the International Labor Organization involved encouraging some of the national delegations openly to support communist causes, a general diversion of attention from the purposes of the organization. This led to the temporary disaffiliation of the United States, to the devaluation of the ILO and, therefore, to the general devaluation of the Soviets' covert activities there.

One of the purposes of encouraging and discouraging foreign groups and individuals may be to affect the likelihood of coups d'état. It is relatively simple to foil a coup merely by revealing the plan, sowing dissention among the plotters. It is more difficult to help a coup succeed. People not directly involved must be mobilized to support it; yet this must be done so as not reveal the ultimate goal. It may be difficult to decide whether the foreigners who are preparing the coup are also the right ones to run the coup. Are they capable of doing it? Could they govern if they did? Would their takeover bring improvements which justify the risks and the costs? To make responsible assessments one must know the conditions of the country as well as the coup plotters themselves. Without such knowledge, meddling in coups amounts to mere "destabilization" which, in most cases, is irresponsible. Of course, mere *Zersetzung* makes sense when the target country is about to do something dangerous and one wishes to throw its leaders off track. But, if one cannot know whether an act of destabilization will move the target regime in a direction desirable in the long run and if one is not prepared to deal with the entire gamut of plausible results, one would be well advised to refrain from playing the sorcerer's apprentice with coups. The disastrous results of the coup against Ngo Dinh Diem in Vietnam in December 1963 attest to this. It could be argued that the wave of political violence in the Western democracies in the past decade has not pushed them in the direction of accommodating the stated goals of the terrorists but has been a catalyst for a consolidation of attitudes against those goals.

Finally, foreign authorities' decisions may also be affected by violence or the threat of violence against officials and supporters of the regime. Certainly, a number of factors are needed fully to explain the events of the last decade in the Third World. But, surely, the fear of violence is one of them! How many officials of foreign countries have canceled visits of American ships to their ports because they had reason to believe that they themselves would be the target of violent demonstrations or acts of terrorism! How many officials in the world today are receptive to the PLO (even to the extent of not referring to it as a terrorist organization) because they fear for their lives? How many government, business, labor, and professional leaders have been killed to help or hinder political developments! Violence is all the more effective politically if its perpetrators cannot be linked directly to the country on whose behalf they act. Without such linkage the target public cannot focus its anger on something outside itself, and may turn in upon itself. To the extent that a country which fosters political violence in another does so covertly, it escapes retaliation. However, in practice, this matter is more complex. It is perfectly obvious that certain countries, Libya and the Soviet Union, to name but two, train, equip, shelter and rescue terrorists whose violence, far from being senseless, is calculated to support their foreign policy. These countries do not advertise the fact that they do this but, nevertheless, they are not entirely secretive. Their partial discretion serves two purposes: first, since their targets are democracies, over-obvious support of political violence could provide a rallying point for public opinion and make retaliation inevitable; second, even a thin veneer of secrecy is a useful excuse for leaders of target countries who know full well who is behind the terrorism but who are afraid to retaliate for a variety of reasons. The amount of secrecy required to avoid retaliation from a target country decreases along with the target country's power. For the utterly weak, no pretense is needed.

Influencing the Character of the Target's Body Politic

If one nation has built clandestine networks in another which allow it to influence significantly another nation's decisions, and if it exercises that influence repeatedly, then, willy-nilly, that nation will change the other's political landscape. If it so wishes to direct its efforts, the one may even be able to change the other's very culture.

Let us begin our look at how one nation may alter another's government by considering puppets, and how different types are made and managed. Few political leaders can bear to think of themselves as puppets. Some such as Pierre Laval, or perhaps some contemporary Finnish leaders, may convince themselves that they are true patriots, engaged in the thankless task of getting the best possible deal from the dominant power of the day. The price of latitude, such people argue, is the covert acceptance of the superior power's policies and the promulgation of those policies, somewhat modified, in one's own name. If a nation wishes to try to build this kind of puppet—assuming it is not in the situation of Germany vis-à-vis France in 1940-44, or of the Soviet Union vis-à-vis Finland today—that nation must convince foreign leaders or potential leaders that it is riding the wave of history. The potential puppet must believe that the best course for both himself and the nation is to accommodate slowly to the other nation's superior power and that any policy of forceful resistance would be both impossible to organize and harmful to execute because it would make the superior country's demands harsher. He must also believe that his accommodation is "buying time." But the test of his intentions is whether he proposes doing anything during that time to promote his country from the condition of inferiority. The fateful first step in the process of building a puppet is to induce him to make a major issue in his country of the relations between the two countries, preferably of a treaty which grants the other a commanding advantage, and then to cooperate in an effort to "sell" his own people on those relations or on that treaty. This habituates the foreign leader to regard his own countrymen who oppose him as more alien or dangerous than the foreigners who support him. Thereafter, the growing reality of one's superiority can make the relationship stronger and lessen the need for covertness. But that need will never disappear because there is a natural resentment of foreign domination.

A different kind of puppet can be made from the leader who is trying to climb up or to keep on top of the ladder of success, and who is not particular about where he gets help in doing it. If one provides such help, the puppet's dependence can grow with his power and usefulness. Covertness of support is most important as the relationship of dependence is established and as the puppet gains strength. So-called liberation movements and would-be artificers of coups d'état are candidates for this role. While such puppets are out of power, keeping control is relatively easy; rebellious ones can be destroyed by exposure. During this period one can try to build relations with more than one faction in the puppet groups and/or to make sure that in the process of coming to power the group will alienate enough elements, foreign and domestic, to require one's own assistance to stay in power. Of course, these processes must be covert. But their success hinges not so much on covertness as on the right choice of the puppet and the skill with which he (or it) is managed. Finally, there is no substitute for the capability and the will to crush rebellious puppets militarily.

Building up or tearing down the influence of certain parts of the target nation's body politic may be done overtly as well as covertly. But no such efforts are without some veneer of secrecy. Even when the Federal Republic of Germany decided to build up the Portuguese Socialist Party and its associated groups in order to forestall a communist takeover of Portugal, it funneled most of its advice and assistance not through official government organs but through the governing Social Democratic Party. The veil was thin, but proved sufficient. The stronger and more willful the country, the thinner the veil may be. The Soviet Union, for its part, has publicly argued that it cannot be held responsible for the assistance it provides to communist parties around the world because that assistance comes from ostensibly private groups in the USSR, including the CPSU. Similarly, although the Italian Communist Party rather openly benefits from commercial transactions between its associated trading companies and East European governments, both these governments and the Italian Communists deny the obvious, that these activities are designed in large part to build the Soviet Union's influence in Italy and the political power of the Italian Communist Party. Similarly, in the recent past the US government has sponsored the current land reform in El Salvador in order to diminish the political and social influence of that country's wealthy landowners. The US Embassy in San Salvador has issued denials that it has "directed" the program along with affirmations of "support" for it. Yet, the "support" follows detailed joint discussions with the ruling military-civilian junta regarding which farms are to be seized and which appointments are to be made. Is this covert action? The question is obviously irrelevant.

Attempts to change the character of another political system or culture can be much more covert. The Soviet Union's long-term clandestine support of left-leaning academics throughout the Third

World has given these countries a legacy of universities which are reservoirs of pro-Soviet activities. All sides can count on demonstrations for or against any given cause depending on the Soviet Union's attitude. But because the universities train journalists, broadcasters, etc., one can observe that in a number of countries public dialogue now reflects the notion of class struggle and the code words of Soviet foreign policies such as "imperialism." As for the US, covert support of a newspaper in Chile after 1970 allowed that newspaper to survive the Allende regime's efforts to silence all opposition and thus provided a focal point for forces opposed to the regime.

When governments restrict political, economic, or cultural activities for the purpose of diminishing or destroying certain social or political tendencies in their own countries, these may survive only with help from abroad—which often can best be delivered covertly. In such cases, though the help is covert, the activities fostered are simply ones which normally occur in democracies and which would occur in the target countries except for repression. For example, in the late 1970's, the Italian Communist Party was powerful enough to exercise near-hegemony in broadcasting. To counteract the political and cultural consequences of this, a group of Italian journalists began to broadcast television programs into Italy from the Principality of Monaco. The Communist Party succeeded in having the Italian government forbid Italian business from advertising on that station, thereby cutting it off from normal commercial support. The station managed to survive because it was tied to a successful newspaper. No government opposed to the Italian Communists was forced to consider helping. But had private support been forcibly dried up, some foreign government might well have faced the choice. Similar choices abound in today's world. In fact, a majority of the world's countries do suppress the hallmarks of democractic public life, a free press, free trade unions, expressions of dissidence, of ethnic identity, and others. When democracies covertly attempt as it were, to feed intravenously such tendencies in these regimes, regardless of their motivations, they are reshaping the world in their image.

Nothing has greater effect on the character of nations, especially democracies, than changes in public opinion. Even totalitarian states recognize that despite the powerful apparat for social control which they possess, the spread of an idea, be it as simple as "people live better elsewhere," can change the parameters of politics. That is why they so carefully censor what their people may hear, and attempt to discredit the West's official and semi-official radios which bring them news of the outside world. That may also explain why, in totalitarian countries, ideas which travel by word of mouth or from hand to hand spread across certain networks, e.g., ethnic, religious, labor, almost as fast and much more effectively than the official statements of Voice of America or Deutsche Welle.

The democracies are not without possiblities for shaping public opinion in totalitarian countries. These countries are full of nationalist, religious, ethical and economic concerns which, if encouraged, spread and amplified would have great political effect. But the democracies have not seriously sought to shape public opinion in totalitarian countries for almost a generation. Totalitarian countries, however, have worked hard to bring about long-lasting changes in the Western world's thinking. The themes of Soviet propaganda are familiar enough: "The West is responsible for the Third World's poverty." "Any physical plant or installation belongs to the people of the country in which it is located, regardless of who built it or what contractual arrangements there might be." "Nuclear war is unwinnable and would result in the destruction of mankind." Therefore, those in the West who advocate military preparations are irrationally leading the world to destruction. Imagination does not have to wander far to realize how different the politics of the Western democracies would be if those propositions were not so commonly accepted. Few of these themes are of Soviet invention. Mostly, the Soviet Union spreads and amplifies, both overtly and through agents, ideas propounded by citizens of the country it wishes to influence. The acceptance of these themes has also strengthened the hand of those in the West who have propounded them.

Another way to strengthen a faction in a foreign country is to provide armaments. To weaken other factions, one can instigate, supply, or otherwise aid war against them. The H'mong people of Laos, covertly armed by the United States, held the northwest corner of Indochina for a decade against the North Vietnamese and indigenous communist forces. Of course, the Soviets and North Vietnamese at first covertly, then overtly armed the Viet Cong in South Vietnam. The US covertly armed the successful rebels against Jacobo Arbenz and the unsuccessful ones against Fidel Castro. Cuba is arming the anti-American FALN in Puerto Rico and on the mainland of the US. A number of Western countries are supplying the rebels in Afghanistan and Angola. Under the circumstances, it hardly seems sensible to arm them with Soviet-made weapons obtained elsewhere. The question naturally arises why even try to keep such activities covert?

The very fact that such current projects are the daily talk of the world press attests to the fact that since arms are meant to be used, and can hardly be used quietly in any quantity, armed assistance can only be partially covert. Of course, it can be quite covert in its details, even as the Allies' attempts to supply the French resistance forces during World War II were trumpeted in the newsreels but were covert in detail. Certainly secrecy should protect the beginning of such programs, their details and their eventual scope. But one can argue that the Western democracies have harmed the causes they have supported militarily by wrapping their efforts in excessive secrecy, thereby not explaining to their own people soon enough the circumstances and the reasons for what they are doing. As a result, the people of the western democracies have received most of their information about such matters from the communist side. Another consideration can be understood by examining the Soviets' efforts on behalf of the North Vietnamese. The Soviets never denied they were helping "the Vietnamese People" but, though anyone who cared to check knew that the North Vietnamese Army was in South Vietnam, Soviet propaganda always asserted that only American forces were intruding. Ultimately, during the Paris negotiations, the United States was forced to accept the legitimacy of the North Vietnamese Army's presence in the South. Ironically but instinctively, it was forced to do so by political pressure built up among American citizens in part by the boldfaced claim that the North Vietnamese Army was not in the South, or not really in the South, because the Vietnam war was really a revolt of South Vietnam's people. One could want no better example: The adequacy of cover depends less on secrecy than on policy. By the time the North Vietnamese Army rolled into Saigon, the propaganda, of which the denial of the NVA's presence in the south and the semi-covertness of Soviet assistance was a part, had served its purpose, precisely to justify that presence and that assistance. The combination of covertness and propaganda shielded North Vietnam's military effort by keeping the US from applying its military power effectively. The details are complex, but the principle is simple: the degree of openness or covertness should depend entirely on the political use which can be made of the information.

One argument for hiding the fact of one's military assistance to foreign factions is as valid as it is limited in scope: of course, complete secrecy protects one from retaliation. But in such matters secrecy is almost never complete. Nevertheless, it is also true that the stronger one's position is the less one need fear retaliation. As it became clear to the Soviet Union that the US was so afriad of Soviet reaction that it would not try to punish the Soviets for their supply of the North Vietnamese effort, the Soviets' role became quite open. As the Western democracies have shown greater reluctance to displease either the PLO or the Soviet Union, the relationship between the two has become less and less secretive. Nevertheless, the Soviet Union is still sufficiently wary of possible reactions in the West to employ basic covert techniques to foster terrorism. The western democracies know what the Soviets are doing but, because the injuries are not unbearable, and Soviet involvement is secret enough not to add insult to injury, and further, since the Soviet Union is now so powerful that it is dangerous to provoke its anger, the leaders of the democracies have chosen the lesser evil of suffering in silence. If and when the Western democracies' weaknesses lead the Soviet Union to believe that the West would silently suffer an even higher level of terrorism, its support might well become broader and more substantial.

Vulnerability and Resistance of Different Regimes to Covert Action

Because each kind of regime has its own peculiar strengths and weaknesses, each can be expected to respond differently to covert attempts to influence its policies or its character. It must be kept in mind, however, that influencing another regime's internal affairs is almost always a job far too big to be accomplished exclusively, or even primarily, by covert actions. If the exercise of such influence is the goal of policy, then all the tools of policy, overt and covert must be coordinated for its achievement.

Clearly, if possible, policy should aim to affect the ruling part of the target regime. If, for example, that regime consisted of a figurehead presidency and an army that is powerful both politically and militarily, it may be a waste of one's resources to try to influence the president's counselors or, even more, to support a palace faction in a coup d'état. The presidential palace might be won but could be useless. In such a regime, the more logical focus would be the army. Yet the world is full of totalitarian regimes whose ruling parts have, as it were, armored themselves against influence from the outside. It makes little sense to expend energies trying to support one faction of a disciplined, nearly inaccessible, communist party against another. It makes much more sense to concentrate on those parts of the society less influential but more easily influenced.

Let us now look at the role which covert activities can play in influencing various kinds of regimes, and to facilitate this examination divide the world's regimes into three groups.

(1) At first glance, one might deem the Western democracies vulnerable to every kind of covert action, and immune to none. Western democracies, including Japan, are indeed open to every sort of agent of influence. Given the lack of internal security measures it is relatively easy to sow "illegals" and not impossible to implant "moles." To buy access and influence is a straightforward task. But consider the structure of Western democracies. The organs of government are widespread and tied together by constitutional and legal frameworks. Therefore, the usefulness of any individual agent even highly-placed can only be small, since no one official may transgress the bounds of his authority. Western governments and societies enjoy a kind of compartmentation; each compartment may be easy to breach but there are so many! Moreover, though a foreign government may indeed succeed in influencing decisions through agents of influence, it cannot afford successes that are too evident. Ultimately, the sovereign element in a democracy is public opinion. Outraged public opinion can wipe out in a few months the work of decades.

For the same reason, covert violence is of limited use against democracies. For example, in the 1960's, the Italian Communist Party, acting with very little cover, orchestrated carefully controlled riots and threatened violence. By these means, it affected the choice of government ministers and policies. It even affected the choice of leaders in the Christian Democratic Party. But in the late 1970's, Italian public opinion turned so strongly against violence of any sort that the Communist Party was no longer able even to hint at, much less to carry out, violence. Also, because of its former association with violence, it lost influence everywhere. Moreover, unlike the successful fascist violence of the 1920's, the unsuccessful communist violence of the 1970's did not aim directly at the conquest of power but, rather, at breaking public resistance to subtle political maneuvers. Totalitarian groups trying to subvert democracies may well avail themselves of a few wholly clandestine selective assassinations or of full-scale covert war. But violent measures in between risk raising uncontrollable public reaction.

The logical focus of efforts to interfere in democracies is public opinion. To this end, foreign powers and factions use a number of common techniques. Journalists, academics, clerics, legislators, indeed anyone in a position to influence public opinion in a country, are likely to receive invitations aplenty from abroad. Those who show sympathy for their hosts' viewpoints are likely to return. By this rather open association, the journalist or academic becomes known as an ''expert.'' There is no clear line of demarcation between this sort of cooperation and conscious activity to foster certain ''lines'' of thought. But it is certain that if the notion even becomes widespread in a democracy that foreign elements are somehow ''behind'' an individual or a line of thought, these are likely to be spontaneously rejected more fully than they could be by any official act. Long ago, de Tocqueville noted that in democracies public opinion can shut out dissonant thoughts far more thoroughly than the most elaborate censorship ever could.

(2) The second category includes the monarchic governments of the Mid-East, military juntas, and personal dictatorships such as are found through much of the so-called ''Third World.'' Such regimes may have a single political party, but they are to be distinguished from regimes like that of Cuba and Angola which are built on a single, highly-organized party, after the Soviet model. Regimes in this second category are unaffected by elections. The people who ''matter'' are few, and usually are under few constraints with regard to one another. Neither royal families nor juntas nor dictators control their entourages, much less society in general, in the same way totalitarian regimes do.

Because the power to make decisions is usually restricted, the number of possible agents of influence is small. Yet most of those who are candidates for this role are usually easy to approach, and often receptive to personal inducements. In most regimes like this, except old royal families, loyalty to fellow members of the ruling group is low. Therefore, it is relatively easy to find persons or factions ready to accept help in building their own influence. Similarly, in such environments, little may be required to cause one faction to increase its suspicion of another. Coups d'état are frequent.

In such regimes the armed forces necessarily play a significant role. The Soviet Union long since recognized this. One cannot read *World Marxist Review* without coming across exhortation after exhortation to communists and ''progressives'' to overcome their prejudices and work with any member of the armed forces, no matter how junior, so long as that member shows the slightest promise. That sort of cultivation has paid handsome dividends from Guatemala City to Addis Ababa.

In such regimes, public opinion is of limited but real importance, although there is usually no public opinion on most questions of policy. In most circumstances, it is even difficult to conceive of public opinion on the question of how the country should be governed. Granted also that, except in places like Saudi Arabia, the vast majority of the public has little access to rulers. But, on religious or ethnic questions, public opinion is often very powerful. The Soviet Union's campaign against the Shah of Iran was based in part on accusations of infidelity to Islam launched by the Soviet Union's clandestine radio station "The National Voice of Iran." Palestinian agents, who had been armed and trained by the Soviet Union, operated in Iran under "Islamic" cover.

The fall of the Shah is a good example of the role of covert activities in such regimes. The Soviet Union's covert activities were not fully responsible for what happened. Nor is enough information yet available on the full extent of its activities. Yet one can only marvel at the sight of crowds led by Mullahs, brandishing AK-47 rifles, and shouting un-Islamic slogans which sounded as if they could have been written in Moscow. The sight of Palestinian guerrillas leading Iranian militants certainly leads one to think of those who brought them together. One can also marvel at the sight of tight-fisted bazaar merchants dispensing millions of dollars' worth of food—without charge—to the crowds of anti-Shah demonstrators. One does not have to be a profound student of the subject to contend that covert propaganda, financing, supply, and encouragement of Khomeini's forces placed a major role in the Shah's downfall.

(3) There has been all too little discussion of the possibilities of covert action against the Soviet regime, and against the regimes of Eastern Europe which imitate it. During the late 1950's, the US engaged in some covert activities in these countries but did so in a amateurish way and, therefore, at great cost in lives and in the confidence of potential assets. Yet our failure even to think about covert action there has less to do with the difficulty of the task than with the lack of an overall policy toward these areas. The American public was shocked in 1976 by State Department Counsellor Sonnenfeldt's pronouncement that America's interests lay in the Soviet Union's undisturbed hegemony over Eastern Europe. Yet, except for a brief period about thirty years ago, the American foreign policy establishment—officials, businessmen, publishers—with the notable exception of the AFL-CIO, has done nothing, and has said nothing that might disturb that hegemony. Worse, (with the exception of Cuba before 1968) there is little evidence they have intellectually entertained the possibility that any area conquered by a Communist Party might return to freedom.

The stock-in-trade of the American foreign policy establishment has been to foster the normalization of relations between communist governments and Western states. Though the foreign policy establishment has often used both overt and covert acts to combat the expansion of communist rule to new countries, it has not contemplated either form of action to try to eliminate communist rule once it takes hold anywhere. Not surprisingly, American policymakers have neither anticipated the development of serious dissidence within the Soviet Union, Poland and Cuba, nor the desperate flight of millions of Indochinese. Indeed, American policymakers have felt embarrassed by developments which should rightly be regarded as indications of plentiful opportunities for both overt and covert activities. Clearly, the autonomous actions of oppressed people to regain a measure of freedom do not appear to fit into our foreign policy. The official acts or pronouncements of the Carter Administration during the Polish crisis in 1980, like the Sonnenfeldt Doctrine, surely conveyed to the Soviet empire's subjects the feeling that the Free World wished *them* to remain unfree. American statements during the Polish crisis were full of gratuitous advice to the Polish people not to seek too much freedom.

Far from destabilizing the Soviet empire, American acts have contradicted those struggling for freedom by telling them their efforts are doomed in advance, and inherently dangerous to the world's peace. This sort of message, by all rights, should be financed by the KGB, not by American taxpayers. Until American policymakers decide that their objective really is to bring about the downfall of communist regimes, they will continue to be embarrassed by these regimes' self-destructive tendencies, and will be unable to think about how they might be helped along. Worse yet, they will be unable to deal with the dangers, as well as the opportunities, brought on by the Soviet empire's internal decay.

Helping the Soviet empire to self-destruct does not mean reckless activity, quite the contrary. That empire depends upon the cohesion of the Communist Parties involved, and on the military might of the Soviet Union. At this time, the military "correlation of forces" favors the Soviet Union. The immediate objectives of our policy toward the Soviet empire should be modest—as modest as our military ability to deal with its military power, should that become necessary. Nevertheless, present actions can bring pressures to bear on the Communist Party and perhaps begin to undermine its cohesion. Thereby, they could lay the groundwork for policies which can be pursued when and if the "correlation of forces" changes enough to permit the US to limit the damage the Soviet Union could do to its rebellious subjects and to foreign states which might help those subjects.

The Soviet government does not believe itself invulnerable. The Soviet leaders' obsession with security is not paranoia, but rather results from a realistic assessment of their predicament. Soviet leaders realize that their party is permanently at war with its people, that it is working against the grain of family, religion, individual justice and ethnicity, that the claims and promises which are the currency of official public discourse are patent lies, and that, after years of Communist rule, society follows the party out of a mixture of compulsion, habit, and the self-interest of hordes of petty leaders. Moreover, the Party's leaders are acutely aware that they are engaged in constant high-stakes struggles against one another. The West is not without means of affecting the Party's relationship with its subjects, and even with itself.

Overt broadcasts and statements of policy must play an important role. In regimes characterized by outrageous claims, truth is corrosive. They are the principal means of "going over the head" of the Party to feed the social and religious aspects of life which communist internal propaganda seeks to snuff out. It would be both irresponsible and unnecessary to incite armed resistance thereby. News of the outside world and news of what is happening within the Soviet empire is inflamatory enough to the empire's subjects. It can provide them with one of the means of liberty routinely availabe to citizens of free countries. Public opinion *is* important in the Soviet Union. That is why the Party spends so much time and effort to shape it. In order to do some of the other things that free people do—such as communicate and organize—subjects of the Soviet empire may need certain things, such as money and equipment, which might best be provided covertly from outside. Thus, covert action could supplement overt means in helping people in disadvantageous circumstances to enjoy, albeit precariously, some of the freedoms we take for granted.

There are widespread networks of religious, ethnic and political dissidence in the Soviet Union. While normally it would be too dangerous to the group themselves for foreign governments to help them covertly, private Western organizations certainly could help overtly, to a certain degree. The fund set up with the royalties from Solzhenitzyn's books is a good example. Of course, the authorities can always arrest and attempt to discredit those who openly receive money from abroad. But Western governments can place powerful disincentives on this sort of thing. Party officials treasure few things so much as travel and business abroad. Another means of combating Soviet attempts to discredit their Western-oriented citizens is for Western governments to broadcast to the Soviet people the names of party faithful who enjoy the benefits of foreign travel.

Although it is very difficult and very dangerous for foreign help to be channeled covertly, it is not impossible to build networks even within strong totalitarian states. Such networks would have to be based upon strong underlying resentment of the totalitarian state, such as those which arise from ethnicity and religion. Covert activity could not be used for routine purposes, but would have to be an investment in the future; when the totalitarian system faltered, these networks would be invaluable.

The Party is the focus of power. But so long as the Soviet Union does not face the prospect of defeat, one can have little confidence in an effort to encourage one faction of the party against another, by any means, overt or covert. Two generations of Western statesmen have believed that there existed "soft" and "hard" factions in the Kremlin, and that by concessions to the Soviet Union, they could help the former prevail over the latter. But, Westerners have never possessed either enough information about what factions really exist in the Soviet leadership. Above all, Westerners have never had the means of manipulating such factional struggles. The latest attempt, Kissinger's scheme for addicting a whole class of Soviet leaders to the benefits of trade with the West, seems to have achieved less a Soviet lobby for a soft policy toward the West than a Western lobby for soft policy toward the East. This does not mean that the Party is immune. Much of its leadership is involved in business abroad. Indeed the privilege to travel abroad is almost synonomous with status in the Soviet Union. Given the suspicions which exist among these people, nothing would prevent the West from using these foreign dealings to stir up trouble in the party. Of course, one would first have to study the Party carefully.

Covert violence might, at times, also serve a useful purpose. In the third volume of the *Gulag Archipelago,* Solzhenitzyn recalls how the spirit of prisoners, and their living conditions, were raised by occasional acts of violence against the most oppressive trustees. The salutary effects of Robin Hood's band in the reign of usurping Prince John are part of our folklore. Who knows whether a small measure of justice might not be introduced into the captive nations by selective violence against the Soviet Union's most zealous servants? But, such things cannot be decided abstractly. Policy made without thorough and timely knowledge of the area for which it is made is scarcely responsible.

All the world's totalitarian regimes are imperfect imitations of the Soviet Union. Their party discipline, as well as security arrangements are not as tight, and their societies contain sectors not thoroughly penetrated by the party or secret police. Furthermore, their military forces often have serious deficiencies. The Angolan regime might well collapse if Jonas Savimbi's guerrillas were supplied. But if the Cuban Army in Angola doubled in size, or if the Soviets sent several divisions there, covert supply alone would do as little good as covert supply of Soviet dissidents might do.

●

This brief consideration of the vulnerability of totalitarian states to covert activities serves to illustrate perhaps the central point of this examination: covert activities are valuable servants of policy, but they are not a substitute for policy. A country cannot neglect its ability to fight and win wars, or its political relations with its allies, and then look for salvation to even a first-class capability for covert action.

Even the finest apparatus for influencing views abroad, for contacting and encouraging foreign dissidents, will be of little use to the country which possesses it if that country does not have plans for pursuing political goals that are appealing, and which, once achieved, can be defended by whatever means necessary. Usually, people will not make sacrifices for murky goals, or if they believe that what they gain covertly may be taken away overtly by superior forces.

Discussants

Dr. Paul Seabury: I respond to Dr. Bozeman from within the petrified forest that she described my discipline as consisting of. I simply want to note that she has attacked three fundmental maxims of contemporary social science. The first one is: if you can't count it, forget it. The second is: do not travel abroad without taking your model with you. And the third is that if reality doesn't fit your Procrustean bed, find a more compatible reality. But she implies more. Let me try to specify those implications. I think the study of comparative politics as we do it today in this country has been dominated by certain code words for certain kinds of attitudes towards the world.

The concepts of modernization, mobilization regimes, emerging nations, developing nations, structural convergence, technotronic societies, and many others like them float from the typewriters of many scholars, including President Carter's former national security advisor. They come also from academics who call themselves structural analysts. Robert Conquest once remarked that if one applied this particular mode of analysis to the realm of zoology, one would discover that dogs and wolves are furry quadrupeds who have tails, claws, ears, mouths and teeth, and they bark and bite. But, structuralists aside, it is in our interest to be able to distinguish a dog from a wolf. I suggest that we explore to what extent the planners of American foreign policy and of covert operations have been influenced by these esoteric conceptions. I am sure that many operatives have never spent sleepless nights pouring over Almond and Verba's book, *The Civil Culture,* as a way of finding out what the Dervishes are going to do tomorrow. Nevertheless, Almond and Verba have had their effect.

There is, however, on one particular point on which I would differ with Dr. Bozeman. Much innocence about the external world may have come not from abstract social scientists so much as from the reformists of the 1970's who came into the intelligence community to impose a Boy Scout code of honor on it. Those reformers, as we well know, were anxious to establish a universal standard of conduct for a discipline not known for its ethical purity. I, like many from the outside, have no idea how much damage this purification actually caused.

I would like to underline another important issue. It is implicit in Dr. Bozeman's paper that in dealing with alien civic cultures, there is a danger of being deceived by facades. How does one penetrate beyond the facade? Clearly analysts like Almond and Verba mistook facades for reality because they were concerned with political development and understood political development occurring only in a kind of Western context. For example, they saw the Hilton Hotel towering over Addis Ababa, and mistook it for the tower of the future. Suddenly, that turned out not to be the case at all, because a few people were working diligently not to make it so.

I remember, two years before the Shah's overthrow talking with the Iranian Consul General in San Francisco who had just got back from home leave in Tehran. And he said, "I really can't recognize my home town any more. It is totally unrecognizable. Gigantic supermarket complexes are being built up," and so on. But the supermarket complexes were not the agency which forced the collapse of the Shah's regime.

The question for top policymakers concerned with political action is: who are the people best capable of penetrating these facades? When everyone got interested in Afghanistan last year, I picked up my copy of Kipling's *Kim* and discovered that Kim was a model agent, but it was very clear that he did not have an advanced degree from the London School of Economics; probably he was able to swim within the culture because he had not. And I am not so sure that this is a quality that can be picked up in academic circles where even the foreigners with whom we deal are typically very, very Western themselves.

We should do certain things to correct this intellectual imbalance. Dr. Bozeman has suggested some philosophical problems. I would like to point out a practical one. If the American university cannot recover its once distinguished record in teaching people how to speak foreign languages with great skill, languages will have to be taught to professional operatives by their parent organizations. As American culture has evolved in the past ten years or so, the study of foreign language has practically collapsed, and America's ability to operate abroad has diminished. How many of our students are studying Japanese? Yet the ability to penetrate Japanese culture seems to me absolutely essential. Every now and then, you hear of somebody who does that.

Finally, and I would like to underline my last point here, we simply must realize that Adda Bozeman is pointing to a fundamental feature in our own culture. And I came across an illustration of that difficulty the other day when looking into Montesquieu's *Persian Letters*. I would like to read to you a remark from that work of the early 18th Century:

One thing has often astonished me: and that is to see these Persians sometimes as well informed as myself on the customs and affairs of our nation and to the point of knowing the most subtle details and knowing things I am sure would have escaped Germans visiting France. And I attribute this to their long stay here without insisting on the fact that it is easier for an Asiatic to learn about French customs in one year than it would be for a Frenchman to learn Asiatic customs in four. That is because one group is as open-mouthed in its relations as the other is closed-mouthed.

In conclusion, we must also explore how, after all, one begins to live by one's wits, like a Venetian, when one has lived for so long by virtue of one's cultural energy and dynamism and power. We must surely learn to live by our wits, because our power is diminished.

It was not only Nietzsche who pointed out these qualities of dissembling, persiflage, obfuscation are the secret weapons of the weak. And it was said of Persian diplomats in the 20th Century, that they were successful because they were the best liars and obfuscators. But it does not sit well with us because we are not accustomed to that way of life. As we reconstruct our capability for covert operations, as we develop these qualities and skills, this craft, this art, we can at the same time make it very clear to ourselves that these are not the attributes of our own domestic culture. I am optimistic enough to believe that this can be done because we've done it in the past. The exercise of power does not necessarily corrupt. The craft of intelligence can have as its practitioners those who were able to maintain their integrity while being liars and obfuscators.

Dr. Richard E. Bissell: Early in her paper, Professor Bozeman implied that comparative studies must have covered the entire society in question to be useful for covert action. She bespeaks a very ambitious goal. In a sense, the whole paper is very ambitious. One can draw two conclusions from this.

One is normative: yes, this is what we need in order to understand other cultures. But I think the second necessary conclusion is that our covert action, based upon the available intelligence, will necessarily be imperfect as well because we will never or almost never have that kind of comprehensive understanding of cultures, particularly cultures going through change in all the dimensions she lists. Given necessarily imperfect knowledge, there are sure to be failures.

I think that the American people are largely unprepared for failure in covert action. In a sense, Dr. Bozeman has shown that such will happen if only because we don't have full understanding of other cultures. It also may be that we must understand that there will be mistakes along the way.

Another point applies to Dr. Codevilla's paper as well. Neither raised the question: How long should covert action remain covert? The quarterback sneak is fine, but after running off a little, the quarterback must display the ball to show he has it. Should covert action ever become public? It is simply a problem to be raised.

My second major point concerns Professor Bozeman's contention that other cultures are very different and operate differently, and that we in this country do not seem capable or willing to adjust our vision to these radically different circumstances. This is an over-statement. There are people in our society who, in fact, do under-stand covert action. Take, for instance, the Mafia whose members have performed effectively in affecting other societies. They under-stand well the dynamics involved. I would suggest a second group. A number of our politicians in Philadelphia are in a good deal of trouble for dealing with "Arab Sheiks" and money that may or may not have been passed on their behalf. The people connected with this scandal seem to understand what covert action is. I think that they would happily apply their skills to other societies if, in fact, they were handed a briefcase and told to go to another country and influence their political system. In short, significant groups of people involved in politics do understand well what covert action is about.

I thought the most useful part of Professor Bozeman's paper was the part which dealt with the need to ask the right questions about what we call the Third World. She listed a number of issues that have to be considered. It may be I can add something here as one who studies African politics because, in fact, her examples range from India to Persia to Venice, but do not include Africa. I think, for instance, one of our great weaknesses in this country, among students or academics, is that their knowledge about American covert action in Africa is limited largely to John Stockwell's book. It is curious we don't read books by Africans about covert action. There is material there. We don't even read American scholars who know well how covert action has worked in Africa, for instance, Professor W. Scott Thompson's book about Ghana. Perhaps even more pertinently, one could read a book almost unknown in this country, by John Okello on how he led the crew of fifty men in a couple rowboats to take over Zanzibar in 1964. The book describes the dynamics of African politics from an African point of view which is rare and valuable. Dr. Cod-evilla mentioned how easy it is to penetrate African societies. It is indeed easy. They are small; they are very open; they are poor. The political systems of Africa are fragile.

On a third point, I take issue with Dr. Bozeman. She contended that foreign policy is a reflection of the inner order of values. I have trouble identifying much in the way of long-range inner order in most African political systems. Politics is a superficial superstructure in most African countries; and, as a result, so are the foreign policies of African countries.

My last point concerns an issue that Dr. Codevilla raised directly, that is, the legitimacy of covert action. There is much to be studied about legitimacy. It is an issue not only for Americans, but one that arises in any country in the world. We as Americans do not have a uniform notion of cultural bounds. Some Americans think of themselves as being part of Western civilization. According to "world order" studies, the whole globe is within our cultural bounds. But the legitimacy of covert action, it seems to me, is related to one's sense of one's own cultural bound. Most people believe that you don't need covert action as long as you are operating within your cultural bound because within this bound there are rules of behavior that allow you to deal with conflicts in an overt way. When you are operating outside your cultural bounds, you are necessarily going to engage to some degree in covert action, to the extent that that other culture is an "enemy." The issue of legitimacy is a key one, but it goes back to a more fundamental issue of perception—our perceptions of who are we dealing with. Are they friend or foe? Are they "us" or are they "them?"

General Discussion

The discussion focused on three areas where there was general agreement: The absolute necessity for covert activities to be part of national policies broadly conceived and pursued by a variety of means, the importance of detailed knowledge of and sensitivity toward foreign cultures for those using covert action, and the necessity for weaker states to "live by their wits."

Participants agreed in recent decades the United States has not had a coherent foreign policy. In the words of a former US intelligence official: "We stumble from crisis to crisis, improvising while we are stumbling. But stumbling is not a good position from which to improvise." A former US official agreed with Dr. Codevilla's contention that covert action is often seen not as one among many means of pursuing policy, but as a substitute for policy. For example, he noted in the early 1960's, President Kennedy expressed his opposition to the Castro regime not by concerting the US government's many resources to bring down that regime, but merely by ordering the CIA to run covert operations against it. And because many other covert operations have been run under such circumstances, they have been wasted.

A former foreign intelligence official and a Congressional staffer pointed to another factor. If a covert activity succeeds in altering a certain foreign situation in the desired way, but the United States is not ready either to exploit the opportunity thus created, or to protect the gains thus created, then the US is likely to suffer a net loss. For example, although popular revulsion against communism in Poland was not produced by US covert action, it may be instructive for the US to ask what sort of responsibility it would bear for, and what interest it would have in the further development of the situation. Overt political and military power, plus the willingness to use it effectively make covert action much more meaningful.

There was also broad agreement that covert action cannot be a "quick fix." A participant recalled Churchill's observation that military buildups yield nothing in the first year, and do not come to full fruition until the fourth. Capabilities for covert action, he said, necessarily take even longer to build. He noted that deeply rooted habits must be changed to convince assets and above all to develop a cadre of people who can think creatively about situations and see opportunities in them. Therefore, given that the CIA's capabilities for covert action have almost ceased to exist, the CIA cannot be expected to supply the US with a "quick fix" during the coming period of military inferiority. America may build its covert action arsenal, but will be in no position to expend it.

The importance of detailed knowledge of the target for policy, for the formulation of plans and for their execution was clearly recognized. One participant said that we should have learned by now that unless one has a policy based on known facts, then to plan covert action is to play the sorcerer's apprentice. But another participant added a note of caution: detailed knowledge is needed in inverse proportion to the assets available. He pointed out that in 1954 the success of Guatemalan forces favorable to the United States was due less to their subtle understanding of Guatemalan society than to their preponderant political and military power.

There were several views on why Americans who plan covert activities have been generally insensitive to the environments of the areas where those plans must be carried out. A former intelligence officer noted the often-stated reason that American policymakers are too busy to learn about such things. But, he said, since these are the factors which make the difference between success and defeat, they should have the time or make the time. Another former official commented on the level of knowledge of planners and practitioners. A standard two-year tour abroad, he said, is inadequate for apprehending the essence of foreign cultures. All agreed that it would be difficult to imagine successful covert action planned or carried out by people who do not even speak the target country's language. At this point some criticized universities for having abolished language requirements while others blamed the CIA for failing to demand that its employees master foreign languages.

The discussion then turned to the quality of academic instruction in area studies. An intelligence official complained that when the government turns to the academic community for enlightenment about the Soviet Union, it most often finds a combination of social science models which bear little relationship to reality. Seldom do academics turn their attention to Soviet realities such as the International Department of the Soviet Communist Party's Central Committee or the KGB. He concluded that practitioners of covert action cannot expect to have learned much from their graduate studies. The academic "data bank" on foreign countries is quite poor. An academic explained that this is due to academic bias against area studies. Professors who know languages and focus on actual events have not always faired as well with regard to rank and grants as have those who specialize in model building.

The question regarding the importance of a people knowing how to live by their wits was first framed in these terms: Heretofore the US has been strong and has not had to rely for survival on surreptitious measures, but now that we are relatively weak in the world we will have to learn to live by the arts of the weak, being sensitive to foreign cultures and turning foreign events covertly our way whenever possible. But it was pointed out that historically, reliance on wits, on stealth, depends not so much on a nation's weakness as it does on that nation's perception. Venice, for example, used covert activities well both while weak and while strong. The reason seems to be its preoccupation with strategic designs. The United States, on the other hand, has made relatively little use of covert action while strong, and does not seem to be on the brink of change even though it has become weak. Perhaps it was speculated that is because the perception of America's weakness is not yet widespread, or perhaps because Americans are as yet unused to thinking strategically.

CHAPTER THREE

The Uses of Political and Propaganda Covert Action in the 1980's

---

Paper:

Vernon A. Walters

Discussants:

Dr. Ray S. Cline

Dr. Abram Shulsky

Almost since the dawn of organized human society governments who feel threatened by actions or apparent intentions of other governments have tried to find out as much as they could about those other governments and then to influence their course of action in ways favorable to themselves. They have used bribery, threats, cajoling, deception, diplomatic activity. When these did not produce the desired result and when the situation did not seem to demand open military action, they often turned to more discreet ways of attempting to change the course of events to fit their wishes. Then governments have resorted to what we now call covert action.

When a nation decides that the actions of another nation, either at home or in a third country, constitute a serious threat to the interests of that first nation—or to the security of its friends and allies—it then seeks to weaken its adversary and defuse the threat before it becomes an open military one. The more general form of covert action is to seek to alter in the long term the thinking in the target nation in such a way as to make them perceive that their interest does not lie in hostility to the first nation. If this can be done, then those responsible for the formation of public opinion and the key decisions may be made to see things quite differently from their original views and this can be done at considerably less cost and less loss of life than one day of open warfare. The most successful action of this type takes place without anyone in the target nation being aware of it. Most important, there is no armed clash.

In my view, most effective covert action has been carried out by the Soviet Union against the United States. It has been done with great sophistication and profound understanding of the American national character and of the "American dream." I can almost hear in my mind the Soviet long-term planning group in 1948, noting that

115

the US emerged from World War II practically undamaged—with very small losses in manpower compared to the other major belligerents—its industrial plants unharmed by bombing or sabotage, producing half the world's goods with six percent of the population, and with a nuclear monopoly. The US had decided to insure the financial and industrial recovery of western Europe and Japan through the Marshall Plan, an act Winston Churchill once called the "single most unselfish act in human history." No other nation had ever financed its competitors back into competition with it and then, still worse, from the Soviet point of view, the US was preparing to cover this recovery with the military umbrella of NATO.

I can imagine the gloom that must have permeated that group until one member who knew us well said, "Ah, comrades, that is all true but the American giant has an Achilles' heel that will enable us to lay him low, despite all of the advantages you have listed. What we must do is so broaden and deepen that streak of guilt, which is an essential part of the American character, that we will paralyze them through their own conscience when we move to advance our interests and help our friends. Already they feel guilty for the very reasons you have mentioned. They know that they have suffered far less than the British, Poles, Germans, Chinese and French. Their factories are undamaged by bombs or fighting. Their people have all they want to eat. They are rich and prosperous; everyone else is poor and hungry. We have the means to enlarge and deepen that streak of guilt until these proud, hard-working, confident people who are so sure that they have the solutions to all the world's problems will become confused, unsure, disorganized, divided among themselves, unable to resist our steadfast march to the mastery of the world. If we act correctly, measure their weakness and take the actions that are necessary, then we will be on the way up and they will be on the way down." I can hear now as well the objections of those who must have said, "You are mad. They are only six percent of the world's population; they are producing half the goods in the world; they have unlimited access to the storehouses of raw materials and energy; their infrastructure is untouched; their will to greatness is enhanced by the recent victory. How can you possibly achieve the results for which you hope?"

Then must have come the reply, "We must study their society and all of its vulnerabilities. We must study the resentment of their allies at being helped by them. Britain and France were only recently proud and mighty nations—now they are destitute and they resent it bitterly. They regard the Americans as nouveaux riches and uncultured

barbarians. This will give us the opportunity to drive a wedge between them and their allies. But is must never be seen as 'our
wedge'.''

"The United States is a different country from the other nation
states. It does not have a single main ethnic root. They think of
themselves as a melting pot. Well, comrades, we must make the pot
boil. There are enormous possibilities for us to stir that ethnic mix.
Now, their immigrants are proud of being Americans and in a great
measure of want to forget the 'old country.' We must reawaken their
deep racial pride. We must make each of those minorities feel discriminated against. We must provoke friction between them, as well
as jealousy and a feeling that they are being discriminated against.
But they must never be able to prove to one another that we are
behind this reawakening.

"There is a background that will help us. They have discriminated
against their Blacks, orientals, Jews, Indians—ah, they feel particularly guilty about the Indians—and we will work that theme. His-
panics, too, will be ripe for agitation. This must be done subtly and
in such a way as to make the whole development seem natural and
logical and, above all, without any external connections. The fertile
ground for this effort lies in the fact that they know that in the recent
war these minorities fought for them and sustained casualties at least
as heavy proportionately as the Anglo-Saxons. Already they feel
ashamed of their treatment of the Americans of Japanese origin,
locking them away in concentration camps. They know that they
have discriminated against their Blacks, who do not have rights like
other Americans, who are low on the economic and educational scale
and do not have the vertical mobility that other Americans enjoy.
We must make these minorities acutely conscious of this discrimination and injustice. We must help them organize to demand full
equality and there we will have the beginnings of mutual mistrust
and, if we play our cards well, hostility between the various ethnic
groups. We must stimulate pride in ethnic culture and memories of
the 'old country'.

"Politically, Americans are like children. We must educate them
and make their young people as politically conscious as are the
Europeans and Latin Americans. Now their youth is interested only
in sports, girls and jobs. This we can and must change. A small
number of academics, properly placed, largely unaware of what they
are doing for us could act as leaven and cause the dough to rise. It
is important that we use a minimum of recruited agents and a maximum of discontented idealists. Some of those in academia think that

they are the best educated and the most intelligent citizens in the community and their salaries are incredibly low compared to those paid by American industry. We must give them the feeling that a society which does not recognize and reward them must of necessity be rotten and doomed to fall. Once we get that snowball rolling, comrades, the task will be easy.

"America is a country of idealists. They always want to help others. We must make them understand that they have developed the most terrible of all weapons in history and they have used it on people of another race. What an opportunity there is here to increase their guilt. We must mount anti-nuclear campaigns in the United States and throughout the world. This will serve a double purpose. It will increase their feeling of guilt and prevent them from using this weapon—or even threatening us with it—during the period while they still enjoy a nuclear monopoly. Soon, thanks to our intelligence agents and Americans who 'felt guilty,' we will have it too. We must stir their feeling that it is unfair for them to have it and for us not to have it. We must never cease to emphasize that they used it and we did not.

"Then there is the problem of their immense industrial production. This production has not been achieved without damage to the countryside and the atmosphere. We must invent terminology that makes them feel guilty for their industrial production, rather than proud of it.

"They are a young people and, like all young people, they are violent. We must point out their violence and make them feel ashamed of it. We must make them understand that this America which they still regard as the 'last best hope of mankind' is tainted, marked with discrimination, materialism and injustice. When they move to help their friends we must point out the faults in their allies— the fact that they do not live up to the ideals the Americans preach but do not practice.

"Our whole effort must be to arouse doubt, anxiety and guilt. When this has been done, the great consensus will be broken and they will be ripe for the next stage, division and mutual hostility. They have always been uncomfortable with large armies in peacetime. We must increase that discomfort. What will be done to the Americans will resemble acupuncture. We will press invisibly on a thousand pressure points producing reactions in entirely different parts of their body politic.

"This, comrades, represents only an outline of my idea of how we bring them down to our size. Guided by the wise directives of the party, we can carry out such a program over a long period of time. Unlike them, our leaders and experts remain at their posts and carry out their programs over many five-year plans. Their whole political structure is thrown into an upheaval every four years and their leaders do not remain in power for periods comparable to ours. Perforce their policies are less stable. They know vaguely what they want. We know exactly because, through Marxism, we know what is inevitable and that is the triumph of the party of workers, peasants, soldiers and sailors. Their convictions are more diffuse and their certainty of right is less and must be made even smaller.

"Their attitude toward intelligence is typical of their guilt-ridden state. They have always been ambivalent toward it. When they do not feel threatened, they regard it as immoral or else disband it entirely. Just think, comrades, during their Civil War, the federal government had no intelligence service. President Lincoln had to hire a private detective agency to get information on the South. They have never been a monarchy and so have no idea or what is meant by *raison d'etat*. They think that in politics it is wrong to lie or dissemble. When the time comes, we can use loyal Americans who think intelligence is immoral and un-American to cripple, blind and deafen them, and those who will have helped us will believe, truly and sincerely, that they have done something noble. As a people, they want to do the right thing and this is one of their principal vulnerabilities if we handle them correctly. Whatever it is we want them to do we must make it look like the right thing to them and there will be no difficulty in getting them to do it.

"It is not that the task is so difficult. But it will require enormous patience, continuity of effort on our side and skill, so that our hand will not be seen and all of the developments we want to bring about in their society will seem natural and normal developmental changes that were inevitable anyway if America was to become a better and more just society. We must study them continuously to see which tactics work and which do not. We must be flexible in our tactics and extraordinarily inflexible in our strategy.

"Comrades, this is an unique opportunity in history to apply judo tactics. We must use the enemy's strength to get him off-balance and then pin him down. The harder he struggles, the surer will be his fall. But, above all, we must have patience. Time, history and, in the end, the Americans will be on our side if we handle our plans properly. We have a sense of historic inevitability; we know that time works for us.

"What I suggest may take thirty, forty, fifty years. Meanwhile, we develop and strengthen the base of the revolution here in the Soviet Union while eroding the values of their society, family, Judaeo-Christian ideals, sense of rightness and destiny. We must make them understand that their apparently limitless power does have limits. We must reevaluate our plans continuously, reinforcing ideas that work for us and discarding those that do not seem to be producing effective results. We must constantly monitor key areas to see if we are getting results. We must also carefully apply our resources to those areas and remember that an effective agent of influence is far more profitable from our point of view than spies, open propagandists or members of the American Communist Party. For us, the CPUSA is a liability and offers us no hope of effective action. Above all, we must not attempt to implement the program I have described through the CPUSA. Above all, comrades, constant study and patience—patience.''

•

This may not have been the scenario at all. But, if we look at what has happened to this country since the end of World War II, it could well have been. In any case, such a scenario is a prototype of a plan for political action by one country against another. Such a plan must be based on a thorough study of the target country's history, habits, differences, problems, hopes and ideals.

Such covert action requires special skills, special contacts and long-term experts who have won the confidence of those who must assist them in the country where the covert action is planned. So much of the success of such plans must be based on a degree of confidence that can only be built up over the years. Covert action programs cannot be turned on and off like faucets.

No covert action should be embarked upon without the expertise, the confidence and the knowledge necessary to carry it through to a successful conclusion. And, to be successful, it must live up to its name and be covert, that is, it must not become public. Moreover there must be an awareness of the difficulties involved, and an understanding of the other side's capabilities to respond to such an action.

Once a plan is adopted, it cannot be tinkered with. If some part is removed or changed, then the whole plan must be reviewed. One cannot eliminate some essential part and then say, ''Oh, go ahead and carry out the rest of the plan.'' What happened at the Bay of Pigs made that self-evident. Once the decision had been made to remove the air strike, the whole plan should have been reviewed or changed.

All of this is as true of kinds of covert action which do not require military action as it is of kinds that do. Covert actions aimed only at moving public opinion can have tremendous effect. Often covert action may require nothing more than making certain information available to our friends or helping them to get it to the public's attention. Sometimes it may involve organizational or financial help and this must be handled only by those who have an intimate knowledge of the country and its traditions, customs and politics.

Through the communist parties, the Soviet Union has a ready-made vehicle for covert action in almost every country but they are far too shrewd to use only those who are openly and unconditionally favorable to them. In most respects, then, this world is neither more nor less favorable to the Soviet Union's political action than it is to the political action of any other country. Agents of any country engaging in such action must choose influential people whose views are not totally in agreement with theirs but who are moving in essentially the same direction in which they wish to see the situation evolve.

Anyone seeking to act covertly must select certain key influential personalities in each country who may be useful. Then they must study the desires, ambitions, prejudices and vulnerabilities of such people to see how they may be manipulated. Some, by a misguided idealism, some by the lust for power, others for money or other material ambitions. Some are motivated by a desire for revenge for some real or imagined hurt. Some, may be manipulated through blackmail because of past misconduct or irregularities in their sexual lives. Therefore, biographic intelligence is of the highest importance.

First, one must identify the key figures whom it seems desirable to manipulate, and, to do this, one does *not* have to recruit them as agents. Then one must find out, after careful study of all of the biographic intelligence available, what courses of action are most likely to succeed with this particular individual in inducing him or her, knowingly or unknowingly, to support certain courses of action. One also surveys the powerful media and sees what agencies or personalities can be of assistance to their projects. Here again, the subject may be witting or unwitting. For all of the foregoing reasons, data on the vulnerabilities of key personnel must be tirelessly collected. The most serious problem is the highly-motivated individual who has been intelligent enough to realize that there must be no vulnerabilities in his life that would expose him to blackmail or other forms of pressure. In the words of the poet Hafiz, ``The heart of the most powerful tyrant trembles before the man who wants nothing for himself.'' However, such men are rare indeed. Money is sometimes useful, but history teaches us that well-organized and carefully-planned operations have often been run on very small amounts of money.

In covert action, success is only a matter of luck unless all of the ``pressure points'' have been carefully identified and evaluated. Areas where success is improbable or highly unlikely should not have resources—human or material—squandered on them. Priorities must be designated and it is upon these that the main effort must be carried out.

Here the question of language skills and country-knowledge enters the picture. In delicate matters, it is essential to be able to communicate directly with those whom it is desired to influence. The Soviets have understood this and have at their disposal large numbers of highly-qualified linguists, many with native fluency. Native fluency is hard to achieve, because when someone reaches 96 percent proficiency, there is little to push him to make the effort to go the last four percent of the way. At 96 percent, he is being congratulated for his extraordinary fluency. Yet the extra few percent can make a big difference. The extraordinary effectiveness of people like Oleg Troyanovsky, the Soviet Ambassador to the United Nations derives in significant part from their ability to communicate directly and subtly with influential people from a number of countries. Unfortunately for us, the United States has few Troyanovskys. The US is today the only major country in the world in which it is possible to get a college diploma without the knowledge of a foreign language. Study of foreign languages in the United States is at an all-time low.

What is true of language is also true of history. As a people, few of us are conversant with the history of foreign countries. One must know the history of a people to understand what made them the way they are and how they became what they now are. The study of history must be supplemented by close physical acquaintance. This is important not only because it is essential to know the broad outlines of a people's character and consensus, but also because the outcome of any action, overt or covert can easily depend on awareness or ignorance of what we have often call foibles. There are a million-and-one such national foibles and anyone who is thinking of covert action in any form whatever had better be very well-informed of them.

One of the most dangerous assumptions concerning people of another country is that, because they speak our language well, or went to school in our country, that they are necessarily friendly. Consider Haile Mariam Mengistu in Ethiopia or many of the Iranian militants who are graduates of US institutions of higher learning. Americans often make this mistaken assumption. But the Soviets tend to err in the opposite direction. The Soviets are often suspicious of any non-ethnic Russian who learns Russian. They want to know why he studied Russian. They are not alone. The Dutch, who are marvellous linguists generally react with scarcely disguised hostility to any foreigner attempting to speak Dutch to them.

Native speakers of French in many cases think they have been the victims of linguistic imperialism by us, that we deliberately set out years ago to replace French with English as the world's great international language. This arouses resentments of which we should be aware. The Germans tend to feel privately that Americans regard them as second-class allies, not like the French and British, and therefore often perceive a slight where none is intended. Every Mexican child growing up reads in his history book that the United States took half Mexican national territory. It is true, and inevitably colors their view of Americans. Every Colombian child learns in school of American perfidy in tearing away Panama from Colombian sovereignty. This, too, is true.

The Third World is an important arena in the struggle between forces of freedom and those of totalitarianism. Consideration of policy is an area where personal relationships far outweigh others. This is a difficult concept for Americans to grasp. We do everything because it is either in accord with policy or it is not. In the Third World, friendship and trust are far more important. These are often won and lost not by national criteria but by personal involvement and the management of attitudes. The world is full of prejudices and predispositions. Many of these work not against us, but against our adversaries. For example, there are in Eastern Europe deep prejudices against Russia and profound resentment of the thirty-five-year occupation of their countries by Soviet troops. At any rate, knowledge of something like a road map of the world's prejudices is absolutely essential to anyone who would plan political action, overt or covert.

There are those who will say that trying to influence events or opinion in another country is immoral. But no one can deny that the first duty of any official personnel in another country is to increase the number and importance of the friends of their own country. In fact, it has been said that diplomats during their service in a foreign country should be judged by the measure in which they have increased the number of their country's friends and decreased the number of its enemies. Morality does not require that friendships and the efforts made to gain them be broadcast to our enemies.

Covert action that aims at affecting public opinion or political events in another country is part and parcel of overt policy. It differs above all in that for successful execution it requires human resources of the highest order. It requires superb intelligence—economic, political and military. It requires biographic intelligence at a level above that which we have heretofore considered adequate. It requires friends who trust us and who know that we have the ability to keep their identities secret. It requires a degree of patriotism and motivation of the highest order. It requires patience and imagination and, above all, it requires will on the part of the decisionmakers. It requires discretion from us and from the friendly parties we may be assisting.

We cannot face the coming years and the ever-growing threat without such a capability. If we do, history may not forgive us. If we have such a capability, and it is known, we may save a large part of the world from the long "Red Night." The possession of such a capability carries with it an awesome responsibility to use it sparingly and well, never capriciously or lightly, and we need also the ability to recognize when covert action is being used against us and the means to thwart it.

Discussants

Dr. Ray S. Cline: I thought General Walters was ingenious for putting himself in the mind of a comrade-planner in the KGB. I suspect, however, that the Soviet experts have observed that they don't need to expend any effort to cause Americans to handicap themselves by a deep sense of guilt; it comes naturally. It was built into the territory perhaps by our Puritan ancestors and perhaps by our 20th Century investment in psychiatry. Somehow we do ourselves all sorts of damage in this field. Any assistance from Moscow is simply icing on the cake. Rather, I think the Soviet Union's concept of covert action is a little different. I would recommend it to our attention.

Covert action or special activities or political and propaganda covert action are not a last resort. Rather, they should be one of the first resorts to supplement strategic planning and policymaking. I believe General Walters agrees, and was saying that paramilitary action is a last resort. My point is that we should be thinking strategically all the time about all of the weapons or means available to our government. If we had a strategy in foreign policy which we have not had for a number of years, it would be very useful to supplement that routinely by a persistent effort in every part of the world to conduct what I call covert political action.

Covertness is often useful because the information given, the money passed, the influence built up by whatever methods is not directly attributable to the US Government. In 1952 we coined the word "covert" to mean not "clandestine," because everybody can see what is happening, but rather to refer to something that could not be proved to be coming from the US Government.

I think that this kind of covert activity should be a routine part of the human resource activity of the intelligence services. It became bureaucratically isolated and separated somewhat accidentally. Then, because of the preoccupation of former Senator Church and some other well-meaning persons with paramilitary operations, it became intellectually separated and isolated. However, in my own view this intellectual separation is mistaken. The Bay of Pigs came to seem to most critics to be the typical covert action of the US Government. In fact, the Bay of Pigs operation was not a covert action at all. It did not reflect any of the qualities which we have all recommended should go into covert action.

I would like to stress that covert action will almost automatically result from the existence of an effective intelligence network of human resources in the trouble spots of the world. If we are able to collect clandestine intelligence, to conduct espionage knowledgeably and selectively and with targets aimed at key opinion-making and decision-making elements of the societies we are interested in, we will almost automatically have the basis for the subtler forms of covert action, covert political influence on decisions in those countries. This is because the same people who often are collectors are also covert political actors. In fact the best ones I think are usually both. So I would like to suggest that covert action is probably an inappropriate term, but ought to be part of the thinking of the US intelligence officer, both the analyst and the secret operator, and that it should be part of our standard armor to try to influence events in key parts of the world which our strategic policy tells us are important.

It is my view that if we didn't make such a shibboleth of conducting special activities or covert action and simply went about explaining American values and the facts of life of our friends abroad, especially the facts of totalitarian and hostile intelligence life by all means possible, we would buck up stabilizing elements in in-between nations subject to both US and Soviet influence.

The values of our society ought to be taught better in our universities, along with special knowledge of languages and foreign areas. This sort of teaching certainly has atrophied in a disgraceful way in the last twenty years. We ought to be bringing that knowledge of foreign societies and of global geopolitical considerations into the ken of policymakers. The best way I know to do it is to sensitize intelligence officers to such considerations, especially those who operate abroad and collect key missing links so that analysts at home can make a complete picture. Therefore these perspectives would also reach the minds of the analysts who ought to be able to be persuasive with their political bosses.

To accomplish this not everybody need be superintelligent. The answer is to have a working institutional framework leading from the collector in the field and the covert actor in the field, through the analyst in Washington to the decisionmakers in Washington. These decisionmakers are the key. They somehow must have an appreciation of the importance of objective information, and of the importance of using that information almost spontaneously and naturally to convey our attitude, our values, against hostile values and forces in any area in which we consider we have an important international interest. None of this is strange. We all conduct covert action every day with everybody we know. Why shouldn't our nation do it too?

Dr. Abram Shulsky: I will briefly try to transpose General Walters' hypothetical discussion of the kinds of covert action the Soviets could run against us to the kinds of things that we perhaps might want to consider doing vis-a-vis the Soviet Union in the eighties.

Let me first point out an introductory premise which will explain a little of what I will say later: I assume that it is quite unlikely that any covert action that we might undertake will remain really covert for long. In other words, we don't really have the means to keep a covert action covert throughout the various parts of bureaucracy that would be involved in carrying it out. There is enough resistance to covert action that I think one simply has to assume that it would hit the media sooner or later. Therefore, any covert action must be such that its revelation will not cause tremendous domestic problems for the Administration nor cause a foreign policy disaster. Of course, this depends heavily on what the publicly stated policy is regarding the area in which the covert action takes place. The covert action must be consistent with the policy.

Revelation of covert action then would result in showing that the government is doing is more or less what it said it is doing; but that it just hadn't explained exactly how it was doing it. I think it is important that any covert action be seen to be centered on the one goal that could maintain public support for covert action: that is, the defense of freedom against totalitarianism.

Throughout the Carter Administration and the tenure of the preceding two Presidents, reference has been made to a policy of détente, defined as a combination both of cooperation and competition. But, as far as the public was concerned, all the emphasis seemed to be on the side of cooperation. The SALT negotiations were described as the centerpiece of our foreign policy, meant to enhance cooperation. Then what is meant by enhancing competition? What kind of practical meaning has been given to that? Very little. However, nothing prevents us from talking publicly about "political action," or "active measures." Perhaps we could even adopt the latter term, the Soviet term, which is "ideological struggle." This, the Soviets say, goes on even in the period of détente and peaceful co-existence. Why can we not publicly proclaim we are conducting a struggle of the ideologies even while the other part of the policy is attempting to avoid nuclear war and so forth?

I will just divide this "struggle" quickly into two general categories: First, actions that might be directed against the Soviet Union, Soviet bloc countries, and secondly, other kinds of action that might be applicable elsewhere.

When we look at the Soviet Union and the Soviet bloc countries, and if we use the perspective of General Walters' paper, we see that there really is a big problem: Because the Soviet Union is expert in this kind of activity, it has largely designed its own country to be invulnerable to it. There are tremendous internal controls on what people do, what they are allowed to say inside the country, tremendous inaccessibility to the influential people in the regime. To be allowed out of the country, to visit Westerners, is already a great privilege and something that one has to earn. The Soviet professor, even to be able to have access to foreign visitors to the Soviet Union, must use controlled channels. Therefore, we usually don't have access to the professors in the Soviet Union unless they have passed some sort of ideological test. And, of course, if we did have access, the kind of influence that we could have over them is quite limited. The domestic censorship, the fact that the struggles within the Soviet government are not publicized and are papered over by means of a large propaganda apparatus, all designed to show a kind of unity. This makes it extremely difficult to have some of these ordinary means of covert action used against the Soviet Union.

On the other hand, there is a clear vulnerability, I think, of the Soviet bloc countries which results from the loss of ideological belief on which so much of the country's governing powers were vested in the past. There is a kind of openness to new ideas among the population and even among the leadership, deriving from a certain cynicism toward Marxism/Leninism.

I think our key goal in political action vis-a-vis the Soviet Union and the Soviet bloc is to play upon that vulnerability by essentially providing Soviet citizens true information about their country. In other words, the people, although they don't believe the official line, simply don't have the information available to come up with any other ideas. They are starved for information about their own country. Solzhenitsyn commented on this rather acerbically in his 1979 *Foreign Affairs* article. He complained about the Voice of America saying, "What do they do? They broadcast about America; in fact, they broadcast silly things about America." He mentioned a program on collecting beer cans. What we should be doing, he says, is to broadcast about the Soviet Union. That is what people in Russia really want to hear. They want to know about their own country. And we can provide that kind of information. Again, all true information; I think that is sufficient.

One doesn't even have to embellish the truth. We could go far by mentioning a few simple things, for example the casualties that the

Soviet Union and Cuba are incurring in Afghanistan and Africa. That information is not available to the Russian and Cuban people. They are probably able to forget about the war. Compare that to the American population's inability to forget about the war in Vietnam during that period because of what was coming on the television screen every evening. By telling the Russian and Cuban people the facts, we would permit them to assess the costs of their government's aggression. What are the costs in money? What are the costs in the lost development opportunities in their own country, and the opportunity to solve domestic problems within the country?

Much more can be done just by giving the people facts routinely available to citizens of democracies. What is the crime situation in Russia? How can one expect people to know that they have a real problem when the government officially ignores it? And another example, there were strikes in the Soviet Union in the Spring of 1980 apparently caused by the lack of food supplies. Again, it was reported that the government handled these strikes by rushing food supplies to the area. It seems the Soviets have supplies scattered around the country, and when the situation goes critical in one city, they rush food there and calm the situation down. Clearly this couldn't work if every city knew that this is how you got more food. Much would happen if we simply explained that situation.

At the end of the first major strikes in Poland in August 1980, one of the concerns of the Polish workers was that the government allowed the broadcasting of a mass on Sunday morning. That is in one sense very good, but, on the other hand, why haven't we been broadcasting masses into Poland for the last thirty years? Why haven't we been broadcasting religious programs, say, from the Polish churches, Russian orthodox churches, and so forth, into those countries all along?

In other words, there are lots of healthy tendencies in these countries. They can and should be supported. Nevertheless, I don't believe this could possibly have the sort of success against totalitarian countries that General Walters was talking about for the Soviets' hypothetical programs against us. On the other hand, we probably can help healthy tendencies, and we can do this in a way that I think really raises no moral problems whatsoever. And so we can be sure if it comes out next year that certain broadcasts were being made without saying, "This is information coming from the USA," it would be clear to everyone what had been done was in no sense dubious, in no sense immoral, and so forth. We would simply be providing the truth and providing information that by any standard anyone in America believes should be available to the people of a given area.

Outside the Soviet bloc, I think we have certain opportunities that come about primarily because of the shift in what the Soviet leaders call the "correlation of forces." The result of that shift in forces is a kind of Soviet adventurism that is running up against all sorts of other resistances in the world, as for example in Afghanistan. A lot of support can be given to these various kinds of resistance movements. Again, there is really little moral question about such support. In January 1980, it was reported that we were giving arms in some manner covertly to the Afghan rebels. There was no outcry about that. Why? I think partly because it was such an obviously reasonable thing to be doing, and therefore it was very hard to object. So that there can be any number of organizations or groups throughout the rest of the world that will be involved in resisting this kind of Soviet adventurism. Certain kinds of support can be funneled to them.

Finally, another trick we might try to pick up from the Soviets is the ability that they have to separate out what is being done on the official level and the state level from what is being doing on unofficial levels. The Soviets use their relations with the world's Communist parties to conduct much of their foreign policy.

Others can play a similar game, if not on the same scale. The West German Social Democratic Party, for instance, already has started moving in this direction with its aid to Socialist parties in other parts of the world. The AFL-CIO is giving material support to the Polish unions in a way that the CIA cannot do, and without the dangers that would come about if the CIA did it.

Therefore, I conclude that there are opportunities that come to the fore in the context of publicly stated policy that can be justified should they become public.

General Discussion

Two themes emerged in discussion: The relationship between contemporary US political action and secrecy, and the conditions under which covert activity by intelligence agencies is to be preferred to overt activities of the American Foreign Service.

At the outset, several former US intelligence officials objected to Dr. Shulsky's suggestion that, henceforth, covert activities must be planned on the assumption that they are likely to be disclosed. One said that in thirty years' experience no operations in which he was involved were leaked either by the intelligence community, the press or a Congressional committee. Dr. Shulsky replied that he was not necessarily speaking of the past, but that based on US experience and culture, in the future covert actions had better be justifiable in terms of policy. Another former official disagreed with Dr. Shulsky, maintaining that the intelligence profession's tradition of secrecy has not really broken down even though he acknowledged that retired intelligence officers are now writing books about their activities.

A Congressional staffer suggested that Dr. Shulsky's point was misleading. After all, prior to World War II President Roosevelt had taken part in British covert action on American soil which was inconsistent with stated American policy—neutrality—and of American law. But Roosevelt's actions were quite justifiable in terms of the defense of freedom. Covert activities, he suggested should be justifiable in terms of things more solid and worthwhile than policy.

The second theme was discussed in terms of two questions: Is covert action an intelligence function or a foreign policy function?; and when is overt action preferable to covert? One former intelligence officer contended that covert action is very much an intelligence function because in most cases the very same assets useful for collection are the ones best placed to exert political influence. But another former intelligence official maintained that a "cultural" prejudice has developed according to which the activities of the Foreign Service Officers to influence local politics are permissible, while the activities of clandestine intelligence officers are considered beyond the pale, unless specifically authorized, even when they accomplish worthy ends. This, the official said, is the result of acceptance of the "debased" morality of the US media. He suggested that secrecy does not necessarily affect the moral worth of any action one way or the other.

Another former intelligence official maintained that there is no abstract rule on the basis of which to choose the proper mixture of overt information policy, open diplomacy, covert propaganda, and covert political action. Rather, in his view, policymakers must first decide what they wish to accomplish. Only with reference to specific missions can one judge the appropriateness of means—overt or covert. The appropriateness of US radio broadcasts to Hungary prior to 1956 cannot be judged abstractly, but rather must be seen in relation to what senior American policymakers were and were not willing to do with regard to Hungary. Several participants maintained that overt and covert means must also fit with senior policymakers' policies with regard to domestic public opinion. For example, no major political action programs toward the Soviet Union, be they overt or covert, can be expected to succeed unless some attempt is made to explain to the American people that we are fighting for our survival against the Soviet Union and that we are right to try to prevail.

CHAPTER FOUR

The Uses of Paramilitary Covert Action in the 1980's

Paper:

Theodore G. Shackley

Discussants:

Mr. Daniel Arnold

Dr. Frank N. Trager

The Challenge

As the decade of the 1980's opens, Cuban mercenary armies sustain dictatorial governments in two large African nations, Angola and Ethiopia. In the Western Hemisphere, Cuban and Soviet-trained revolutionaries rule in Nicaragua. Their comrades threaten to seize neighboring El Salvador. Guatemala is in turmoil for it knows it is next in line to receive priority attention from Havana's and Moscow's guerrilla movements. In the Middle East—the energy treasure trove of the Western world—the southern tip of the Arabian peninsula has become an armed camp for the military forces of the Soviet Union and its allies. From this base they have attacked an intimidated North Yemen and pose today a threat to an eastern neighbor, Oman, the country that controls the Strait of Hormuz through which over half the free world's oil supply moves in giant vulnerable tankers at the rate of one every 15 minutes. The importance of free access to this vital sea lane has been forcefully underscored during the early days of the Iraqi-Iranian war which started in September 1980 and quickly commanded the attention of a world concerned about access to oil supplies.

A Soviet Army is engaged in conquering Afghanistan which is only 300 miles away from these important straits. Meanwhile, the nation in between, Iran, is racked by revolution and engaged in a war with Iraq. Farther east, beyond the Bay of Bengal, the Soviet-supported armies of Vietnam are rooting out native resistance in Laos and Cambodia while simultaneously menacing Thailand.

These then are some of the areas where communist-trained and supported forces are engaged in open combat. This indicates that the challenge of the 1980's is not all nuclear—in reality it is a mixture of conventional warfare and insurgency played out against a nuclear backdrop.

135

Elsewhere, such as in Honduras and Namibia, Soviet-supported guerrilla movements are arming and training, waiting for the moment to pounce on weak or isolated governments. What business, some may ask, is this of ours—of the Americans?

The answer lies in the reality that Soviet-supported nations and insurgencies are increasingly clustered in areas of importance critical to the survival of the United States. The fateful chain of events which led to this situation may have links that reach back into the histories of the nations involved, but the actual threat to our interests is the product of the last few years—the same years during which the United States, as a matter of policy, abandoned the use of covert means to support its friends, and then turned away from opportunities to help its sympathizers in countering insurgent movements.

History teaches us that no nation, since the age of steam and steel, has been able to hide within a shrinking world. Nor can a great power avoid the responsibilities of its position. If a nation foreswears the use of power to protect its allies and interests, then it misuses that power as surely as if it employed it for aggression. During much of the last two decades, Americans have been caught up in a dilemma. What is our role in the world and our national destiny? How do we weigh this against reality? Some say we should disdain the use of power abroad—come what may—because it is inherently immoral. Is this self-interest? Or is it simply self-expression. In any event, the world is not listening, particularly the Soviet Union and China.

The Kremlin has clearly dedicated itself to expanding its influence and dominion over others through clandestine means. This is hardly news. Yet there are those in America who have forgotten that over the years, the tools of political warfare—propaganda, deception, "agents of influence," bribery and secret financial support—have been used to advance and protect Soviet interests in both developed countries and in the Third World, whenever other means were tactically inappropriate. Where the situation required it (often as a result of the methods just mentioned being successfully applied), the Soviets have turned to more direct means: fostering insurgency and guerrilla warfare—and outright invasion.

Failure to confront and repel the challenge posed by these techniques of international political warfare is dangerous, recklessly so. Indeed, such failures might well lead ultimately to a nuclear confrontation between the Soviet Union, controlling much of the world, and an isolated, embattled United States turning to its nuclear arsenal in convulsive desperation.

In fact, Kremlinologists say this is pretty much the way the Soviets see the possibility of nuclear war. But we still have the option to combat expanding Soviet influence through political warfare, counterinsurgency and irregular warfare so that the balance of world power—the Soviets call it the "correlation of forces"—is never so favorable as to lead them to the ultimate temptation—or us to the ultimate desperation.

Probably the most effective form of political warfare or covert action is the clandestine sponsorship of armed insurgency and its antedote, counterinsurgency. The Soviets call these insurgencies when they sponsor them "wars of national liberation." It should be noted, however, the United States also has the option of assisting insurgents when they request our help; Jonas Savimbi of the National Union for the Total Independence of Angola (UNITA), for example, asked for such help from America as recently as November 1979. The insurgents in Afghanistan who are valiantly struggling against Soviet domination have also sought our assistance.

The focus of this paper, however, is on that aspect of paramilitary operations that deals with combating Soviet-backed wars of national liberation in the 1980's that could be one of our most pressing requirements. Unfortunately the trauma of a lost Vietnam forced senior policymakers in the United States to retreat into a narrow unimaginative range of choices when considering post-1975 foreign policy options. The question of how the United States should project power into distant lands was accompanied by much paralytic hand-wringing and self-examination. A debate about which options the United States should have available to deal with challenges abroad took place both in public forums and Congressional hearings. Before Congress, William Colby, then Director of the Central Intelligence Agency, accurately summed up the dilemma in which the nation had locked itself; the nation had two options short of a nuclear confrontation in coping with international crises. We could send in the Marines. We could do nothing.

Senior intelligence officers like myself, who had experience in irregular warfare operations, insisted the United States should also consider *the third option, the use of insurgency and counterinsurgency techniques and covert action to achieve policy goals.*[1] In our view, paramilitary skills would give the United States an additional arrow in its national defense quiver. Others, equally articulate and at the same time politically more influential, argued differently and shrilly, that the United States has no right to interfere in the internal affairs of sovereign states, no matter what the provocation or danger. Until now this view has prevailed. The net result is that the United States now has less paramilitary capability than our vital interests demand. The time has come, therefore, when there must be a testing of political cross-currents in a country that is shaking off the malaise of the post-Vietnam period. This should tell the nation if its elected officials at the apex of national security decision making have, or lack, the will to pursue policy goals through techniques that have preserved our interests in diverse areas such as the Philippines, the Dominican Republic, Venezuela, Bolivia and Thailand, just to cite a few success stories. That will seems to have been rekindled in the land. One can conclude, therefore, that in the 1980's, we will see paramilitary operations once again an integral part of the arrows that are in the nation's quiver of national security options.

Paramilitary Operations

The covert action sphere can be subdivided into various functional parts. One of these is paramilitary operations which is the furnishing of covert military assistance and guidance to unconventional and conventional foreign forces and organizations. This definition coincides with the views of French military strategists like Roger Trinquier[2] who have written that "modern warfare" concerns itself with combating an "armed clandestine organization" whose essential role is to impose its will upon the population. In essence, this is revolutionary warfare and paramilitary operations. Depending upon which side of the conflict the United States is on, it can be devoted either to fostering or defeating revolutionary wars.

Guerrilla Warfare

Guerrillas are lightly armed indigenous forces operating in an area controlled by a hostile central government or a foreign occupying power. The guerrilla is basically an offensive weapon of war who harnesses superior terrain knowledge and the element of surprise to mount hit and run operations against conventional forces. The guerrilla disengages as soon as he has struck the enemy and before the latter recovers from the shock of the attack. In breaking off the engagement the guerrilla withdraws in an orderly and preplanned manner to base areas where conventional troops have difficulty in pursuing him due to his adroit utilization of natural terrain characteristics. Experience indicates guerrillas operate most effectively in rugged mountains, dense jungles, swamps or desert areas.

The guerrilla warfare concept is also influenced by the following factors:

- Being an indigenous force, the guerrilla lives off the land. This makes him dependent on the local population for food, medicine and clothes.
- Guerrillas should have the support of some segment of the local population in order to obtain intelligence on the tactical actions of the government or occupying forces.
- Modest levels of success against the enemy must be achieved and sustained if the guerrillas are to perpetuate themselves or expand through the acquisition of new recruits.
- Guerrillas can use terrorism and reprisals to obtain needed levels of support from the local population if all other techniques fail.
- Weapons and ammunition are obtained from what the guerrillas can capture from the enemy, steal, buy or receive from a foreign sponsor.
- Communication between guerrilla units is usually by courier or dead drop.
- Radio communications are used primarily to maintain contact with a foreign sponsor who provides guidance, funds, weapons, evacuation of wounded personnel, and international propaganda support.

The most likely uses of a guerrilla movement by the United States in the 1980's are to:

- Provide indigenous resistance to a superior invading conventional force. This would be done to slow down the invader, make him pay a price for his actions, and to buy time for the defending armed forces so that they can properly mobilize.
- Initiate guerrilla warfare as part of an orchestrated effort to overthrow an oppressive government.

Counterinsurgency Operations

The Soviet Union, China and Cuba have developed a capacity to engage in a variety of paramilitary activities. Perhaps the most important is their support of "wars of national liberation." The initiative rests with them to pick the next battlefield for, despite tomes of evidence to the contrary, the birth of a Communist insurgency is really very simple. First, there must be an element in the population of a given country which has been impregnated with thoughts of revolution, and a desire to oust an existing government or to resist a perceived foreign invader. Subsequent developments generally depend on the presence of two "midwives":

- The Soviet Union concludes (or a surrogate power such as Cuba concludes) that the potential gains of clandestine intervention in a particular country exceed the risks.
- Intelligence officers are able to spot, assess, and recruit enough qualified candidates for political indoctrination and guerrilla warfare training to form a revolutionary nucleus, or cadre.

This puts the counterinsurgency practitioners in a defensive mode. In essence, counterinsurgency is a passive form of warfare in which the government is reacting to threats or the battlefield moves of its enemies. Experience in such diverse areas as the Dominican Republic, Guatemala, Cuba, Laos, Vietnam, the Congo, and Angola have been variegated enough to provide some basis for generalizing about how wars of national liberation unfold and what the practitioners of counterinsurgency skills should do to combat these challenges.

Cadre Phase

Experience indicates an insurgency is most likely to originate in an environment of harsh economic and social injustice, political repression, and pervasive corruption. Other factors, such as nationalism, a desire for regional autonomy or a rejection of standard values in a predominantly urban society, can also contribute to creating a climate that enables a small elite to ingratiate itself with important sectors of the population.

It is clear, therefore, that one effective way of nipping an insurgency in the bud would be to encourage and assist threatened nations to undertake lasting social and economic reforms, thus justifying hopes of the population for a better future. One technique successful in the past: local civic action programs which deny the insurgents the allegiance of people in given areas.

Successful civic action programs have tried to meet the people's aspirations for improved educational, health, or transportation facilities. When a government has come close to satisfying the needs of its constituency in a particular village or district, then guerrillas have been unable to flourish.

If a government has not been reform-oriented when political unrest develops, the birth of an insurgency takes place with the creation of what is called a "cadre." All "wars of national liberation" begin with a phase in which the local communist party or the *rezidentura*[3] of the KGB, Cuban or Chinese intelligence service are spotting and assessing candidates for guerrilla training and political indoctrination. At the same time, disaffected groups of individuals who are in an emotional state of revolt have decided to solicit foreign funds, weapons, training and guidance to violently pursue their own political aims.

The end result is that the communist recruiter and the potential insurgent eventually meet. There ensues a "feeling out" process during which the potential recruit is evaluated for intelligence, motivation, character, psychological stability, leadership qualities and charisma. If the evaluation is positive, the candidate is asked if he or she is willing to work for "the revolution." If the answer is yes, the new recruit is sent for training to the Soviet Union, Cuba, China, East Germany or Czechoslovakia via a devious clandestine route. A Peruvian travelling to the guerrilla warfare school of Cuba, for example, might fly first to Paris. There contact is made with an intelligence officer from the Cuban Embassy who exchanges the recruit's passport for a Cuban travel document. This, plus an appropriate legend or cover story of who he is and why he is travelling enables the cadre candidate to fly from Paris via Prague to Havana. The pages in the Peruvian's·*bona fide* passport do not reveal travel to Cuba. After three to six months training, the insurgent reverses his steps and returns to Paris where he picks up his valid passport. He then returns to Peru, now one of the hard core cadres charged with preparing the insurgency.

Civic action in and of itself has not stopped insurgent movements from developing. Governments have had to take other measures to protect their very existence. The following eight steps, if taken in time, have been effective in combating an insurgency in its early, or cadre phase. These steps, while obvious and apparently childlike, are often ignored. They are:

Who is doing the recruiting? The security and intelligence services of the menaced country bear primary responsibility for uncovering the identity of those enlisting potential revolutionaries. They should be assisted by American experts to the extent that they need and ask for help in this mission. The local services should use surveillance, photography, informants and listening devices to establish who in the communist embassies is doing the recruiting of cadre candidates.

How are they doing it? What procedures are used in selecting cadre candidates for training? Each nation's intelligence services often employ different—and sometime specific—techniques of tradecraft or how they go about the business of espionage. Much of this tradecraft is commonplace. Once it is recognized for what it is, the trail is not at all difficult to follow. Unfortunately, many of our friends in the Third World lack the experience and operational background to detect this tradecraft. If it is in our national interest to do so, we should provide them the advice and tools to protect themselves—as well as *ourselves*. Such expertise can include how to install telephone taps on embassy personnel, our own debriefing of Cuban and Soviet defectors, information acquired by our own agents in the enemy camp, stolen documents and the interception of communications.

Penetrate the spotting (who is the target?), assessment and recruitment organization to identify the candidates selected for guerrilla warfare training. An agent appropriately placed in the other's camp is worth his or her weight in gold. The source cannot always identify cadre candidates by name, residence and occupation. But often the penetration agent, if in the ranks of the hostile intelligence service, may have access to its support apparatus or the local communist party that can provide enough data concerning age, physical description, educational level and family status so that the local security service backed by worldwide United States resources can identify the target candidate.

Once a positive identification has been made, legal action can be taken against the recruit at the appropriate time and place. It is important to note, however, that not all such potential terrorists or guerrillas should be arrested. There are advantages in tracking a cadre candidate until he leads the authorities to others in his cell or, for example, to arms caches.

What to do about it, or how to selectively disrupt by due process the cadre phase of insurgency operations. Numerous options are available if reliable information exists about what hostile intelligence services are doing to recruit cadre candidates. For example, the recruiting officer can suddenly be declared *persona non grata* by the country to which he is assigned. His expulsion can negate his recruitment accomplishments. The cadre candidates can be detained, denied passports, and prevented from leaving the country for training. More sophisticated approaches can also be used if the host country has the manpower and skills to use them. One such approach is to have the security service recruit the cadre candidates themselves. This starts a double agent operation and the security service has a penetration of its opposition.

Don't hide it. An aroused and well-informed citizenry is an effective deterrent to the type of spotting and assessment that has to take place if the Soviets and Cubans are to recruit cadre candidates. The people should be told what they can do to cripple insurgent activities. Afterall, it is their society which is at stake. Radio, television, and newspapers should be encouraged to launch a campaign exposing how foreign powers are attempting to recruit cadre candidates from among their audience. This can seriously impair recruitment efforts.

How we can help: or how the US can assist in the establishment and maintenance of an effective security agency in the target country. The first line of defense in any counterinsurgency effort is an effective internal security service. This organization must be staffed with intelligent, dedicated and incorruptible officers who have been trained to use counterintelligence techniques to penetrate the cadre phase recruitment cycle. In most underdeveloped countries quality manpower is in short supply, and what little there is often seems to be snatched away by high profile, more prestigious units such as an air force. Given the sink or swim realities of internal disorders, leaders must put a greater percentage of talented young men in intelligence than they have in the past, and they must be paid accordingly. It is no secret that corruption is rooted in poverty and inequality.

The security service should have arrest powers properly supervised by judicial review. What's more, it should have the modern capability to maintain computerized records on citizens travelling abroad. If required, the United States should help the country develop this record keeping system. The service must also earn the respect and confidence of its fellow citizens. There can be no violation of the accepted norms of human rights, or the service becomes seriously disadvantaged.

Internally the service must keep a clean house. Security standards within its own ranks must be rigorous enough so that foreign liaison services can feel comfortable exchanging sensitive data. There must be minimal risk that such information will be compromised by indiscretion, corruption or treason. Without such assurances, there can be no mutually beneficial exchange of intelligence and counterintelligence data.

Guide governments in the preparation of anti-subversive laws. It is critical that a government be able to neutralize Soviet or Cuban-supported revolutionaries—not by sending them into exile—but by putting them in jail. Unfortunately, when the cadre phase begins to unfold, many countries find they do not have laws on the books to deal with the threat. As a result, the party in power must pass such laws promptly or mount an education campaign to rally public opinion in support of laws that will permit the government to arrest and convict subversives. If these laws cannot be obtained, then the government must use executive orders in order to obtain convictions. It is better, however, to take legal action against subversives on the basis of a *law* rather than an executive order.

Assist the host country's military or police forces to establish and train an elite anti-guerrilla unit. Once the cadre phase has begun, a country must accept that it may not be able to prevent the insurgency from advancing to the next, and more dangerous stage. To prepare for this development, the friendly government should organize a special anti-guerrilla unit, staffed by elite military or police personnel. The strength of the unit should derive, not from its numbers, but from the quality of personnel, their training and leadership, from mobility, fire power, communications and tactics. Initially, the size of the unit should not exceed one 550-man battalion.

This elite strike force should be formed as soon as the cadre phase of insurgency has been detected. Later, there will be scarce time to build it when the guerrillas "war of national liberation" actually begins in earnest. Experience has shown that the selection and training of personnel who will conduct combat operations should be completed at least sixteen weeks before there is an actual need to use them in the field. Emphasis in training should focus on the unit's ability to move and attack with lightning speed without telegraphing the punch.

The Incipient Phase

An insurgency enters the "incipient phase" once cadre have been trained and begun to build the subterranean infrastructure required to mount sustained operations rather than acts of terrorism. To lay this hidden foundation the cadre establish bases within defined operational areas. Arms, ammunition and explosives must be purchased or otherwise acquired from foreign supporters then cached. Meanwhile, channels for resupply of both material and recruits must be opened, broadened and protected.

Most important, the revolution must attract ever-increasing manpower—for this is the life-blood of prolonged struggle. Without new recruits, combat losses cannot be replaced, cadre cells—the core of it all—cannot be rebuilt if exposed and shattered by security forces.

If properly done, political indoctrination and guerrilla warfare instruction abroad have equipped returning cadre with an intimate and working knowledge of how to use the basic tools of terrorism and revolution. They are familiar with firearms and explosives, how to compartmentalize insurgent teams so that one does not know of the existence of the next and thus cannot betray it. They have learned countersurveillance to prevent disastrous penetration. They have learned how to conceal and support themselves in either the rural or urban environment where they are to function—to swim as a fish in the sea, Mao called it. They also have at least rudimentary knowledge of clandestine communications.

Ideally, at least from the standpoint of their sponsors, they have pledged themselves to a fanatical, revolutionary morality that justifies killing the innocent and destroying society, and a zeal that enables them to pass on the germ of insurgency like so many "Thyphoid Marys." It matters little whether their slogans bear no relation to reality. What is important is that *they* believe. And they are able to persuade others to believe.

Typically, cadre slip back into their homeland in small groups at different times and by various routes. Some, more reliable, will have been provided with avenues through which they can communicate with their often impatient foreign sponsors. Frequently-used channels include agents within the local communist party, or in some noteworthy cases, intelligence officers working out of Soviet, Cuban or East European embassies. Sometimes clandestine meetings are arranged in a neighboring country where they are less conspicuous.

Customarily cadre divide into cells of no more than five to ten people. The first critical task for the cadre is to neutralize the area in which it has chosen to operate, then develop a sanctuary in the form of a base area or camp. The selection must be made wisely. A misjudgment on location, the attitudes of its inhabitants or terrain can be fatal.

A rural operational base must be carefully scouted. What about concealment and water? There should also be several different ways by which guerrillas can enter or flee. Once established, the guerrilla must cultivate the goodwill of the peasants in the surrounding area, usually within a radius of a six hour march—enough warning time of approaching security forces to allow insurgents to flee. From villagers close by the guerrillas can acquire an intimate knowledge of terrain, local trails, water holes and hiding places that will permit them to survive. In time, and if won over, peasants may offer logistical support such as food and medicine or volunteer as porters—to say nothing of serving as the insurgents' eyes and ears. And peasants will be a source of indispensible intelligence when planning operations, evading or ambushing government forces.

Once they have mastered their new environment and gain confidence that they can survive and prosper in it, the guerrillas organize civic action programs such as assisting the local residents to dig wells or repair their homes. But nothing comes free. Along with such assistance local villagers can expect a steady diet of political indoctrination. This widens the guerrillas' support horizons as the audience increases. But it inevitably brings them into conflict with those who object and will not be bamboozled by sheer rhetoric. The insurgents soon turn to assassinating and burning the property of such cynics.

This in turn tends to polarize political views in the operational area. There is muscle behind the talk after all. As the terrorizing of "doubting Thomases" intensifies, so do the bonds of commitment of supporters. Gradually the band gains new recruits. They may have grievances against the government or they may simply seek adventure. Whatever, they are by now convinced that these insurgents in their midst mean business. The band cleverly exploits these diverse motivations and as new recruits are enrolled, they are trained and equipped. By addition of local recruits, the band gains more tactical flexibility. Many can farm by day and play guerrilla by night. The insurgency begins to emerge from the incipient phase once the cadre cells have consolidated their bases, cached arms and supplies, and have significantly increased their numbers through local recruiting. When the band successfully employs force against government installations and survives, the initial retaliatory measures of police and conventional military forces, it is finally free of its "incipient" stage cocoon.

There are specific actions security forces can take to prevent this newest of insurgency metamorphoses; among them:

Identify the guerrilla cadre as they re-enter the country or quickly thereafter. If security services unmasked a trainee scheduled to go abroad during the first, or cadre phase, but failed to prevent the journey, an efficient travel monitoring system still may spot the subject when he or she returns. Penetrations of the local Communist Party can result in advance word of travel plans. Intensive surveillance of the Soviet, Chinese, or Cuban embassies using previously described techniques may also lead the authorities to newly returned cadre.

Locate the urban and rural safehouses that the cadre have established to support the incipient phase of guerrilla operations. At first glance this seems like finding a needle-in-the-haystack. Actually, no magic is required—if the security service is moderately competent in counterintelligence techniques. Safehouses can be located through surveillance of the identified trainee once he has returned home. Additionally, safehouses can be uncovered by recruited agents from among local Communist Party functionaries or if one is very, very lucky in the local *residenturas* of the Soviet, Chinese or Cuban intelligence services. Another productive source can be rural and urban informants that the local service has seeded in enemy operational areas. Residents can detect changes in a community's living patterns. New or suspicious tenants are noted instantly. An unexplained transfer of property becomes a subject of gossip—all should be tapped. Agents locally "in place" are in a position to hear even the grass grow. Their contributions are pearls of intelligence.

Identify and disrupt channels for arms and ammunition. In most countries the government requires citizens to obtain permits to own or buy firearms, thus the acquisition of five to ten weapons is a major project for a guerrilla armorer. Generally speaking, weapons must be smuggled into the country by covert channels run by the local Communist Party. The diplomatic pouch of a foreign supporter like the Cuban DGI is one popular ruse. But, if aware of the dangers, customs, border patrol, police and military forces can often throttle off the supply of weapons. Obviously, interdiction of arms supplies can be like shooting ducks in a bathtub if—and this is a big, capital IF, your own agents can be inserted into the smuggling chain, the Communist Party, or the hostile intelligence *residentura*.

Gain intimate knowledge of terrain which appears best suitable for a guerrilla base. Analysis by maps, aerial photography and information from local authorities, can pinpoint potential base camp locations. Where, for example, are the waterholes, rivers, clearings, and main trails? What about potential ambush locations? These can all be triangulated and then pinpointed, predicated on the assumption that guerrillas generally operate within a reasonable day's march from a base site. In short, one can now know what an enemy will do and how he will go about it—even before he does. Once that is done, drop zones or helicopter landing areas should be marked for later use by the government's elite anti-guerrilla unit. So, you have managed to prepare the battleground to your liking, not the guerrillas'.

Establish informant networks in potential guerrilla operational areas. Don't wait for the enemy's arrival. Have selected informants planted in villages throughout the chosen area. The number of informants required depends on such diverse factors as terrain, population density, type of agriculture that is practiced in the area, and the means of transportation in and out of the district. The broader the society, the more varied its life style, the greater the number of "in place" assets needed. A network of this type can be controlled and serviced by local police units. The key to its very existence: to provide advance word that a guerrilla band has moved into the area. Once that fact is established—plus what security forces have already gleaned about the area—the network can provide the tactical intelligence needed to make the government's anti-guerrilla unit combat effective.

Organize effective civic action programs to encourage and reward loyalty to the government among the local population. Civic action can be important if it delivers what it promises. It can convince the people that steps are really being taken to improve their life. Programs should be designed to attack social, economic and political evils. Corrupt, repressive and incompetent local officials *must* be removed. Next comes the improvement of the local economy: the digging of water wells, building bridges and hospital dispensaries; schools must be opened and professionally staffed. New agricultural techniques can be taught and harvest increased tenfold through the use of seed stock programs.

Initiate anti-guerrilla operations with the elite unit as soon as tactical intelligence reveals the presence of a guerrilla band. Nothing is so effective in stopping the development of an insurgency as neutralizing those who, having finished training in the Soviet Union, China or Cuba, take to the field for the first time. Pressure, increasing pressure, must be applied—raids on guerrilla base camps, ambushes, sustained pursuit and the denial of water and supplies. Pressure, pressure, pressure. Often the guerrillas—weakened by constant pursuit and harassment—will turn and fight. Thus brought to bay the government must concentrate all the firepower necessary to destroy them if they choose not to surrender.

The preceding techniques must be used simultaneously, not piecemeal, to attack the incipient phase of an insurgency. In the aggregate they are cost effective, because they can save a significant loss of life in later phases of an insurgency—not to mention the independence of a sovereign state.

Operational Phase

If, despite aggressive counter-measures, an insurgency is able to grow to multiple bands of 20 or more men in a single district or province, then the movement has escalated to the next and most violent of all stages. Now the insurgency threatens the survival of the government itself.

In the operational phase, guerrillas surface to confront security forces in open combat. Their tactics are now more of hit than run. The risk is often worth the gain if they have accurately calculated their strengths—and government weaknesses. They can drive out security forces to the point where authority must abandon the region, leaving guerrillas in sole possession of the population. If this falls short of the mark, they try at least to own the night. The tempo of recruitment increases. The delivery of arms by foreign importers or through raids on government installations reaches a feverish peak. Meanwhile, civic action and political indoctrination programs among the populace intensify.

The increasing aggressiveness of the guerrillas in the form of more frequent and large-scale assaults acts further to open the desperate government's jugular. Combat widens and escalates. But all caution is not thrown to the winds. To guard against the possibility of their forces being wiped out in one costly firefight, the insurgent bands remain organized in separate units. However, they now know of each other's existence, many for the first time. To maximize the impact of operations, they coordinate through clandestine communications—couriers, dead drops, meetings in safehouses, coded radio messages and the like. The longer the guerrillas are permitted to operate at this level, the more they consolidate control over an area, the stronger they will grow. It becomes easier to receive fresh supplies, security is harder to pierce. Indeed, at this stage the guerrillas may have added anti-aircraft weapons to their armory, endangering airborne or helicopter assaults by government forces. The flow of intelligence and recruits dramatically increases, for at least in this region they are the government—and the people know it.

Legal authority *must* respond promptly to defeat the insurgency lest it grows to an even greater danger. Here are the steps necessary which can still be taken at this late moment in the struggle by the central government and its American advisors—assuming of course they are on hand.

Accurately determine the guerrillas' strength, disposition and intentions. Quality, timely intelligence is indispensible to defeating any guerrilla force. It can best be gathered from deep penetration agents who have managed to have themselves recruited by the guerrilla bands. The difficulty lies not so much in finding these assets. As the insurgency grows, guerrilla forces must run the risk that less reliable recruits will be attracted to the movement. For them the glamour may quickly fade as hardships in the bush increase. And when it does, government talent spotters must be ready to pounce. The real problem lies in receiving communications from such a double agent so he can warn the security service of his unit's next move in remote areas; the problem is significant. Yet, it can be solved with ingenuity and technology.

Intensify counterintelligence operations against the guerrillas' support apparatus. The secret supply lines through which the guerrilla receives food, medicine and arms is perhaps his single greatest weakness—if security forces are sufficiently informed and equipped to shut them down. As all roads once "led to Rome," so do supply pipelines to an enemy's camp. Assume that security agents learn that a particular peasant is found routinely larding a food cache near his village for the guerrillas. The agents then can slip a signal beacon into the supplies which will enable them with proper US equipment to track the movement of these supplies to the guerrilla base camp. Once that occurs a tombstone for the group is as good as carved.

Devise psychological warfare operations to keep progovernment resistance alive in guerrilla-controlled areas. If guerrillas control an area by night, the government should use radio and television to convey messages of hope aimed at persuading listeners and viewers that the guerrilla occupation is temporary. This must be done subtly so the campaign does not propagandize the guerrillas' cause by revealing government weaknesses. No promises should be made that cannot be kept.

Start an "open arms" program which appeals to the guerrillas to lay down their weapons in return for amnesty. The "open arms" program must realistically show insurgents what a brighter future can hold for them, their families and the nation. For those who respond, it is critical that credibility be fortified by sending them to centers for vocational training and political reorientation. When the re-education process is completed the government should publicize success stories of guerrillas who have rejoined the government so that their former comrades-in-arms still in the bush can believe that their own defection can be successful.

Expand civic action programs in the areas adjacent to those where the guerrillas dominate. Civic action programs, begun in the incipient phase of an insurgency, should not be abandoned because the insurgency has reached the new plateau of its operational phase. Spread more health and economic opportunities to as large a segment of the population as possible. The emphasis should be on those programs which prove that cooperation with the government will pay off with better economic and social dividends than those guerrillas offer.

Step up the intensity of anti-guerrilla operations by the elite anti-guer-

rilla unit. If organization of the elite anti-guerrilla unit began in the cadre phase, as it should have, the unit should now be at its full strength of 550 men. It should be fully deployed in platoon formations against the twenty-man guerrilla bands. Superior equipment, training, leadership and motivation will soon be felt.

A proven reality of irregular warfare is that guerrillas buckle under sustained pressure in their operational areas. If, acting on reliable intelligence, the anti-guerrilla unit makes contact with an enemy unit in a raid, ambush or patrol action, it must not relax its grip until the enemy surrenders or is defeated. Tactics are critical. Night vision devices, helicopters and gunships—plus advice from a one or two-man American unit—can keep the enemy force pinned down or on the run. In either case, contact should not be broken. Better communications, mobility and fire power will inevitably lead to the defeat of the individual guerrilla band. Each victory should be widely publicized in all of the media throughout the country for defeat is propaganda that guerrillas can ill afford.

Establish population controls. As guerrillas become operational they normally must vanish from society, their homes and favorite haunts. It is at this point that population controls are needed, particularly in the districts adjacent to the guerrilla operating area. The key to a population control system is an identification document issued within a limited period of time to all residents of a given area. The card should exhibit a photograph, a fingerprint, a basic description of its holder. And, it should be tamper-proof. A by-product of issuing the document is an accurate census of everyone living in the district. Suspicious shifts, increases or decreases, can quickly be noted. Meanwhile, guerrilla movement is restricted. Without such a document he can scarcely run the risk of a check by security teams.

Organize local self-defense forces. A local self-defense force, or citizens militia should be recruited in the districts adjacent to the guerrilla operational area rather than in them. These forces are trained in light infantry weapons, how to defend their own villages, if and when the insurgency spills over. If this force is motivated, well-led and supplied with reliable communications equipment, they can be effective indeed. But more conventional forces should be kept close to cover these local forces by artillery support or air power. A village protected by a tough self-defense force becomes a springboard from which government forces can mount their own offensive operations.

Coordinate conventional military forces with the elite anti-guerrilla unit. When the presence of guerrilla units in an area is detected, sweep and encirclement operations are one time-tested way of finding and eliminating them. Conventional forces should carry out sweep operations. Meanwhile, the elite anti-guerrilla unit can take up blocking positions across likely routes to or from suspected guerrilla locations. As sweep operations get underway, the guerrillas will flush and slip away toward safe areas or their base camps. A nasty surprise will await them if the anti-guerrilla unit has been properly positioned. Again, superior training, equipment and fire-power should smash the scattering guerrillas.

Keep the enemy off balance. Mount raids against sanctuaries or supply depots in nations bordering the operating zone. If the guerrillas are receiving logistics support or sanctuary from a neighboring country and if their depots can be pinpointed within ten kilometers of the border, then hit and run commando raids should be launched against them. It is a high-risk and politically sensitive operation, and the raiders should be carefully chosen from regular military forces. The goal is to wreak as much havoc as possible among guerrilla personnel, destroy a maximum of equipment. Such raids send a clear political message to the neighbor who is interfering in the internal affairs of another state.

Establish an interrogation capability that can promptly exploit guerrilla prisoners. Each revolutionary movement has its own jargon and idiosyncrasies. It is essential that the government train specialists who can speak the insurgent's language, recognize his weaknesses. In short, know him better than he knows himself.

Covert War Phase

Some mystery surrounds what point in time an insurgency shifts into top gear, the covert war phase. One key indicator is that the insurgents begin to coordinate their attacks in battalion strength, simultaneously in two or more large regions. Not always do they strike as a battalion, however. Often companies from these battalions will appear in different locations to harrass government forces, police the battlefield for weapons and further dramatize government weaknesses to those living nearby. Elsewhere, neither the elite anti-guerrilla unit nor conventional forces of the government are able to prevent the guerrillas from cutting vital railways and highways. This means the government is no longer able to halt expansion of the insurgency with the forces it has on hand.

The presence of a few advisors, a couple of dozen sophisticated aircraft and limited amounts of other selected equipment will not help. Time is running out. Will the US provide military equipment and other assistance on a large and diverse scale? Or do we pull back and write off an ally?

Assuming we decide that it is in our best interests to prevent the beleagured nation's collapse, we should jointly do the following:

1. *Establish force levels for the government's conventional forces to be supported by United States equipment.* Based on a mutual intelligence assessment of the threat, a joint force level should be agreed upon. The agreement should specify the total size of the force, its organization and equipment, and a time-table must be set for combat readiness. Usually the remaining time available will not allow us to fully re-equip the nation's army. So, both parties should concentrate on upgrading roughly a fourth of the country's forces. These, then will become a spearhead against the insurgency which is now in full bloom.

2. *Provide an airlift capability, usually under commercial cover, to move supplies and personnel to staging areas.* Given the emotions in the Third World, our target nation may wish to avoid the impression that it is being kept glued together by a Western power. In this case, airlift under commercial cover is one effective disguise. The civilian aircraft should deliver American supplies directly to the regions where the forces are fighting, not to a central depot in the capital. This speeds delivery of equipment to those who need it most. It also cuts the hemorrhaging of material which can occur from a single arms dump.

An infrastructure to support the airlift must also be built. Landing strips must be established. Fuel bladders must be on hand to service the aircraft when they arrive. And once prepared, the landing strips must be protected. For if they are to be of any use, they must be located near combat zones. Crews must be prepared to parachute supplies—around the clock if necessary—to government forces deep in the bush, or cut off from relief. This means a careful mapping of the terrain, split second timing between drop crews and troops on the ground. Only then can constant pressure be brought to bear on the enemy.

The airlift can provide medical services to the combat troops. Nothing will buoy morale more than certain knowledge that they will be promptly evacuated to hospital facilities if wounded. The airlift, when not providing support to combat forces, can be used for high visibility civic action missions designed to push in the right direction those who remain unconvinced of the government's determination to not only win the war, but to improve the lives of its citizens.

3. *Furnish instructors to expand specialized military training programs.* When sophisticated equipment is supplied to conventional forces locked in a guerrilla war, lack of qualified training personnel limits their effectiveness. This problem can only be overcome by qualified instructors from Western nations who can teach such specialties as demolition, disarming of booby traps, sniper tactics and ambush defense. They need not be Americans, for qualified professionals can be recruited by the host nation with US help from third country governments. A few experts can triple the effectiveness of any training program. Preferably, the training should be done in host country facilities. There are circumstances, however, where the training must take place abroad or in nations close by.

4. *Selectively employ "volunteers" as combat troops or advisors.* The supply of high quality manpower is limited in any country, even more so in a besieged Third World nation. Rather than stand by and watch these units bled white, the use of skilled volunteers should be considered. They can be elite combat units or advisors who accompany local forces in the field. Combat leadership is indispensable. How, then, to recruit them? The volunteers can be reservists from a neighboring country who have just finished tours of military duty and are hired to fight on fixed contract terms. Obviously, their own government must be sympathetic and well aware of the dangers of the insurgency becoming a threat to their own security. It is a wise idea, however, not to allow their friend-in-need to fall into the trap of relying on such aid—at the expense of shouldering their own defense burdens.

5. *Appropriately expand earlier programs from the operational phase which are proven successes.* In the midst of a full-blown covert war it is unrealistic to focus on furthering innovation—stage programs. No time exists. Survival is what counts. Emphasis should be placed on improving existing programs. Here are some examples which US advisors and government officials should consider:

- Continue to widen intelligence collection on guerrilla strengths, dispositions, plans and intentions.
- Step up counterintelligence operations against guerrilla support operations.
- Do not relax psychological warfare operations that keep alive the spirit of resistance to the insurgents in guerrilla-held areas.
- Expand the "open arms" program to encourage less-committed guerrillas to surrender under provisions of amnesty.

- Broaden the scope of the civic action programs, functioning in areas neighboring those the guerrillas operate in or control by night.
- Keep hitting the insurgents in their base areas with small, elite anti-guerrilla units. Use booby traps.
- Maintain population controls to read the movement of people and commodities, both in and out of guerrilla-held areas.
- Further strengthen local self-defense forces.
- Plan more combined operations in which the conventional forces continue to coordinate with elite anti-guerrilla units.
- Intensify raids on insurgent supply depots across the border in neighboring countries which support guerrilla operations.

As in the earlier phases, success or failure will determine if the insurgency moves on to the next and final phase.

Conventional War Phase

The final phase of a "war of national liberation" is reached when guerrilla forces decide their military strength is sufficient to confront government forces in a decisive battle. At this point, the dilemma for the government is very simple: either it survives, or it does not. They are no longer confronted by bush guerrillas. They must deal with an army. The insurgents now have such luxuries as long-range artillery, anti-aircraft weapons. And they know how to use them. Ask the French who, in 1954, hoped to suck Viet Minh "guerrillas" into a meat grinder called Dien Bien Phu.

Can nothing be done to avoid a defeat of this magnitude? If it begins to appear the guerrillas might win the key battle, thus the war, the United States must reassess its own commitment. There are two options still available. The first is to abandon the counterinsurgency program entirely. This is a painful option, for it resurrects the unpleasant specter of defeat.

Inevitably, the second option arises: is the United States prepared to intervene with conventional military forces? This choice was exercised in both the Dominican Republic and in Vietnam. One was successful, the other became a national controversy.

Assume, then, that we consider the cost of doing nothing too great. The President and an informed Congress commit our conventional forces. Once done, there can be no turning back. There can be no alternative to victory in a conventional war in a Third World setting against non-nuclear powers.

Thus when the decision to intervene has been made, the conduct
of the conventional war becomes the responsibility of the Department
of Defense which controls both the tactical and strategic resources
needed to achieve victory. At that point the insurgency has shifted
from the covert to the conventional phase, and there must be passage
of the Field Marshal's baton from CIA to the senior American military commander in the field. This exchange of responsibility must be
accompanied by the prompt and unequivocal implementation of a
new Command Relationship Agreement which when invoked must
clearly define the roles of the Ambassador, the senior US Military
Officer in the field and CIA. While a sensible command relationship
evolved in our last war, Vietnam, there is a need to learn from this
experience. A key conclusion which emerged was there should be
preparations *in advance* for potential wars that will see our paramilitary cadres relinquishing command over a covert war to the defense
establishment as the war moves into a conventional confrontation.
This is a crucial area of neglect which merits immediate attention by
Pentagon planners, the State Department and CIA.

As the command lines are restructured, a concept of how best to
conduct the conventional war must be agreed on. The only choice
here is the "one war" theory. This doctrine grew from America's
experience in Vietnam. Its strength lies in simplicity. All host government agencies must contribute to winning the war by a total
reshaping of their missions to one goal and one goal only: taking the
battle to the enemy. This means that intelligence and security officials, and their American advisors, must place their resources at the
timely disposal of the military commanders. Essentially, they become subordinate to the conventional military structure.

In the "one war" theory, host country intelligence and security
forces, aided by their American advisors, should concentrate on:

- Producing positive intelligence of high quality in a timely manner
  on the strength, location, plans and intentions of the enemy's
  military and political forces.
- Mounting counterintelligence operations designed to protect
  United States and host country military units in the field by
  identifying, neutralizing and manipulating the enemy's intelligence agents and their collection capability.
- Establishing escape and evasion capabilities using host country
  personnel operating behind enemy lines as guerrillas. The mere
  existence of such a force will contribute significantly to the
  morale of both American and government forces.

- Developing a resistance movement behind enemy forces. In addition to collecting intelligence, such teams can harass the enemy through low-cost, high-visibility sabotage operations. Examples: sniper attacks; booby traps. Thus, if the enemy wants to maintain security of his rear areas, he must tie down more and more manpower and equipment—all are assets that would normally be deployed against us in direct combat.
- Utilizing irregular forces developed from the elite anti-guerrilla units to launch high-intensity raids and ambushes against enemy forces scattered in areas near the combat zones. For maximum impact these operations should be coordinated with attacks by conventional forces. The objective of these combined operations is to tie down enemy forces in flank security tasks, lower morale, bleed off personnel from units fighting our conventional forces.
- Mass psychological warfare operations designed to keep alive the flame of resistance throughout society. This can also help maintain stability within the host country government and its military forces in a time of great stress.

These steps are not sufficient in themselves to turn the tide of battle, but they are an indispensible part of the larger effort. Whether this formula produces or not, the first principle of conventional war is that once the United States commits its national prestige through its conventional military establishment against a second or third-rate power, it *must* pursue that decision to its logical conclusion—the military defeat of the enemy. Anything less than military victory cannot serve United States' national interests.

Infrastructure

The preceding sections have outlined the challenges, concepts, and techniques of paramilitary operations. There must be an organizational structure, however, within which these concepts and techniques can be harnessed as an effective instrument of power. The CIA's clandestine service is the proper home for paramilitary operations. In recent years, however, CIA's ability to handle this task has been severely diluted by management decisions made during Admiral Stansfield Turner's stewardship of the Agency. In short, the limited capability that now exists is not adequate to the challenge of the 1980's. This capability must be rebuilt in a prompt and professional manner.

The reconstruction effort has to be guided by several broad principles. They are:

- Policymakers need to understand that CIA's staff officer personnel cannot be brought from behind their desks in response to a bugle call to run a "Guns of Navarone" commando raid or to mount a "Lawrence of Arabia" attack on railroads. In short, these men are not soldiers or leaders of men in combat.

- CIA's paramilitary experts must be viewed as skilled organizers of insurgency and counterinsurgency operations. They must be people who develop irregular warfare concepts, test new techniques for conducting operations, plan force structures, recruit, train and equip the indigenous forces that do the actual fighting. These paramilitary specialists must be keen students of leadership and as such be able to identify local personalities who can provide combat leadership for local forces.

- CIA's staff personnel who are paramilitary specialists must be augmented by a select cadre of third country personnel who can be activated as needed for training tasks or operations that require brave and skilled non-American irregular warfare experts for short periods of time.

- Stocks of basic infantry weapons and ammunition must be maintained at levels that could sustain a serious counterinsurgency effort or guerrilla warfare operation for at least six months. The stockpile should place heavy emphasis on the Soviet AK-47 assault rifle as it is the basic weapon of either the guerrilla or conventional forces that American-supported paramilitary operations would be called on to fight. Given this reality, it would be prudent to be able, in part, to fight with the material that one would expect to take from the enemy. Additionally, the weapons stock should place great emphasis on ground-to-air missiles like the Soviet SA-7 and handheld anti-tank weapons. Stockpiles should be maintained at a level that is commensurate with anticipated contingencies.

- CIA must have plans in being for the prompt acquisition by lease or charter of aircraft and maritime resources needed to do the job which has been assigned to it at any point in time.

- Liaison between CIA and the Department of Defense must be strengthened so that the lessons learned in paramilitary operations concerning weapons, techniques or tactics can be passed to the military for application in their anti-terrorist operations, strike force concepts, or in their wartime planning for unconventional warfare.

Bottom Line

In the final analysis, the decision to use or ignore the potential of paramilitary operations as a force for peace or as an instrument of power will not be based solely on challenges, concepts, techniques, paramilitary manpower skills or weapons stockpiles. The decision will be made by those elected officials who have, or lack, the will to pursue policy goals through paramilitary techniques that have protected our interests in such diverse areas as the Dominican Republic, Venezuela, Bolivia, Thailand, Malaysia, and the Philippines—just to cite a few success stories.

The will to take these decisions has been rekindled in the land. One can conclude therefore that in the 1980's we will see paramilitary operations become once again an integral part of our defense arsenal.

Notes

1. For a fuller exposition of the views herein, see Theodore G. Shackley, *The Third Option: An American View of Counterinsurgency Operations,* (Reader's Digest Press and McGraw-Hill: New York, 1981)
2. Roger Trinquier, *Modern Warfare, A French View of Counterinsurgency* (Frederick A. Praeger: New York, 1964)
3. The field unit of a Communist intelligence service operating under diplomatic or commercial cover from offices in an embassy.

Discussants

Mr. Daniel Arnold: As Mr. Shackley has noted, American security is increasingly being threatened by a combination of Soviet paramilitary support for Communist-dominated insurgencies and direct military action by Soviet and surrogate armed forces in parts of the world vital to the interests of the United States and the rest of the non-Communist world. I have been asked to go somewhat beyond this to address the subject of coups and countercoups.

The suppression of covert action as a policy instrument does in the political sphere what the strategy of massive retaliation does in the military one. I submit that by reducing the range of American options in foreign policy decisionmaking, it has hindered the ability of the United States to respond effectively to the many different kinds of threats which the United States and the non-Communist world face today. A paramilitary operation gives policymakers one kind of intermediate step between merely political and conventional military action. If we were to reconstruct the American covert instrument incorporating the principles that are discussed by Mr. Shackley, we could create a well-prepared, professional, competent, covert, paramilitary force which would add and open up foreign policy alternatives not now realistically available to the United States.

Covert support of coups and countercoups must be justified both pragmatically and morally as a tool of foreign policy. Given the complexity of the international situation, the choices involved are often not reducable to simple cases of black or white, but instead to varying shades of gray. Yet, when action is called for, sound judgments and hard choices must inevitably be made for or against action.

Paramilitary involvement should be designed to affirmatively influence the outcome of a contest which might otherwise be lost to the Soviet Union. American covert support for local political forces may, at a minimum, equalize the local political equation by providing the resources to permit friendly elements effectively to contest for power. This relates in turn to the moral element in the policy equation. Is it more moral for the United States to stand aside while Soviet-backed forces subvert a society than to covertly intervene to support far more benign forces with which we share a common interest?

It is important that the consequences of any US effort include the enhancement of long-term freedom and justice in the affected country. This may occur as it did in Chile when a Soviet-oriented leftist government is overthrown by a rightist coup. Conservative authoritarian regimes, though in themselves undesirable, may at least hold out the prospect for subsequent amelioration of political conditions and thus have a restoration of political freedoms. But the undermining of democratic institutions at the hands of a Marxist/Leninist regime is likely to be irreversible once its control is solidified.

Such intervention should never be taken lightly or arbitrarily, but is warranted by only the most critical and threatening of circumstances. American involvement in cases of lesser danger would be both unwarranted and unjustified. But, circumstances can exist where, by acts of legitimate self-defense, the United States can covertly intervene overseas in a way that enhances the prospects for long-term social justice and stability in the target country. In other words, the means chosen—in this case the use of coups and countercoups—must be appropriate to the circumstances and to the desired end. Such action should be undertaken only when there is a reasonable prospect for success.

As part of this calculation, it must be asked whether the operation being contemplated is best suited to covert action or could be better handled through more overt channels where greater operational resources are available. This question must be asked in particular in the case of a paramilitary action where the possible need for continuing or large-scale supply may be at odds with the need to maintain plausible cover.

Time and circumstances here are not appropriate to address the question of how one brings about a coup or countercoup. However, I believe that there are as many variants and approaches as there are situations that oblige such action. Absolutely essential is a significant body of current intelligence and a profound appreciation of the dynamics of the local situation. A second essential is good communications; and third is the capacity and the will to act decisively. Timing is almost always critical to the success of such action. The resultant action may be as simple as a one-on-one interaction at a critical juncture. That is, to encourage an individual or a group to action. And conversely, the action could require the covert orchestration of diverse forces up to the level of paramilitary or regular forces.

As with all foreign policy questions, covert support to coups and countercoups as policy tools should be compatible with the values of a just and free society. If this is the case, such action may in appropriate circumstances be a legitimate weapon of that society to defend itself and its interests worldwide.

Dr. Frank N. Trager: I regard Mr. Shackley's presentation as a model of concise and clear exposition. However, as I read his paper, I found myself with a growing sense of déjà vu.

What Mr. Shackley has given us is really a distillation of one special well-defined concept of covert action. His analysis flows from a single basic judgment—namely, that the US in the 1980's will be a reactor or a counterpuncher. Hence, our main thrust in effect will be on counterinsurgency. I disagree with this judgment. Everything in my own experience and everything that I have tried to do in terms of policy, intelligence, counteraction, insurgency, counterinsurgency, has been to avoid this notion that we have to limit ourselves to reaction. I have tried to make it possible to recognize the signs of situations in which we will be the actor, the puncher if you will, rather than merely the counterpuncher.

If we accept that that 1980's will be a time for us to react and to counterpunch, then the kinds of emphases that Mr. Shackley gave to his analysis of revolutionary warfare is a standard one. It is in all of the literature which he has well synthesized and really requires no greater amplification. And the only thing to do is to do it.

But, let us ask: Must we wait until revolutionary war appears on the horizon, until we enter the cadre stage, incipient stage, operational stage, covert war stage, conventional war stage, and really large-scale war with regular military forces? I submit the answer is no. This session has already underlined that good intelligence as well as good policy must always be forward-looking, and must be based on accurate evaluations of what is hostile or friendly, as well as plans for dealing with them to advance our interests at home and abroad. It is quite possible for us to identify hostile areas, hostile powers, and to estimate their moves. That is what intelligence is for. We can anticipate where blows might come. And by preparing for them, it seems to me that we then can utilize quite a number of instruments before the cadre stage becomes even evident.

In the case of Laos and Vietnam, in March 1962, for example, eight years after events really got underway, President Kennedy, through General Max Taylor, issued an instruction to all of the upper-level and middle management schools of the military and civilian departments of government to introduce, even in a one-year course of instruction, a two-week extension to teach officers and civilians about counterinsurgency. And at that time, the kinds of analysis presented by Mr. Shackley was at least in major outline available for instruction.

But that was at least eight years after events had started in Vietnam. In 1955, on the other hand, Ngo Dinh Diem, aware of what was happening after the Geneva 1954 agreement, had already set up his anti-Communist organization that had the job of doing the kinds of things that you would call incipient stage one. And data was then available on which our respective ambassadors presumably could have acted. Some of them tried in a variety of ways to anticipate the further effort that the North Vietnamese were making across the border at the 17th parallel.

Given our history, we now can pick out the likely spots where there are events such as the ones which were occurring in Vietnam in 1955, and begin to do better now what we failed to do well in the early days. Then, it seems to me, the other paramilitary activities and what you call the economic and political aspects of counterparamilitary and covert action can be undertaken either overtly, or where necessary covertly. Nothing would have prevented us from undertaking the kinds of action Mr. Shackley proposes later on as early as 1955 and 1956. (And I am sure that some CIA officials proposed such measures officially to the government at the time.)

In short, therefore, it seems to me that Mr. Shackley's judgment about what we can do is a overly pessimistic—that we can only react and can only counterpunch. Our judgment can be elevated a notch by looking at the world through the eyes of American interests as well as through the eyes of hostile threats. And we can arrive at policies that are—call them what you will—overt, covert, paramilitary, but which begin punching and acting long before we have to counter or counterpunch or react.

General Discussion

The discussion focused on technical matters and considerations of the legitimacy and morality of paramilitary covert action.

An academic noted that the Soviet Union has enlisted a number of its allies, such as East Germany and Cuba, in its execution of paramilitary acts around the globe. He questioned why the Western democracies could not similarly divide such labors amongst themselves for their mutual interest. A former intelligence official answered that in some cases this division had occurred, but that he knew of at least two such arrangements which had been terminated by the Carter Administration.

Another academic, presuming the Carter Administration had acted out of ethical concerns, asked whether it was really necessary to deal with matters of high national interest in the language of law and ethics. There was no argument against the proposition that law and ethics bear on the use of paramilitary means, but there was wide agreement that stategy must be the primary consideration. Two former intelligence officials strongly suggested that the most ethically repugnant results of paramilitary operations have come about because of the absence of strategic considerations and of firm policy. They pointed to ethnic groups in Southeast Asia who had fought against North Vietnam with the United States' encouragement, and who had since been abandoned to either death or squalid refuge. One of these officials emphasized that a commitment of paramilitary assets, no less than a commitment of regular forces, involves decisions about life and death. The other former official pointed out that the long-term implications of covert paramilitary action must be thought out in advance, and action should not be undertaken without a commitment to carry it through to a worthwhile conclusion. A contemporary example was offered: The anti-Soviet rebels in Afghanistan are seeking American help. It is in our interest and in our power to help them. But it is probably not within our power to help them enough to actually liberate their country. Therefore, he said, help should be offered with this caveat, and with contingency plans for taking care both of Afghan refugees and of neighboring Pakistan which provides them safe haven.

A former foreign intelligence official, citing long experience in counterinsurgency, stated that unless a country is on the strategic offensive, it is difficult, if not impossible for planners of paramilitary actions to be "punchers" instead of "counterpunchers." Because the geographic areas of Western interest are broad, he said, it is unlikely that there will be enough detailed information on enemy revolutionary activities to permit paramilitary preemption. A former American intelligence official, citing American inability in Vietnam to do anything except react, agreed, saying that we cannot expect the US now that it is much weaker, to do more than it did at the height of its power. An academic agreed strongly with both propositions. We should not limit ourselves to our losing experience in Vietnam. He suggested we consider going on the offensive. As for capabilities, we should identify the ones needed to produce victories and proceed to get them.

Another academic initiated a discussion of the political legitimacy of paramilitary covert action. He remarked that such discussions are usually carried on in peculiarly narrow, American terms. A former intelligence official, while not disagreeing with this, noted that in every country, including the Soviet Union, paramilitary projects must receive approval, at the highest political levels. The problem, he suggested, is a political, not a moral or intellectual one. Another former officer agreed, saying that an earlier paper had clearly placed secret activities in the intellectual framework of international relations, political theory and law. Political legitimacy, however, must constantly be built up. An academic remarked that what is true of secret activities is also true of many other aspects of contemporary US policy. He noted that incompetence in languages has increased despite the periodic institution of new language programs. That is, he maintained, because such programs wither on the vine for lack of support from all concerned. People simply see no reason to devote time and money to activities which they do not believe justified in terms of a worthwhile national purpose. Paramilitary action may well be covert and politically approved, but it will lack political legitimacy unless it serves a purpose the public well understands and supports.

CHAPTER FIVE

Trends in Soviet Covert Action

Paper:
Donald Jameson

Discussants:
Mr. John Barron
Mr. Herbert Romerstein

For my purposes, covert action is a term used to describe those actions covertly conducted by one government or institution with the intent of influencing or countering the policies of another government or institution without revealing the first government's role. In addition, I shall restrict covert action to actions short of terrorism or insurgency. Perhaps the most difficult line to draw lies between covert action, "grey propaganda," and other activities in which the role of the sponsor is sensed, but not proved or at least not admitted. It is particularly difficult to draw such a line with regard to Soviet covert action because of the panoply of front groups and publications that they sometimes involve. I only note, however, that such a line exists and has a certain importance for the analytical treatment of covert action, especially Soviet covert action.

The problem in drawing a line between the essentially attributable and the fundamentally non-attributable actions of the Soviet Union is rooted in the origin of the Soviet regime. Its origin as a covert operation, its massive use of political warfare, which is perceived as necessary for survival and the unlimited ambition of its leaders to expand their power, have led to the creation of a system in which covert action, propaganda, and related activities play a role in state policy that is qualitatively different from their role in other societies. The Soviet regime began as a covert action operation of the German General Staff and then became a government. This sinister birth (in all three senses of the word) led the Soviet Government to regard propaganda and covert action as normal from the outset. E. H. Carr pointed out:

> The initiative in introducing propaganda as a regular instrument of international relations must be credited to the Soviet Government. . .[during the revolution]. . .the principal element of strength in their position was

169

their influence over opinion in other countries; it was natural and necessary that they should exploit this weapon to the utmost. . . . Soviet Russia
was the first modern state to establish, in the form of the Communist
International, a large scale, permanent international propaganda organization. Since the end of the Middle Ages, no political organization has
claimed to be the repository of universal truth or the missionary of a
universal gospel. . . . So revolutionary did this innovation appear that the
Communist International purported at the outset to be wholly uncon-
nected with the power of the Soviet Government. (*The Bolshevik Revolution,* V. 1, pp. 137-38.)

In addition, the centralized nature of the Soviet government's control
over all of society's activities had led to an integrated style of projecting influence abroad. For the Soviets, covert action is always
part of a general policy, not (as has been the case in the United States
at times) a separate line of activity tactically unrelated to other types
of activity directed toward the same country.

The Soviet Union's covert action campaigns are peculiar in a third
way: the regime's enduring dedication to the aggrandisement of its
power without apparent limit. The patience of the Soviet leadership
is great, but the goal of world domination remains its ultimate
aspiration.

At the apex of the Soviet covert action and propaganda system is
the International Department of the Central Committee apparatus
and the ancillary International Propaganda Department. From this
height, the Politburo's policy toward other countries and groups of
countries, such as NATO and the Common Market, is translated into
orders for all elements of the Soviet system that have foreign connections. Trade policy, diplomatic policy, military policy, covert
action, intelligence collection and so on all originate within the Central Committee apparatus. While suggestions for operations from
subordinates to implement policy are reviewed there, the basic function of the Central Committee's apparatus is to direct and verify the
execution of assignments by operating elements, a rather effective
form of oversight. By way of contrast, the committee of the US
National Security Council that reviewed covert action proposals in
former administrations and, presumably does so today, was designed
to screen out proposals contrary to policy or otherwise inappropriate, but rarely to assign tasks or programs to elements of the
executive branch of government, or to monitor the effectiveness of
performance.

Moreover, in the US the numerous private, public, academic,
social, religious, commercial and political organizations that engage
in activities influencing foreign countries are, of course, almost en-

tirely beyond the reach of government. In the Soviet Union, all such organizations have their assigned role in campaigns to influence other nations. Below the International Department, which has broad responsibility for all aspects of foreign policy, is the International Propaganda Department of the Central Committee, a newly formed part of the apparatus that reflects, as does the current role of the International Department itself, the increasingly bureaucratic, administratively tidy evolution of the organs of power in the Soviet Union. The International Propaganda Department is well staffed with specialists from the media. Below it are spread the organizations which act as the operational elements of foreign policy, including covert action.

This includes not only the KGB but also committees, institutions, the media, the publishing houses, front groups, such as the World Peace Council, and the World Federation of Trade Unions, research institutes such as the Institute for the Study of the USA and Canada, the Rodina Societies that keep in touch with emigrés of all nationalities of the Soviet Union, Communist parties, Radio Moscow, TASS and Novosti. In addition to their roles as organs of overt Soviet propaganda, virtually every one of these organizations has a covert action role as well. In analyzing the Soviet covert action effort, parochialism can be left behind. It is one big ecumenical effort.

The KGB, unlike the CIA prior to 1967, does not fund and manage radio stations, or large international organizations. These matters are handled by the Central Committee and front groups. The KGB infiltrates its officers and agents into these organizations for spotting, assessing and recruiting spies and other types of agents and for counterintelligence monitoring. The burden of management lies elsewhere. The KGB's principal efforts in covert action are deception, penetration, disinformation, agents of influence, manipulation of Western media and the like.

In the 1980's, the KGB is likely to continue its basic programs but with greater sophistication. Among the most significant differences will be a continuing shift in the type of personnel used by the KGB and, indeed, by the other organs of Soviet covert action as well. The founders of the current program, from Willy Muenzenburg to Richard Sorge came from a broad, internationally-minded cadre of Comintern revolutionaries. Most of the best were intellectuals who had grown up in the West. With the purges and the coming of the Second World War, these men almost disappeared from the ranks of Soviet officials. With them went the style and knowledge of the world that made

Soviet political warfare so effective before World War II. With the war's end, Stalin's men emerged to take their place.

They were reliable Russians, not too *salonfähig*, perhaps, but more reliable, or so Stalin thought, than the pre-war, snobbish, foreign, intellectual cadre that kept the Soviet Union's reputation as an enlightened, exciting, dedicated nation untarnished even when Stalin was murdering millions of Soviet citizens. After the war, Stalin's henchmen revived the fronts. Many had profited from the atmosphere of wartime cooperation, which predisposed so many Westerners to friendliness or neutrality toward the Soviet Union. However, the isolation and rigidity of Stalin's operatives took their toll. Soviets abroad often were heavy-handed, dogmatic boors, ignorant of foreign countries and contemptuous (or afraid) of foreign ways.

In the late 1950's a new type of official began to appear abroad. These were the first products of the intense educational program for officials serving abroad that was instituted after the war. Although still subjected to much Marxist-Leninist dogma, the graduates of the program of the Institute for International Relations excelled in languages and received serious courses of instruction on the areas in which they specialized. To the West, the prototype of the new breed was Alexander Kaznacheyev, who defected in 1959 in Burma. A polished, well educated young man who spoke fluent English and Chinese, he was also the Soviet Union's first student of Burmese. From his time on, we have seen a whole new generation arrive to man the *rezidentura* in the West: well trained in the languages and cultures of other countries, well read and capable of taking part in wide-ranging discussions. For the most part, cynical, selfish, and competent, these new officers whose qualities have become increasingly distinct from their predecessors, will continue to influence the way operations are carried out and the kind of operations that are planned.

In addition to the significance of the change from the wartime generation to the current one, one must also note the difference between them and their professional grandfathers, the Comintern agents. But the grandfathers believed; the younger generation do not. They are professional intelligence officers of the Soviet Union. They pursue power. Most of their grandfathers thought that they were serving mankind. Directives from the Center may still emphasize ideological motives, but these men don't care. The liberation of the working class is left to socialist students or to the Cubans. They focus on campaigns that weaken and confuse other countries. They recruit agents that hate their own countries and worship power, attitudes they understand and often share, attitudes that are reflected in the operations they run.

Tomorrow's strategy, so far as I can see, is likely to remain the same as today's: to divide the industrialized West and to reduce the military and political power of the parts, beginning with Western Europe and Japan and finally the reduction of the power of the United States. In this strategy, the Third World is a tactical target, most significant for its impact on the industrialized nations, and most attractive because of its vulnerability.

I find it useful to divide Soviet operations into two groups: thematic campaigns and enduring targets. One example of the thematic campaigns was that against the modernization of theatre nuclear weapons in NATO nations. Whether there is a significant connection between this massive campaign and the section on CBS TV's program *60 Minutes,* first aired I believe in November, 1980, dedicated to protests and criticism of the plan to base cruise missiles in the United Kingdom, I don't know. Certainly for the Soviets, the program was a welcome contribution to their effort. The enduring targets include defamation abroad and destabilization at home of the government, economy, politics, and social mores of the United States. Other targets include the distancing of West Germany from NATO, China in all its aspects, and the destabilization of the Republic of South Africa's racial situation. The CIA, the US military, the FBI, Western intelligence and police services in general, multinational corporations and nuclear power plants are among the enduring targets of less than national size.

These two types of activities differ in that thematic campaigns often begin with the public announcement of the Soviet position on the issue by the top leadership which then works its way through the Soviet media to the Western Communist Parties and front groups, and their associated media, mass demonstrations, and petition gathering, and from there to the non-communist media and organizations that, almost by instinct, pick up the cause. Such campaigns use all types of propaganda assets from Brezhnev to unwitting American journalists. Obviously, not everybody involved is an equally witting participant or participates for the same motives.

For instance, consider one of Moscow's greatest thematic campaigns, to get the United States out of Vietnam and to exploit the divisions the war had stimulated in our society. No successful campaign can grow on barren soil. It can only enhance and focus the convictions and concerns indigenous to the target environment. For that reason the full impact of the Soviet-fostered effort *per se* cannot be measured, but its existence and the crucial role it played in helping to organize the Vietnam Day Observance Committee and other key groups that put together the main events of protest is clear, if not widely appreciated. The Heritage Foundation's study on the subject meticulously documents the nature of the cadre employed. The CPUSA provided some personnel and expertise, while front groups, Cubans, Czechs and Hungarians, left-wing think tanks and the like, provided more. Through these channels, the Soviets were able to shape generalized discontent into a hard-hitting campaign that paralyzed the conduct of the war and led to America's acquiescence in an illusory, foredoomed peace.

Perhaps the most interesting aspect of Soviet operations in the United States during the Vietnam war was the support given to the Weather Underground, and other extreme left terrorist-oriented groups. That support may well have continued since 1973, but what is now publicly known is that between 1969 and 1973 the Soviets and their satellites, the Cubans, the East Germans, North Koreans and others trained and supported a broad spectrum of revolutionary, violence-prone radicals in the United States with equipment, money and safe haven. The travel bills alone that were paid for by the Communist states to these groups must have been in the millions. This can easily be determined from documents prepared from classified government reports by the defense for the former senior FBI officials Felt and Miller and publicly presented at their trial.

In addition to those mentioned above, typical thematic campaigns of the recent past include the anti-neutron "bomb" campaign, which has smoothly turned into a campaign against NATO's modernization of theatre nuclear forces, and blended well with the campaign to "neutralize" West Germany, and the campaign to weaken the United States' credibility in Egypt. The first of these is well documented in the CIA study: *Soviet Covert Action and Propaganda,* presented to the Oversight Subcommittee of the House Permanent Select Committee on Intelligence on February 6, 1980.

Unfortunately, though understandably, the study omits any reference to KGB activities that took place in the United States. The picture is thus much diminished. Nevertheless, it is impressive. Consider the following. In Istanbul, a Peace Committee demonstrated in front of the US Consulate General; in Accra, a group described as completely out of local character delivered a protest letter to the US Embassy. In Stuttgart, Frankfurt and Dusseldorf, front groups delivered notes to US Consulates; in Bonn, two Soviet journalists were observed at a demonstration at the US Embassy; a front group in

Lima, Peru, sent a protest to the UN; in Tanzania, the World Peace Council delegation sought propaganda assistance from President Nyerere. Brezhnev wrote letters to every western government warning that the neutron bomb was a threat to detente. The Dutch Communists organized an "International Forum" against the "neutron bomb" which imported pacifists and party-liners from all over the world for a march of some 40,000 people in Amsterdam. Finally, though the CIA study omits it, a group of "devout believers" demonstrated in front of the church in Washington where President Carter was attending services. He saw their demonstration, went back to the White House and cancelled production on the weapon. CIA estimates that the campaign cost the Soviets a hundred million dollars over three years. For that much money one could totally rebuild and modernize the facilities of Radio Liberty. The Soviet Ambassador to the Netherlands received a decoration for the way he marshalled the Dutch CP for the cause. We do not know how many others were similarly decorated for their efforts. Whoever sent the gentle souls over to President Carter's church should have been given the Order of Lenin. Maybe he was.

The third example, the Egyptian campaign, has sought through forgeries and press propaganda to sow dissent between the US government and President Sadat, and between Sadat and the US on the one hand the Egyptian people on the other. The chief instrument has been a series of forgeries of US official documents. Some were mailed anonymously to the Egyptian Embassy in Rome while others surfaced through a Baath Party newspaper in Syria. To compare this operation to the neutron bomb campaign is to go from the orchestra to the kazoo, but forgeries can be effective, sometimes in places far removed from the target locale and place. Years later, they can be reproduced or referred to in articles or books and leave a lasting impression.

The second of the Soviet's thematic campaigns is the most serious and the one that has lasted the greatest length of time. Its cover aspects have been briefly sensed here and there through the years, but the counterpoint of overt and covert action is so clear that one can almost hear the missing notes. This is the campaign for the allegiance of West Germany, one of the most crucial issues of the postwar period. The full story of this campaign is too long and complicated for inclusion as an example of Soviet political warfare with a major role for covert action. Among the operations involved have been the publication of far right or Nazi journals, desecration of Jewish cemeteries, agents of influence, including leading members of the parliament and the immediate aide to the Chancellor, and support for terrorist groups. There has also been sponsorship of a magazine, *Konkret*, that mixed pudenda and propaganda together to produce radical political pornography and which was edited by Ulricke Meinhoff's husband. Additionally, there have been instances of close collaboration, if not more, between certain leaders of the SPD and the Soviet leadership, particularly, with key officials on the Central Committee staff. The Deputy Chief of the CPSU's International Propaganda Department is the former Ambassador to the Federal Republic.

For campaigns such as those mentioned above and for attacks on enduring targets, the Soviets through the KGB and others have developed a wide variety of assets in non-Communist media. Depending upon their milieu, these assets can be used to champion Soviet superiority in various fields, replay stories originally surfaced in the Soviet or Communist press, attack western targets such as NATO and the CIA or support causes in the West that serve Soviet purposes, such as the movement against nuclear power. As one would expect, in the course of the past decade the Soviets have increasingly shifted to covert propaganda that does not directly proclaim Soviet policies. Some of it even criticizes peripheral aspects of Soviet policy the more credibly to hammer home its main point. A former Soviet official who was from time to time tasked to write articles to be planted in Western media said that his instructions often included the admonition to criticize Soviet policy in passing while concentrating the attack on the United States.

In exploiting Western media, the general policy is to concentrate on the individual writer, not the newspaper or magazine ownership. In most cases the individual reporter can insert the desired line into his copy more easily than his publisher. Among ways of getting at working journalists and also their editors, the recent case in France of Charles Pathé demonstrates an effective technique. Pathé was arrested in 1979 and confessed to having been a Soviet agent for 19 years. He devoted his talents mainly to getting Soviet-inspired articles into the French press. He favored Soviet disarmament policies, championed Soviet science, villified the United States, and defended French nationalism against American incursions. His major vehicle was a newsletter concentrating on scientific developments but covering economics and politics too. He also prepared background material and articles for journalists. He succeeded in getting his material into almost all of the major press of France, including *Le Monde, Realité* and *Le Figaro*. Although known to have an indulgent attitude

toward the Soviet Union, until his arrest he was assumed to be
expressing an individual preference while preserving an independent
point of view as a journalist. The significance of this case is that it
almost certainly represents in documented form a phenomenon that
is widespread in various parts of the world. In other cases the proof
has not, unfortunately, been forthcoming.

An interesting example of curious happenings in the US media is
a magazine called *Executive Intelligence Review,* a vehicle of the "New
Solidarity International Press Service" in New York. This magazine
celebrates Lyndon LaRouche, a candidate for the Democratic nom-
ination for the Presidency in the 1980 election, and formerly a leader
of neo-Trotskyite causes. *Executive Intelligence Review* does not espouse Soviet causes *per se;* in fact, it favors increased US arms in
certain contexts, advocates expansion of nuclear power, and opposes
"windfall profits" tax proposals. Its target audiences are business
executives, government officials, professional people and the like.
Perhaps they have approached you as they have me at Washington's
National Airport. I have heard of their attempts to recruit readers
and sympathizers in Dusseldorf and Houston. The curious thing
about this militant effort is that the *Executive Intelligence Review*
praises Soviet science, Soviet education, and even Soviet diplomacy.
It calls the Israelis "fascists," prints a tendentious interview with a
retired Italian general (labelled a Communist Party member) on the
dangers of modernizing theatre nuclear weapons in Europe, exag-
gerates the value of Soviet petroleum resources and in other ways
leaves the reader with the impression that the Soviets are tough,
able, willing to listen to reason and, in any event, several cuts above
the Carter Administration when it comes to getting things done effectively. No one item in the publication is too assertive, but the
impact of the whole makes interesting reading for one looking for
new variations on old themes.

A direct Soviet role can be found historically in the growth of
another US publishing endeavor, the Myron E. Sharpe Press of
White Plains, New York. Long a publisher of pro-Soviet materials
of a scholarly cast under various firm names, Mr. Sharpe was a
registered Soviet agent until 1965. Over the years, he has come to
concentrate on translations from Soviet technical and scholarly publications, beginning with a press summary that was widely perceived
at the time as an attempt to drive *Current Digest of the Soviet Press,*
published by the American Council of Learned Societies out of
business. Having lost that battle, Sharpe now produces a large number of journals printing Soviet articles on academic subjects. In

addition, Sharpe publishes books about the Soviet Union and Eastern Europe and a magazine called *Challenge*, a slick paper journal devoted to economics with a list of advisors that includes many of the country's top economists. Although eclectic in its choice of articles, it has a generally collectivist bias, treats Soviet economic theory with marked respect and sometimes lets go with a broadside, as it did in a signed commentary by Sharpe on the award of the Nobel Prize to Frederick Hayek. The exact nature of the relationship between Sharpe and the Soviets these days is unknown, but he has done well in getting the Soviet message to college students, scholars and economists in the United States via intellectually respectable media.

These adventures have dealt with the propagation of the faith abroad. We cannot leave the subject of Soviet influence on the Western press without mentioning the operations at the center. The Second Chief Directorate of the KGB, which is charged with preserving the internal security of the USSR from foreign malevolence has cadres of officers dedicated to suborning foreign journalists in Moscow. Their efforts appear to be rewarding. A reporter does not need to be recruited as an agent to become cautious, although it helps. Some reporters are better able to defend themselves than others. A few reporters are permanent staff members of publications which assure their people that if they are expelled from a country for doing their jobs, they will not suffer professionally. Even these reporters have been harassed. However, the majority of reporters, the stringers whose careers are dependent on staying in Moscow, are much more vulnerable and tend to be much more exploited.

Another technique the KGB seems to value is forged documents as a tool for deception and influence on a periodic basis. The rhythm, which was first noted during the Eisenhower Administration apparently coincides with concern for detente. When the diplomats cool off, the forgers heat up. What does this tell us about the Soviet views? Do they think forgery is so viciously potent that they dare not use it when trying to improve relations, or do they just consider it a gimmick they can turn off and on to impress us with whenever they want to? I can only add that after a lull during Nixon's second term, they went back to forging again when Carter entered the White House and have been at it ever since.

The principal forgeries with which I am acquainted are of official US government correspondence in which something offensive is said about our friends such as the piece that quoted Secretary of State Vance criticizing Sadat, King Khalid and other Arab leaders. One of the most elaborate of recent years was a forged US Army field manual giving guidance on the handling of security problems at bases over-seas. The forgery left the impression that the US military had become involved with domestic political and security matters in other countries. The document was referred to in a left-wing Turkish news-paper in 1975. The full text appeared a year later in the Philippines. Two years later, it surfaced in Spain when a Cuban intelligence officer was offering it around together with an article on the US military by a Spanish Communist. It last surfaced in Italy where it was cited as evidence the CIA had Aldo Moro killed because it viewed him as a dangerous leftist.

Forged documents can be effective in Third World countries es-pecially to reinforce local negative views of the US at times when the subject is particularly apropos. They have also had an impact on left and radical media in Europe and the US. They have even pro-voked serious diplomatic incidents.

The use of agents of influence, people recruited and controlled as specifically as other types of agents, but dedicated primarily to the task of influencing governmental or political policy, is one of the KGB's standard techniques. Because the agent often is a public figure, there are problems in handling and communications, and with the agent's possession of compromising materials. Identification and arrest of agents of influence is difficult. Suspicion and even firsthand evidence often does not lead to official investigation or judicial action for reasons of state. One of the few western countries that has arrested and tried several agents of influence is West Germany. There the KGB and the East German service have succeeded in recruiting the confidential aide to the Chancellor, the secretary of the leader of the opposition, the member of parliament charged with East/West German negotiations, several other Bundestag members and officials on every level of government. Many of these agents have had espi-onage assignments as well as influence assignments. Alas, there seem to be more agents in West Germany than secrets.

In the United States, few people have been identified as agents since the days of Alger Hiss, Harry White and others. There have been three cases at least of agents on Congressional staffs and others who were aimed in that direction, but intercepted before they got there. But in the Carter years, there was a closeness of relations between certain employees of the departments of State and Treasury · and organizations much involved with Cuban officials, some of them identified as intelligence officers. Perhaps this was not without sig-nificance for the Carter Administration's policies toward Latin Amer-ica and Africa.

These considerations lead to what might be called the institutions of influence. These are organizations dedicated to causes whose personnel are, presumably, sincere advocates for causes they espouse. They do not necessarily have any ties to Soviet Cuban or other surrogate services. Such institutions differ from classic front groups such as the World Peace Council by their less evident affiliation with the Soviet Union. In the early fifties, the Institute for Pacific Relations was shown to be a Soviet instrument. Today Washington abounds with organizations that appear to be godchildren of the IPR. The missions of these organizations seem clear and often their connections with Cuban officials with intelligence backgrounds are a matter of record. The basic funds flow through foundations and churches. So far as I know, there is no unmistakably certain Soviet funding source. Indeed, it is probably true that the large bulk, if not most of the money received by many of these organizations comes solely from genuinely American foundations. These organizations' missions, however, coincide remarkably with those of the KGB. Some of these institutions have evolved from authentic American pacifist and radical roots into groups which respond to Soviet influence.

Before turning to the future of Soviet covert action, I must note the ultimate in curious happenings in this shadowland of causes and influences. During the time when Rockwell International was building the prototype B1 Bomber, there was a picket brigade outside the headquarters of Rockwell in Pittsburgh that carried signs protesting the project. Then President Carter cancelled the B1. Three days passed. The same pickets returned. Now they protested Rockwell's contract with the Army to manage the Rocky Flats nuclear research center in Colorado. They objected not only to the business of nuclear weapons in general, they also charged Rockwell with importing 40,000 South Korean fetuses for radiation experiments at Rocky Flats. I have no idea where that idea came from, but as an old campaigner, I can imagine the session where somebody put it together. Then the story hit the Pittsburgh papers and some people may have believed it. (Pittsburgh newspapers attributed the information to Sean MacBride.)

To introduce speculation on the role of Soviet covert action in the future, let me first describe the most arcane example of that art I know—and a harbinger of more to come. In the general campaign against China, the Soviets seek to exploit the minority nationality problems of the Inner Asian peoples, the Mongols, the Uighurs, Kirgiz, Tibetans, and others whose homelands lie wholly or in part in western China. But these central Asians live not only in China and the Soviet Union; there is a sizeable colony also in Saudi Arabia, 65,000 of whom have been there since the 19th century in some cases, some since the suppression of Enver Pasha and the Basmachi in the 1920's, and, most recently since the Chinese Communists drove out the leaders of the East Turkestan Republic who had ruled Sinkiang in the middle 1940's. The earlier groups had been conquered by Russians; these last by Chinese.

Everybody's agent in the Soviet Union, Victor Louis, was commissioned to write a book about the Central Asians. It is called *The Coming Decline of the Chinese Empire* and it says that all the Turkic peoples are one and should unite, including the brothers from over the border in China. This has led to an interesting side effect. The focus of the Uighur exile community is the East Turkestan Refugee Committee in Istanbul, led by the aging ex-president of the East Turkestan Republic. This man and his son had worked for Radio Liberty until the Radio cut off the Uighur program about two years ago. The cut-off of American aid for the Uighur cause and the Soviet Union's assumption of it has turned the Uighurs against the United States. But the Uighurs and their cousins are not found only in China, they and their brother peoples live in tightly knit little communities in Saudi Arabia. By preference, these immigrants seek military and police careers. Many are in the air force and many in the police, including I have heard, the chief of police of Mecca.

About two years ago, the old president of the ETR, Yusuf Alptekine began to respond to the increasing attention paid him by a Soviet Uighur, Ziya Samedi, a writer who originally came from Chinese Turkestan (Sinkiang). Ziya was concerned about preserving Uighur culture in the diaspora and getting support from Uighurs everywhere for the idea of a new Central Asian state or at least freedom from the Han people for the Uighurs. Behind Ziya Samedi there stands Tursan Rakhimov, a former *apparatchik* of the Central Committee who is now using academic cover as a scholar at Moscow's Institute of the Far East. Rakhimov has also raised a young follower in Dias Qadir Ogli Hasanov, a Uighur who has become an interpreter in Arabic, working for Arab delegations that have come to Moscow for Congresses of the CPSU and other assemblies. He is a member of the Soviet-Palestine Society of the USSR Academy of Sciences. A Soviet scholar visiting the West told a friend about a year ago that Hasanov was now in South Yemen. Through these connections, Soviet Uighur literature and even personal correspondence flows out to Uighurs all over the world, including Saudi Arabia. The Rodina Society, which keeps up with emigres of all nationalities (and is used extensively by the KGB), produces through its Uighur section a magazine that appeals to Uighurs abroad to keep the national faith. Beside the publication, the personal contacts, such as that between Ziya Samedi and Yusuf Alptekine, subsidies for Uighur publications abroad, and payments for contributors to Soviet publications keep the channels expanding. The Rodina Society's Uighur magazine has recently printed its first contribution from a Uighur in Saudi Arabia. As a result, the Soviets may well find that a few years from now they will have a solid cadre among Uighurs in key positions in Saudi Arabia, all picked up through a channel that nobody thought to pay attention to. If perchance this effort doesn't get anywhere, its cost as part of the larger effort against China is insignificant.

Soviet covert action is unlikely to change much in the future unless there are major upheavals inside the Soviet bloc or the strategic position of the West shifts dramatically. Therefore, we are speaking about a world caught up in trends, but not calamities. First, let us look at our vulnerabilities as the Soviets perceive them. The major ones are:

- inconsistency, we don't pursue a goal over long periods of time
- lack of centralization, we don't direct everything from the center
- decadence, we are too rich, too self-indulgent
- lack of serious purpose, one must hear a Russian talk about *seriozniye dela,* things that really matter, to appreciate the contempt in which they hold the quick-fix or the superficial approach
- commercial greed, we will do anything for money
- lack of social discipline, we can't enforce proper standards
- hypertrophied legal system, anybody can use the system to defend himself or to obscure his actions
- lack of protection for secrets, anybody can find out anything
- self-contempt, the one factor that fits Marxist theory is the hate that some members of our society bear toward it
- weakened security apparatus, restrictions on the investigative powers of the FBI, CIA and police.

In general, these vulnerabilities are considered to be typical of all of the industrialized countries. Soviet recruitment strategies, their operational planning and their expectations of success to some degree take them into account. The Third World is thought to be even more vulnerable because in addition to the above, they suffer from economic weakness and political instability. In the opinion of several Soviet officials I have met, the only nations who understand the game and play it "seriously" are China and Israel.

Over the coming decade, I think that the following thematic campaigns and enduring targets will receive the most attention from Soviet covert action: enervate and confuse the US; promote disarmament in the West; divide Western Europe and dissolve NATO, and as a corollary, emphasize the national character of the European Communist Parties; reduce US influence in the Middle East; divide China from the US, and divide China from Japan and Japan from the US. Other campaigns will be directed at support of revolutionary and terrorist movements in Africa, Latin America and the Caribbean, efforts to divide and confuse groups of Soviet expatriates and defectors, blunting other anti-Soviet activities and destroying the links between the outside world and the Soviet dissenters.

To further these goals we can expect to see more global campaigns similar to the attacks on the neutron warhead and the B1 bomber, linking Soviet-supported groups to others amenable to influence and sharing goals. The objective of these campagins will not be so much to advance Communism as to weaken the target countries. The anti-nuclear power and anti-nuclear weapons movements and the attacks on transnational corporations will be parts of global campaigns, even more than now.

Economic operations, using Soviet gold and the worldwide Soviet banking system, are likely to be used to weaken the vulnerable business classes in small countries and to gain advantages in Western markets. The Third World will see the coming of age of the first crop of Lumumba University graduates, who are now becoming ministers in cabinets, leaders in industry and commerce, senior officials in governments and parties, and heads of colleges and institutes. Among them are surely some reliable agents of influence who have perhaps lain fallow for years.

In connection with the attitudes of the new generation of officers in Soviet officialdom and the general trends of development, we should expect decreasing stress on ideology, particularly hard line Marxism-Leninism. Instead, attacks will be based on an "objective position", that is, an apparently reasonable point of view. False flag operations, recruitment in the name of some other nation or service, even in the covert action field are to be expected as the Soviet Union's public reputation declines.

In summary, in my view, Soviet covert action will continue to evolve along established paths, probably expanding and improving its techniques as its cadre gains even more experience in the Western world. Preoccupation with Soviet vulnerabilities and operations to counter efforts, real or imagined, from the West to exploit them may take on more significance than I have suggested, but otherwise, it seems that a solidly built, carefully directed huge machine will keep on with what has after all proved to be an effective means to pursue the enduring goal of world dominance. Only when they are faced with serious challenges to their efforts will they try to alter basically the methods that have evolved from over sixty years of unique and impressive experience.

Discussants

Mr. John Barron: I believe the import of what Mr. Jameson says is fully supported by both data that are now in the public domain and by an even larger body of data which may become public eventually. I can only elaborate upon some of Mr. Jameson's observations and judgments. Three very important and valid themes emerge from his commentary. First, the Soviet commitment to covert action, or active measures as the Russians term them, is congenital, massive, and enduring. Barring some transfiguring upheaval within the Soviet Union, I find no cause to think that this commitment, one might say addiction, will diminish, much less vanish. The surface currents of Soviet diplomacy and policy ebb and flow with the perceived expediencies of the moment, but covert action and allied clandestine activities proceed unabated on a grandiose scale. Neither peaceful co-existence in the 1960's nor détente in the 1970's abated the clandestine activities of the Soviet Union. On the contrary, by all objective measurements we can apply, the scope, scale, and intensity of Soviet covert actions and clandestine operations have steadily increased.

Secondly, Mr. Jameson notes, significantly, I think that Soviet covert actions integrate, synchronize, and concentrate all relevent resources of the state into the effort to achieve a particular goal. Let us consider just how these covert actions work, how they function, and see how total this integration is.

The Politburo or the International Department of the Central Committee, which is really a descendant of the Comintern, and Cominform, conceived or defines the objectives. Once they are defined, however, ideas for achieving them, for instigating a particular covert action, may originate in any number of places in Service A of the KGB, formerly the Disinformation Department, now called the Active Measures Department, or within any of the fronts of the International Department, the Afro-Asian Solidarity Committee, World Peace Council, or within the International Department itself. Once an idea is proposed, it is submitted through the International Department and through the Politburo. Incidentally, sometimes the originator will even draft the response for the Politburo so the latter doesn't have to trouble, but need only sign off on it. Then, this order goes out to KGB stations, or *rezidenturas* all over the world, to the agents run throughout the world by the fronts of the International Department. The implementation of this order occurs literally on a worldwide basis.

A former practitioner of Soviet covert action told me it was not at all unusual for the residency to receive in a single day four or five different orders, do this, that, and that. He emphasized that the West must understand that the repetitive, cumulative nature of Soviet covert action gives them their overall thrust. Everybody participates in this. In a KGB residency, there is something called the active measures group. Which concentrates solely on this aspect, but at one time or another every agent within the residency network may become involved. The Soviet press as well as the Ministry of Foreign Affairs' personnel participate. And, as in the anti-neutron bomb campaign, even Brezhnev himself may join in. It is a total, massive, integrated effort. Mr. Jameson pointed out some rather spectacular examples of the anti-neutron bomb campaign, but even relatively plebeian ones which we don't notice go on day after day after day. Ultimately, they have an effect.

The third point is that the practitioners of Soviet covert action are as cynical as ever and much more sophisticated. These two go hand in hand in an interesting way. It is difficult to find any Soviet representative who cares anything about Marxism and Leninism.

One to whom I spoke said that there should be a great red neon sign flashing through the night, "Cynicism Unlimited," over the mansion which houses the fronts of the International Department. But this cynicism, this shedding of dogma, has allowed for much greater flexibility and much greater sophistication in putting active measures or covert action to work. The whole operation shows an ever-greater willingness to work with anti-Communists, in Japan with nationalists, in France with nationalists, people who are anti-American, but may be just as well anti-Soviet. They don't care any more. They were working and supporting the US Weather Underground which was not certainly under Soviet control, and some of whose members were not necessarily sympathetic to the Soviet Union. They didn't care. If they wanted the US Capitol bombed, they didn't necessarily demand that the bombers be pro-Soviet; they just wanted it bombed.

So we see also in this sophistication superb intelligence upon which their actions are based with a prescience far exceeding that of most political analysts. In the mid-1970's they saw the growth of conservatism in the industrial democracies, and they shifted accordingly. Today they are quite interested in developing agents of influence in conservative newspapers, and in conservative circles. I think in this decade we will certainly see even greater sophistication. All our data from inside the apparatus suggest preparations for more covert action. They believe that this instrument is a successful one, and I think they have grounds for that conclusion.

Mr. Herbert Romerstein: I think this paper gives us a good overview of the Soviet covert action effort, and it partially answers one of the questions that was raised earlier: when should we engage in covert action?

The idea that covert action has been used throughout history is an insufficient argument for its indiscriminate use. But, because we are faced with an enemy that desires our destruction and is prepared to undermine us through agents of influence media placements, and other methods, and to divide us from our allies, the United States must also use the weapon of influence and covert action to defend itself. I am not suggesting that our covert action should always be reactive. Very often covert action, should be aggressive, moving against the enemy's weaknesses.

While this paper is a very valuable contribution to our understanding of this subject, one problem Mr. Jameson did not address is the paramilitary mode of Soviet covert action. Obviously, its propaganda role, the agent of influence role, and so on is on a much greater scale. But Soviet support of paramilitary operations both directly and through surrogates in various parts of the world, is something that we must seriously consider. The use of surrogates is an interesting phenomenon. For the most part, the Soviet Union does not give direct aid to terrorist groups, but there are exceptions to this. The PLO, for example, does get direct aid.

While there are instances, significant instances, of direct Soviet support for terrorism, more often the Soviets work through cut-outs. It is the surrogates such as Cuba and the PLO who provide this assistance, that is both the surrogate states and terrorist organizations provide training to other terrorist groups from Europe, Latin America and other places. John Barron in his book *KGB* told us about a group in Mexico who were recruited at Lumumba University in Moscow, brought to North Korea for training, and sent back to Mexico for terrorist activities. The notorious Carlos was a student at Lumumba University when he was recruited for operations by the PLO.

The People's Democratic Republic of Yemen serves as a base for terrorist activities against Oman, Saudia Arabia and North Yemen using Soviet arms, Soviet training, and with Soviet coordination of activities.

Our problem, at least in examining the public sources in this area, is that there is often a gap between Soviet operations and the terrorists in the United States, although, every so often, we get a good example which clearly illustrates the chair of command. One of these is the Puerto Rican FALN which has been responsible for five murders in New York City and numerous bombings. In 1975, in a communique after one of their bombings, the FALN said, "We especially acknowledge the moral support given to our organization by the Cuban people and Government in a speech made by Prime Minister Fidel Castro in August in which he said the Cuban Government would do all it could to support the FALN." The Puerto Rican Socialist Party which serves as a support group for FALN makes no secret about its Cuban relationships. The PSP actually holds some of its major meetings in Cuba and serves as a Cuban propaganda arm both in Puerto Rico and here in the United States. Of course, Cuba serves as the Soviet surrogate for terrorism in the Western hemisphere. Almost every terrorist group in this part of the world has had its cadre trained in Cuba.

I have in my possession several interesting pamphlets that indicate a Soviet role in terrorism against Saudia Arabia. They were obtained at a meeting of the Association of Arab-American University Graduates. An Arab friend got them for me from the table of the Democratic Front for the Liberation of Palestine. These pamphlets are aimed at the destabilization and overthrow of the Government of Saudi Arabia. The Democratic Front is the closest thing to a Communist party that exists within the PLO. It gets its support and training from the People's Democratic Republic of Yemen, which in turn gets support for itself, as well as the wherewithal to support others, from the Soviet Union. The role of Palestinian communists in an operation against Saudi Arabia indicates again the role of Soviet proxies in the terrorist thrust against Saudi Arabia.

Mr. Jameson points out how the massive, Soviet-organized worldwide campaign against the neutron weapon, coupled with similar activities in the United States against the weapon, pushed President Carter's decision not to deploy it.

Mr. Jameson also makes reference to a rather interesting group, the US Labor Party, also called the National Caucus of Labor Committees. A number of people in this room have been approached at airplane terminals and on the streets by their members. The US Labor Party often uses right-wing slogans. But on almost every issue, the bottom line is support for some Soviet need. While the Soviet Union and open Communist propaganda will attack the Polish workers for striking, for trying to organize free trade unions, the National

Caucus of Labor Committees is not quite so blunt. The Polish workers, according to their propaganda, are the tools of British intelligence, the Zionists, and the Trotskyites. They praise the Soviet Union for being very gentle and nice about this Polish problem, because according to NCLC, by all rights, the Soviet Union could just go in and clean those terrible people out. On every issue of interest to the Soviet Union, this group invariably comes down on the Soviet side. NCLC admits they have had frequent meetings with the Soviet UN delegation. They now claim to be a conduit for information from the "good elements" in the Soviet leadership to people in the United States. That, of course, is exactly how an agent of influence works. While they are a relatively small group, they serve to help confuse some of the issues, by using right wing slogans to support any line that serves the Soviet Union.

Finally, the Jameson paper gives us a good overview of the real world out there. A world that we have ignored during the past years of anti-CIA hysteria. If we continue to ignore it, we do so at our own peril.

General Discussion

Before turning to Soviet covert action, the discussion turned on the existence in American society of a "sense of guilt" about our own prosperity. There was general agreement that this feeling has facilitated the Soviet Union's covert political activities against the US and has limited US activities. A former senior intelligence official, however, cautioned that although the Soviet Union has played upon this feature of American society it did not create it. Rather, guilt has been a constituent part of our collective psyche since the 17th century. Another former official distinguished, however, between self-doubt, which he acknowledged is very widespread among the American people, and self-contempt, which afflicts America's intellectual elites. Only the latter, he said, find satisfaction in their country's failures. The major problem is among our elites.

A journalist agreed, saying that self-doubt in society is healthy because it makes possible freedom and toleration. But, society has no doubt it needs a successful intelligence agency. America's political leaders have been astonishingly timid about accepting responsibility for an intelligence service which engages in covert action and counterintelligence. He cited the eagerness of many American leaders to pass off responsibility for intelligence operations to the courts by involving them in a decisionmaking process which is wholly foreign to the judiciary. He concluded that much talk by high officials about America's self-guilt is just an excuse for the failure of the CIA, as well as their own failure, to do the job.

Turning to the Soviet Union, a former intelligence officer made the distinction between the Administrative Organs Department of the Soviet Communist Party's Central Committee and the International Department of the Central Committee. Although the former is administratively responsible for the KGB, the latter is responsible for planning and supervising the KGB's covert activities abroad. This division of labor, he said, is often troublesome for the Soviets. A former foreign intelligence officer agreed, and pointed out that often top Soviet officials, especially in the Ministry of Foreign Affairs, are not cleared to know about their own covert actions, and consequently often cannot tell to what extent the flow of news they get from abroad is genuine or generated by Soviet activities. Thus, he said, the Soviets sometimes deceive themselves. Another participant cautioned, however, that Soviet analysts are trained to look for deception from any and all quarters, including their own.

A former official commented on the growing sophistication of Soviet covert action. During the 1940's and 1950's, he said, individual geographic departments of the KGB carried out individual covert actions and coordinated little with other organs of the state. These actions were of low quality, and were overshadowed by the vast campaigns by the front groups run by the International Department. In 1959, however, the Department of Active Measures was established under General Agayants. Between 1959 and 1974 coordination of all Soviet and East European assets improved significantly. He admonished Americans not to underestimate the East European services. Each major action was rather efficiently coordinated down to the departmental level even of the East European countries. After 1974, the Soviets apparently perceived that their operating environment had become much easier, and therefore gave each of their own officers engaged in covert action greater latitude. Two other participants pointed out that the Soviets have also loosened controls on their allies. In recent years, in both the political and paramilitary fields, the Soviets have loosened their command and control over foreign assets which they support. Since their margin for error is now perceived as greater, they tend to support these assets and let them make their own mischief.

CHAPTER SIX

Strengths and Weaknesses in Past US Covert Action

Paper:

B. Hugh Tovar

Discussants:

Dr. Samuel P. Huntington
Mr. Philippe Thyraud de Vosjoli

I t is no secret that Americans have played the covert action game ever since we learned to walk as a nation. Our first intrusions into the *sub rosa* realm were deliberate and our leaders, starting with George Washington, displayed no apparent need to justify their deviations from the norms of open diplomacy. This self-assurance has withered somewhat in recent years, and in the glare of exposure we seem to be as embarrassed at our successes as we are ashamed of our failures. We have had our share of both over the years, and we owe it to ourselves to look hard at the performance pattern. Some of the reasons for success or failure can be identified. Lessons can be learned and applied to new situations. If indeed covert action has a long history in US foreign operations, it is our post-World War II experience that remains most apposite and germane to the challenges facing us today.

Patterns of Success and Failure

The most impressive achievements in American covert action have developed in situations of strength. The nation at the end of World War II saw itself as powerful. A rival loomed on the horizon, but parity seemed remote. National self-confidence was at an all-time high. Our power, interests and commitments were in a reasonable state of balance. There was strong national leadership and we thought we knew where we were going. These conditions prevailed more or less consistently through the end of the decade and well into the fifties, which some have called the golden age of covert action.

Conversely, the worst episodes in covert history have coincided with periods of national uncertainty, days of transition and confusion, best illustrated by the Watergate years, 1972-1975, when covert action became anathema amid near-total disintegration of national poise.

The Ingredients of Success

Opinions differ on which, if any, of the Central Intelligence Agency's better-known covert action programs were successful. Some were, and the views offered below are predicated on that conviction.

Policy, leadership and continuity—collectively, these are the *sine qua non* of effective covert action. If policy is an articulation of national interest, the people at the top must first have a sense of it, and they must convey its meaning unequivocally to their subordinates. If the people and the policies change frequently or precipitately, the impetus is lost and confusion reigns. Skillful operators cannot prevail against it. President Truman's good years were 1946-1951 and, under his direction, major programs were developed in Europe, aimed primarily at forestalling communist political expansion in the democracies of Western Europe. These were positive efforts to enable our allies to cope with their own problems. For example, Italian trade unions, press and political parties, still weak and struggling against their better-organized and financed communist counterparts, were given material assistance and professional guidance. Over time, the scope of the programs widened to include a host of activities in the covert psychological realm, targeted directly at the Soviets. Paramilitary action in Greece in support of the Truman Doctrine added another dimension to this extensive panoply. Lastly, but overridingly important, the entire effort was conducted against the backdrop of the Marshall Plan and the establishment of the North Atlantic Treaty Organization. Together these were an expression of a national commitment to rebuild, revitalize and sustain Western Europe. Here was policy coordination at its best and biggest, with the State Department, Defense and CIA all marching to the same tune. Somebody in those days was thinking big and thinking comprehensively. The momentum thus generated was powerful enough to carry over into the next administration with no apparent break in continuity.

President Eisenhower's term, 1952-1960, saw the heyday of American covert action and its expansion on three continents. Although the administration had changed, the White House, the Congress and the public saw international life in essentially the same perspective. Our concern was the global challenge of communism as then visualized, to be confronted whenever and wherever it seemed to threaten our interests. There was also continuity of experience and the professional verve and expertise that went with it. This was particularly true of the CIA. Throughout the fifties, and for some time thereafter, the Agency was dominated by a group of able and effective men who had emerged from the war with a sense of mission and who shared many of the same concerns. (For present purposes this applies primarily to the leadership of the Directorate of Plans (DDP), or Operations as it is called today, and to the senior echelons closely associated with Allen W. Dulles.) Their crusading spirit frequently found a response among similarly oriented officials in the State Department and White House. Coordination of policy and agreement on methods of implementation were thus facilitated, albeit rather informally, to a degree rarely achieved in subsequent years. This happy confluence of men and events shows up vividly in a wide range of covert activity.

• In Europe, the operations noted above sustained their impact in the labor, press and political milieux, and expanded aggressively in other areas. Unattributed international broadcasting to the Soviet Union and to the peoples of Eastern Europe rooted itself well enough to survive for three decades. A vigorous challenge by the Soviets in the burgeoning international organizations was met head-on and generally neutralized.

• The Philippines, 1952-1956, where the operators did almost everything right, is also a case study in State/CIA collaboration under ambassadorial direction. More important, it showed how an insurgency could be handled without getting the United States directly involved. The untimely death of Ramon Magsaysay in 1957 was regrettable but it had the side-effect of insuring that the operation never turned sour. Official US dealings with Magsaysay were already offering an object lesson in how not to treat a friend. Had he lived longer, we might well have ruined him.

• The early CIA *spectacular* in Iran, 1953 could have no counterpart today. Quite apart from the threat of exposure, which would be great enough to guarantee against such risk-taking, the wheels of policy would probably grind too slowly to permit prompt exploitation of such a target of opportunity. In fleeting moments, such as the Shah's predicament under Mossadegh, conventional diplomacy is rarely able or willing to move quickly enough. On the heels of success, as we learned during the ensuing years, we then face the nagging problem of how to handle a friendly chief of state who is under obligation to us.

• The Guatemala operation in 1954 was noteworthy for reasons quite apart from its tactical success. Compared to covert action in say, Iran or the Philippines, the effort to overthrow Arbenz was large and of high potential visibility. Policy approval and continuing inter-agency coordination were easy to obtain in the cohesive governmental framework of that day. Nor was there serious danger of leakage by officials who failed to share the enthusiasm of the principals.

• Operations during the sixties show a more irregular pattern. The decade began badly with the U-2 incident and the Bay of Pigs. However, once the Kennedy Administration had pulled itself together by early 1962, the message was conveyed to the covert actioneers in no uncertain terms: Where American interests required intervention, intervene we would. The Bay of Pigs was a disaster but it did not mean permanent withdrawal from the arena. The following cases illustrate the application of this approach.

In 1962, when it became apparent that the North Vietnamese in Laos were violating the Geneva Agreement, President Kennedy decided to give clandestine support to elements of the Royal Lao military, including the Meo forces under Vang Pao. If the subsequent history of the so-called clandestine war is beyond the scope of this paper, several points nonetheless pertain. CIA, of course, carried the main burden. But the Ambassador controlled the program and directed massive participation by other American governmental bodies operating in Laos. At the Washington end, similar mechanisms balanced those in the field. While the policy decisions that evoked and sustained this undertaking remain controversial, it would be hard to match its effectiveness as a coordinated program or its continuity over a turbulent decade.

There are parallels between Laos and the Congo, 1963-1967. Large-scale paramilitary activity dominated the scene in each instance. The Congo program achieved its objective of enabling President Mobutu to impose a modicum of stability where chaos had reigned. Notwithstanding the opportunities for ''rogue-elephantry'' which the Congo offered CIA, the program was managed under close Washington direction, and in the field the Ambassador called the shots.

The first phase of covert operations in Chile, 1962-1967, likewise bridged the Kennedy and Johnson administrations without interruption. The bureaucratic consensus which prevailed in the early 1960's and which was obviously derived from higher authority, made it comparatively easy to maintain effective collaboration among State Department, CIA and Agency for International Development participants. Certainly this was the case during the Chilean elections of

1964 and 1965. By 1970, however, the consensus had broken down and the results proved disastrous.

In brief, then, successful covert action is predicated on clear-cut direction from senior government echelons. This means leadership. It also means that people think they know what they are doing and believe they are doing the right thing. Continuity is vital. In practical terms, there have to be effective bureaucratic mechanisms to translate these abstractions into controllable programs. Expertise is necessary and can be developed only through experience. It helps to have it on hand when the need arises.

The Ingredients of Failure

A good place to start looking for the makings of failure is in the successful operation. Weaknesses, unnoticed at first, often show up later. Or times change, and what looked good in one set of circumstances collapses under new pressures. Some operations contain built-in guarantees of eventual disaster. Operational failure may also coincide with and quite possibly derive from a deteriorating domestic political environment, national uncertainty, a leadership vacuum, and bureaucratic confusion. Generalizations along these lines are dangerous but worth exploring. If covert action is to have any reasonable chance of succeeding, it must bear a coherent relationship to the main thrust of US foreign policy. Once it transcends the latter's premises or begins to probe the limits of commitment its outlook is dubious. Our experience in Eastern Europe and the Soviet Union bears this out.

We have noted above that the years 1948-1951 were fruitful in covert action terms; initial objectives were achieved and operations in Western Europe expanded eastward against the less accessible Soviet and Bloc targets. And yet, while exploiting every trick in the book in the permissive environment of the fifties, we accomplished comparatively little. The explanation seems clear enough today. The Western democracies were allies and their security was traditionally a measure of our own. Covert action was one of many elements of the national policy apparatus geared to support that premise. In contrast, did anybody know how far we were willing to go in Eastern Europe, or to what lengths we were prepared to push the USSR? If, inconceivably, it had been US policy to use all available means short of war to force the Soviets out of Poland, Hungary and Czechoslovakia, our use of covert action during the fifties might have been radically different. Instead, and as became strikingly evident in the

Hungarian uprising of 1956, US policy was vague and inchoate and contained more than a hint of wishful thinking. Covert action was intensive but inevitably spasmodic and led nowhere.

The Bay of Pigs episode represents one of the darker periods of both CIA and covert action history. Once described pithily but simplistically as an immaculate failure, it is better viewed as a messy tragedy that should never have been allowed to happen. In the endless post-audits brought to bear upon it, the event emerges successively as a failure of intelligence, a failure of will, a disaster of military planning, or a shambles of execution. There is an element of truth in all of these interpretations.

Was in an intelligence failure? Undoubtedly, and in the grandest sense of the term. It is feckless to argue about guerrilla uprisings or the legion's survival capabilities. They were ancillary considerations at best. The real question devolved on the idea that Castro was so shallowly rooted in Cuba that he could be shaken by psychological pressures, as Arbenz had been in Guatemala, and then ousted by a comparative handful of troops. It is easy to visualize the sequence. The concept once conceived, probably at a senior level, is tested on underlings whose instincts and training guarantee an immediate can-do response. Momentum develops rapidly. Conceptualizing is superseded by planning. Policy emerges in high secrecy and, before anyone realizes it, the project is a living, pulsating, snorting entity with a dynamic of its own. Scrutiny by a disinterested body is all but out of the question under such conditions. The people at the top get the answers they want.

Once astride the tiger, options narrow and will becomes a factor in survival. The Bay of Pigs invasion, whether we like it or not in the comfort of hindsight, was based on a plan. Certain things were supposed to happen in a given sequence, which was presumably understood by those in the chain of command. When the plan was interrupted at a critical point (as in the last-minute decision to reduce by half the size of the initial bombing strike against Cuban air targets) by the President on the advice of non-military advisors, we are constrained to question at least his judgment if not his will. And, given the totality of the ultimate disaster, one can only wonder if US naval air strikes could have made the situation any worse.

A simpler and less emotionally-charged case that can still teach us a few lessons is the Indonesian uprising of 1957-1958. The operational specifics are immaterial. In essence, it was an intelligence failure of massive proportions, a total misreading of the Indonesian scene and of the meaning of Indonesian political development since independence. How did it happen? Washington, that is a handful of key figures in State and CIA, made its own appraisal of events without consulting anyone who knew Indonesia. Rarely has compartmentation been so rigidly enforced. Command and control remained in Washington. The Mission in Jakarta, including its CIA components, was excluded from all but the most peripheral involvement.

We have noted that even successful covert action may contain the seeds of its own eventual destruction. This is not an argument for *no* covert action. It raises questions, however, that require consideration before undertaking any major operation. If we involve ourselves in the survival of a chief of state, as we did in Iran in 1953 and in other examples in the 1960's, we may find it difficult or impossible to disengage gracefully. Often we hesitate to look a client state, even a willing one, in the face. Indecision or failure to follow through is likely to undermine whatever initial success may have been achieved. The question is not solely one of opportunity but perhaps even more of responsibility. In either event the tiger analogy continues to hold.

Guatemala in 1954 was operationally successful, an example of what might be called brash technical virtuosity. But was the game worth the candle? We played into the endemic pattern of Latin American history, military ouster of objectionable civilian governments. Our success was short-lived. It is difficult not to wonder if the planners had read the history of the region before plunging in.

Even continuity when we achieve it may in time plague us. One of the major elements of our covert political action in Europe and elsewhere in the fifties involved international organizations, labor, veterans, women, youth and students, most of them quite successful in their fields. Weaknesses existed, however, and ramified steadily over the years, primarily in funding procedures which became labyrinthine and cumbersome, and increasingly insecure owing to their reliance on foundations. The *Ramparts* exposures of 1967 marked the end of an era and pointed up our failure to realize that times had changed; what had been acceptable in the fifties became anathema in the late sixties—specifically, the operational use of sensitive categories of people and the nation's private voluntary organizations.

Laos, cited above as an example of successful management, was also remarkable for its tactical and operational success against a backdrop of strategic failure. Much more important as a lesson for the future, and one that far transcends the issue of whether or not CIA should undertake large-scale paramilitary operations, was our failure to realize that we were pushing people beyond their limits: the irresponsibility of the strong partner toward the weaker one, particularly when the linkage between their interests and ours had begun to grow tenuous.

If a government convinced of the worthiness of its causes can both overplay and fail to exploit its successes, one divided against itself cannot engage in rational covert action at all. Chile, 1970-1973, stands as an object lesson in how not to do things. However arguable the case for covert action might have been at the time, the combination of a demanding White House, a strongly opposed State Department and a CIA that saw fit not to question orders, seems in retrospect to have been an assured loser.

On balance then, failure in covert action may have its roots in the same matrix of energy and effort that promotes success. It occurs when responsible people fail to look far enough ahead and assess the likely consequences of their decisions, or when they vacillate in accepting the sequential relationship with the entities they may have created. If there is a prime factor in the pattern which is certain to bring on trouble, it is excessive compartmentation among decision-makers, planners and operatives, particularly in the early stages of development. Bad intelligence guarantees bad covert action, which often leads to disaster.

Covert Action and American Society

If activism has generally characterized the American attitude toward covert foreign operations, we have not been immune to nagging doubts about the legality and propriety of such behavior. We see the old dichotomy between idealism and realism, words and deeds, ends and means. The task of reconciliation is often painful. Our adversaries, in contrast, suffer no such discomfort.

And we do have adversaries, great and small. Some of them we can afford to ignore. Others loom large and their sustained hostility has put American society and American institutions to one test after another. The record of recent years suggests that we have fared rather badly in those tests. It is hard to say whether this is attributable to something inherent in ourselves and our institutions, or whether we can blame it at least a little bit on the *stars*. In either event, we have many strengths to counterbalance it and there are no grounds for pessimism.

Weaknesses

We have of course made mistakes, some of them egregious, and given our unique position in the world, that is not supposed to happen. Even our close friends at times find it difficult to reconcile our performance with our presumed capability. There are indeed enormous demands on our attention, power and resources in the world today. Crises and threats to one thing or another that we hold important arise relentlessly in all corners of the globe. For every political task we take on, others await, often clamoring for priority. If at one time, rightly or wrongly, we fancied ourselves the world's policeman, we seemed then to have available a great deal more in the way of resources and possibly skills to apply than we do today. Conversely, as we balk at the demands levied upon us, the Soviet Union is evidently now ready and willing to fill the vacuum by committing skills and resources at unprecedented levels.

It is no exaggeration to say that the Soviets have used every trick in the book to make life unpleasant for the US in recent years. They have shown a willingness to go for the jugular that has never distinguished American covert action, even during its so-called golden age. We came close once, when we flew the U-2 over the USSR for four years in the most successful clandestine operation ever conducted. Our ensuing embarrassment when Powers was shot down suggests the beginning of a loss of direction or weakening of purpose that has climaxed in recent years. The Soviets find it easy to play tough and preach detenté. We find it awkward.

Our traditional reluctance to take on the Soviets except indirectly is embarrassing in another sense. The situation was dramatized some time ago by Senator Moynihan: the Soviets are permitted to operate within the US on a huge scale and in a manner which not only enables them to collect vast amounts of intelligence but also entails flagrant violation of the privacy of individual Americans. We could take on the Soviets by throwing them out or by reducing their missions to levels comparable with our own in the USSR. Yet most interested agencies, State, CIA, the FBI and ICA, would doubtless oppose such action for certain valid reasons and for others that are essentially parochial. One wonders if such diffidence will be duplicated as our new and presently cordial relationship with China matures.

It would be absurd to pretend that we are in as good a position today to undertake covert action as we were, say, in 1960. More Americans now question the wisdom and propriety of interfering in the domestic affairs of foreign nations. Our power has declined on the comparative scale and we have experienced unwonted setbacks and frustrations. If the resulting climate of exposure and reprehension emboldens our enemies, it also discourages potential collaborators. It may be a sad joke to say that the bookmakers' odds are bad on the survival of our close friends abroad; it is also a fact of life.

The cleavages that mark American society have their counterparts within the government bureaucracy, one reflection of which is our pervasive inability to keep secrets. If there is coherent policy direction, it needs better public relations than it is getting these days. There may well be some good covert action in train at present but it is likely to be in *ad hoc* response to exasperated pleas from the White House. One would like to think that the approach were more deliberate, careful and constructive, with an eye toward the long term.

A notable step in the latter direction would be the integration of the State Department in the development of covert initiatives. There are times when quiet diplomacy is not enough. State's policy planning elements, if they were once to accept the notion that covert action is part of the foreign affairs machinery, could participate actively in looking ahead, analyzing and planning, and preparing for eventualities that might call for covert responses. Unfortunately, there are few indications that the State Department is in the least bit disposed to depart from its traditional role of passive critic with veto power. Alternatively, one wonders if CIA is really equipped and manned to do the job effectively.

The dismantling of CIA's covert action capability, pursued so zestfully post-1975, has doubtless left a vacuum. Today, though we can assume that most of the Agency's overseas resources, given the pressures of the times and the assurances conveyed to congressional overseers, were largely terminated, we would like to think that those pressures have relented somewhat and the process of rebuilding is under way. But there remain some disturbing questions.

In key areas overseas, how long will it take to rebuild the mechanisms and to reestablish the channels, both individual and institutional, through which influence can be exerted? And even if a covert action infrastructure is reconstituted, will it be used actively or allowed to atrophy owing to a continuing reluctance to risk using it?

Is CIA itself really organized and does it have the people to mount aggressive operations in the days ahead? The reductions in force undergone by operating components of the Agency in recent years have presumably brought its personnel strength into line with current requirements, most of these in the intelligence collection realm. Can we therefore expect CIA to expand its effort in the face of new action requirements without a corresponding increase in personnel? Another question is expertise. We have to assume that attrition has been heavy among cadres who have had covert action experience.

Maybe there are a few left to carry the torch but there cannot be many. It would also be surprising if many young officers beginning their careers saw much to attract them in a discipline that has occasioned very little acclaim in recent years. The comers among them are likely to avoid covert action like the plague. Assignments will tend to go, as they have so often in the past, to women officers whom the Agency's ingrained male-chauvinist mentality has traditionally relegated to the back-eddies of career development. Training, always weak on covert action, will continue to give the subject short shrift if only because there is nobody in the instructional mechanism who knows anything about it.

There are two final points, both sensitive, which deserve attention. They affect the total operational capability of CIA, with particular bearing on covert action if we are to contemplate a widening of horizons in the future.

Cover is obviously a central problem; it pervades approaches to all clandestine operations. It is pointless merely to proclaim that if we are to have more and better covert action we must have more and better cover. Cover for CIA field personnel today is a disgrace to the profession. If the worst one could say were that it is better now than it was thirty years ago, that would be nice. In fact, it is not. Moreover, it will get no better until somebody comes to grips with the agonizing relationship between CIA and the State Department. This is the real clandestine war that everybody wishes would go away. But it never does. It plagues the daily lives of personnel in both organizations in utter defiance of the cut-and-paste efforts at amelioration heralded regularly by their seniors as the ultimate in cover solutions.

An isolation mentality seems to go hand-in-glove with clandestine activity. CIA operatives over the years have perforce been shielded from various forms of reality, the better to concentrate on their targets. Many of the younger officers, the more so when they are not under State cover, miss the opportunity to learn from the give-and-take of interagency negotiation and competition. Education, certainly education during the course of an Agency career, is deemed neither essential nor particularly important. Perish the thought that all career officers (DDO, not the rest of the Agency, which generally has a better track record on this than the Clandestine Service) should be assigned for a year to Harvard or Yale or Berkeley; the service colleges are available at much lower cost and never effectively utilized. For that matter, even in-house training, once the basic stuff is out of the way, becomes a perfunctory thing; certain courses have

to be gotten on the record. Language training fares a little better but
it is nothing to brag about. It should hardly surprise us if insularity
develops and the world outside takes on a slightly alien look. Then,
when the roof falls in, as it did during the *Ramparts* exposures of 1967
and the upheaval of 1975, there is widespread shock and amazement
that "this can be happening to us." It would be uncharitable, though
fascinating, to study the reading habits of Clandestine Service officers as they rise in the ranks against the backdrop of a changing
world.

Strengths

And, in truth, the picture is by no means all that bad. There are
real strengths to be drawn upon, not only from within ourselves but
equally from the world around us.

The outrageous behavior of the Soviet Union in Afghanistan and
elsewhere will eventually play into our hands. If we are keeping
effective book on the panoply of intrusion, coercion and manipulation
which the Soviets project far beyond their borders, this should add
up to a long list of untapped opportunities for covert exploitation.
Why, if there is utility in publicizing analyses of Soviet military
spending, can we not exploit just as effectively the realities of Soviet
clandestine activities in countries that mean something to us? Their
cynical use of Cuban and East German surrogates in Africa and the
Arab world has received minimal treatment in the world press. We
ought to be able to tell a better story. Perhaps the names of Cuban
mercenaries killed to date in Africa and the circumstances of their
deaths would edify both Soviets and Cubans.

A large reservoir of good will toward the United States exists in
many parts of the world. True, we have done much in the past ten
years to shatter the confidence of those who were once ready to
cooperate with us. The alternatives available to them, however, are
not always attractive. As it becomes evident that we are regaining
our composure, some of our once-and-future friends will very probably come knocking at our doors. Others will welcome our approaches.

No one doubts that we Americans are naturally ingenious, that our
institutions are resilient and tough. And although it would be fatuous
to say that we will emerge from our recent trauma of self-doubt in
better shape than ever, we have nevertheless learned something from
our mistakes and the signs are encouraging, the existence of this
colloquium being one of them. Another is the contention echoed in
official circles and reverberating on the outside that the intelligence

we are obtaining today is better than it has ever been. If some of us have heard that before, we are still predisposed to accept it; we hope it is true. The prerequisite for an effective covert action program is, if repetition will be excused, a functioning, first-class intelligence collection mechanism. Without the one, there cannot be the other. If in addition we can be assured that CIA has conserved the nucleus of its once excellent paramilitary capability, we can point to one more basic resource available for deployment if needed. The climate of public opinion is changing for the better and, slowly but surely, a more realistic framework for congressional oversight is being constructed.

Some Thoughts on Reshaping American Covert Action

The need today is less to reshape than to regenerate covert action as a vehicle for the pursuit of US overseas interests. Our strengths being many, we can turn them into assets whenever we decide to make the effort. Most of our weaknesses are correctible and they need not inhibit us. Toward those ends, we suggest a few basic lines of advance.

Let us think big and purposefully about our goals and, also, about the suitability of the methods to be used in going after them. While we preserve our own self-image as an advocate of peace and decency in the world at large, we must also recognize that in the minds of our adversaries we are the main enemy, and are thus depicted relentlessly in their propaganda—both internal and external. The fact is, they believe it. We must therefore approach détente with enough flexibility and toughness to insure that we are not hoodwinked or powered into dangerous corners. We should respond to challenges when they are important and we should do so if possible on our own terms. For example, instead of restricting ourselves covert-actionwise to little more than unattributed short-wave broadcasting, we could develop an aggressive program across the board designed to pressure and even manipulate events within the USSR by targeting against Soviet weaknesses and vulnerabilities. As far as China is concerned, inasmuch as we cannot possibly assure ourselves that the latter's aims in life are identical with ours, it only makes sense that we supplement our diplomatic maneuvers with a viable covert capability. It might help to remember the way the Chinese operate in this sphere. For more than two decades the ''voices of liberation'' have emanated by radio from the vicinity of Kunming, addressed to communist guerrilla forces in the jungles of Thailand, Burma and Malaysia, whose governments enjoy friendly relations with Peking. Periodic demarches by the former invariably evoke assurances that the broadcasts have nothing to do with the Chinese government, that they merely reflect the concerns of the Chinese Communist Party for the well-being of fraternal parties in Southeast Asia.

Let us coordinate our thinking about whatever it is that we propose to do in the covert realm. If the American Government is not and never will be a monolith of mind and purpose, it is still a bit shocking that we do not better concert our bureaucratic energies when we target them overseas. Agencies can be made to work together. The collegial approach does not meet our needs; somebody has to give and take orders. The private sector with interests of its own to pursue abroad is generally willing and able to collaborate with government. We should encourage this. One way would be to insure the secrecy of the relationship against unwarranted disclosure. Prospective foreign collaborators would also find this helpful.

Let us try to think ahead. It is true, as a scholar once observed, that in the long term we are all dead. But the program is phased and we are more likely to be remembered if at least a few of our works live after us. Nothing is more difficult for an Agency geared, perhaps inevitably, to a system of annual program/budget justification than to mount and sustain a long-range operation. CIA has a poor track record in this respect, though, compared to most other government entities working overseas, it has been a model of continuity.

It takes time and effort to establish and develop an association with a young foreign contact who is likely to become a person of consequence in his own country. The easier course, one that has become all too common of late, is to assess his potential as a likely source of current intelligence and, if he shows none, drop him and move on. If he turns out to be a useful source, maybe he will also prove to be a good political asset. This is the wrong way to go about it. Agents of influence do not just happen. The good ones are usually the product of development, that is assistance and guidance over months or years. And it is possible to reconcile this approach with the need to respond to pressure for quick and tangible results.

Once in a great while we may be lucky enough to stumble into a potential superstar. More often we will have to build leadership from the bottom up. And when we have done that, it is well to remember that no matter how much we think we have helped, we do not own anybody. Collaboration, not subservience, is the only basis upon which to build a clandestine relationship. As leaders mature, they have to go their own way which, if we have prepared the ground properly, can also be our way.

Leaders obviously must have something to lead. There are many ways to strengthen the institutions through which we expect them to exert their influence and this task should not be neglected. In some instances, those bodies manage very well on their own. Often, however, it is impossible for them to get off the ground against competition or in the face of other local conditions, public apathy, and the like. Discreet support through covert channels may be the catalyst needed to achieve forward movement. One of the key problems for the future will be to find new methods of accomplishing this securely and efficiently.

Finally, let us make certain the American people understand the thrust and goals of our foreign policy. The public should also know that we intend to use our clandestine resources whenever they can appropriately further those ends. If a cover activity surfaces, we should be able to explain it in that context and show that it was important. There is also much to be said for *plausible denial* and for the ancient sport of stonewalling. Should we admit mistakes? Yes, and we should learn everything we can from them. But we should think twice before apologizing and, certainly, before letting our President accept the blame for a blunder. Underlings are expendable and they make excellent foils for preservation of national dignity.

Discussants

Dr. Samuel P. Huntington: I think Mr. Tovar makes a very good case for the proposition that the two necessary prerequisites for effective covert action are, first of all, clear policy direction from above and then good intelligence from below. I would certainly agree with that.

It also seems to me, however, that one has to look at the question of the strength and weaknesses of US covert action in a somewhat broader context. The strength of US covert action clearly has been its relative effectiveness. By and large, the record is very good. One only has to think of what the world would be like if we hadn't engaged in covert action in Western Europe, or the Middle East, or in the Philippines or Central America and the Caribbean. Obviously, it would be a very different—and a much worse world.

There is, however, a basic almost fatal weakness in covert action. This weakness is not ineffectiveness, but the fact that it is perceived to be illegitimate in terms of many prevailing American norms and values. In this respect, even its successes become testimony and evidence of its illegitimacy.

Mr. Tovar has said that he thinks the shift from the good days to the bad days with respect to covert action was linked to the decline in American power. I would register a slight dissent, if by that he means a decline in our ability to act in the world. Rather, it seems to me, that the bad days are linked to the domestic upheaval in the United States in the 1960's and early 1970's. But this, in many respects, was an upheaval which involved a concern with and reassertion of many values, traditional attitudes, outlooks and behavior going back deep into our country's history. It seems to me that what happened in our domestic politics is in many respects a major contributory factor to the relative decline of our national power. We have now moved beyond that particular phase in our history, but I don't think we can entirely escape its effects. Consequently, I think one has to ask: How we can restore some degree of legitimacy to covert action in our society?

Fortunately, part of the legitimacy for covert action derives from the nature of the Soviet threat and the perceptions which people have of that threat. As you are well aware, there is now a new and healthy appreciation among many groups in our society that there is, indeed, some danger out there. However, it also seems necessary to try to build some sort of a bridge between the concept of covert action and American liberal values and ideals which in many respects have forced people to conclude there is something wrong and illegitimate with covert action.

I don't think we can or should try to remake American political culture which has developed over the course of about three centuries. I think we have to recognize that many elements of this culture are very, very deeply rooted in the way in which this country was created in the 17th and 18th Centuries and that the consensus which developed on these liberal values and ideals really antedated the development of a national government. In this sense, we have a very different situation from the countries of Western Europe where you had a tradition of an absolute state and a bureaucratic mechanism in place before the development of the ideology of the late 18th and 19th Centuries.

Covert action will be increasingly important in the 1980's, both because there will be opportunities to be exploited and because dangers will have to be dealt with. Consequently, it will not be what it ought to be unless we are able to create some harmony between the way in which we must act in our foreign relations and the ways in which the American public generally, and elite groups, think about this set of problems.

Therefore, one has to answer the question: Why is covert action deemed illegitimate? I would like to suggest four dimensions of that problem. First of all, covert action is viewed as illegitimate because it violates the norm of the non-intervention in the politics of other societies. This is a norm which is not observed by any government; it is one which, in a world of interdependence, is becoming increasingly obsolete. Intervention is, after all, only the other side of the coin of interdependence. And we all recognize how interdependent the world is at the present time. Consequently, it is highly desirable to attack this dimension of the problem head on and make the argument that intervention and efforts to influence the political processes in other societies is a legitimate thing for a government to do. In previous times in our history, we have viewed political parties, lobbying, labor unions, as being illegitimate forms of political activity. Over the years, we have changed our view. Conceivably, we can change our view with respect to efforts to influence political processes in other societies. And in this sense, I think it would be very useful to think of covert action, not as one aspect of intelligence, but one way of exercising influence together with other ways which are very overt; the International Communications Agency, Voice of America are just a couple of examples.

It seems to me there is a spectrum here, and covert action is simply one way of attempting to produce results in the political processes of other societies. When one puts it in that context, one gets a slightly different picture and one which, it seems to me, makes it somewhat more legitimate in the overall spectrum of American values. Indeed, if one thought of covert action as one set of many among many, one also would be forced to consider trade-offs between one type of means and another for the purpose of developing friendly attitudes to the leadership of another society, or for affecting a governmental decision in another society.

My second point is that covert action avoids the penalty we pay for openness in our society. Our politicians are far more open than those in other countries in the world. This belief in the desirability of openness and shedding light and sunshine throughout all the activities of government tends to mean that the great strength of covert action which is obviously necessary in many cases, that is, its secrecy, is also its greatest vulnerability. And if it is exposed, it becomes rather more difficult to justify its use later on. Americans have always historically had a great penchant for conspiracy. The thought that the American Government is engaged in covert action simply feeds that penchant. But obviously, in some respects and in many areas, covert action is necessary. But the fact is we are going to have great difficulty in keeping it covert.

Point three is the choice of means to achieve our goals. It is, as all the uproar of the seventies indicated, that it is self-destructive to attempt to use means which violate US norms. Mr. Tovar referred to the Chilean experience, which has always mystified me. Insofar as I know from the public record, we intervened so massively in the 1964 election, and then in 1970, after Allende was elected, made a major effort to prevent him from taking office. But we didn't try to influence the 1970 election, except in a very minor way. It seems to me that this was a great failing. And we can do much better at influencing elections, than at trying to organize coups d'état.

Fourth and last, covert action will only work as Mr. Tovar has pointed out where there is a coherent policy, and will only be perceived as legitimate where there is a coherent policy. And in this sense, the policy has to both reflect the security interests of the United States and our ethical and moral values. One can easily cite cases where one or both of these are lacking in our foreign policy in which case, we should stay away from covert action.

Mr. Philippe Thyraud de Vosjoli: It is very difficult to judge, at least for those of us in this group, the strength and weakness of US covert action because we know primarily only of covert action failures. The covert actions mentioned in Mr. Tovar's paper were all unsuccessful as such because they are all known. When covert actions are uncovered, they generally crash very badly. For instance, the coup against Mossadegh was a failure even though Mossadegh was overthrown because it became known, and this knowledge, we know, caused grave long-term difficulties. I believe that a covert action has to really stay concealed, whether or not it is successful in reaching its goal.

In foreign countries, many people really are doubtful as to the ability of the United States' intelligence to undertake covert action. I must say, for instance, Mr. Tovar speaks about success in Western Europe in the early fifties. I don't know if he means France, but at that time, I was in Paris and I would receive almost daily reports on supposedly covert activity. At that time, we all wanted the same thing. We all knew about it. And we all knew where it was coming from. It quickly became very embarrassing for all our American friends, so embarrassing that I remember my boss many times had to call the CIA chief of station and remonstrate with him, asking him to be more discreet. So we were in a situation where we had to cover American covert action.

I disagree with Mr. Tovar's wanting the CIA to control covert action. I believe it is very dangerous. Covert action is a client of positive intelligence. It constantly needs intelligence. But, if the collectors of intelligence also work in covert action, they are putting their intelligence networks in jeopardy. Covert action is highly visible, and easy to trace. This has been one of the reasons why in Western Europe you have had some anti American feeling. For instance, deGaulle's anti-Americanism was partly based in the fact that he knew of American covert action in France.

Mr. Tovar also mentioned the fact that now it is difficult to get cover from the State Department. I really do not believe that anyone carrying out covert action should be a government official in any way. Such persons should not have any official cover. They should not have State Department cover. I think political action should be handled by people who should not be American, but who have been trained in this country. What is important in covert action is to shield the government and to shield the country. And when this is not done, it is generally conduct that brings some kind of catastrophe.

Now, I would also like to say that I know, and many of us know, of American covert action which has been very successful. They have been so successful that nobody has spoken about them. And I believe it is possible to have many more of them in the future.

General Discussion

Mr. Tovar prefaced the discussion by making two points: First, no harm would come from taking responsibility for covert action out of CIA, especially if CIA were made into an overt organization which concentrated on analysis. It is crucial, however, to keep the responsibility for covert action within the same organization responsible for clandestine collection, wherever that might be located. That is, because the two functions involve the same kinds of tradecraft and often the very same foreign assets. Second, Mr. Tovar did not disagree in principle with suggestions that the scope of covert action be carefully limited. But he warned that because individual commitments to covert action are necessarily commitments to people, they must be carried through successfully. If they are not, then covert action will be counterproductive, resulting not just in failures but in turning friends into bitter enemies.

The discussion then focused on the factors which contributed to the success and failure of American covert action. One participant chided the CIA for having worked through the National Student Association and similar unrepresentative American "Leftist" groups. A former US intelligence official replied that CIA sometimes supported conservative forces in the world (e.g. Guatemala in 1954) but that it usually supported the non-communist Left because, he said, the CIA fought where the fight was and in those days the fight was on the Left.

An academic said that although it is clear to students of the subject that covert action is one tool of foreign policy among many, most of today's foreign service officers don't seem to know it. The successes of American covert action in the 1950's and 1960's were due largely to the excellent coordination which then existed between CIA and the State Department's Policy Planning Staff, and the Assistant Secretaries. A former intelligence officer bolstered this point, saying that when covert action was successful, State was the driving force, and even did most of the work. In fact, sometimes State tried to do without sufficient support from CIA. In those cases, the operations failed. For example, in Indonesia, we failed because of inadequate intelligence about the working environment. Another academic elaborated on the point. In both Indonesia and Burma we failed not for want of initiative or coordination but for lack of specific knowledge about who was who, and how much support each of the players had. We dealt primarily with people who spoke English. A former official concluded that the thesis of Professor Bozeman's paper was entirely applicable to those cases.

An intelligence officer asked what might be done to exploit the vulnerabilities which the Soviet Union has created for itself by its actions in Afghanistan and Poland. An academic replied that such a question cannot be answered so long as there is no overall American policy toward the Soviet bloc, and, most important, so long as there is no consensus among the various groups which make up the US foreign policy community on what that policy should be. Another former intelligence officer countered that there is now a broad national consensus on foreign policy, and asked how we might translate that consensus into support for US covert action. The academic replied that, despite the 1980 election, he doubted that there was consensus on foreign policy among American elites. He was not sure that even the Reagan Administration was agreed on a strategy toward the Soviet Union. He suggested that the new President would have his hands full making clear to the intelligence bureaucracy that covert action has a high priority and that money will flow to it. Public statements on the matter should wait until he is ready to articulate a real foreign policy. Another academic urged the audience not to underestimate the attack which certain American elites are soon to make against any serious revival of covert action.

Another former intelligence official, responded to the question regarding the exploitation of Soviet vulnerabilities by saying that it is impossible to develop criteria for the use of covert action in the 1980's because we cannot read the minds of American policymakers who, moreover, are not of one mind on foreign policy. Without a coherent US policy, we cannot develop criteria for counteraction, he said. An academic, however, replied that it is the duty not only of policymakers, but also of the intelligence community to look around the world, to assess conditions and to suggest contingency plans for advancing American interests. The Eisenhower Administration, he said, had some 300 or 400 political contingency plans. He understood that President Carter had designated an official of the NSC to develop an analogous set, but that nothing had ever come of this.

CHAPTER SEVEN

The Necessary Means for US Covert Action in the 1980's

Paper:
Donald Purcell

Discussants:
Senator Malcolm Wallop
Congressman Les Aspin
Congressman C. W. Bill Young

Introduction

The purpose of this paper is to discuss the resources needed by the Central Intelligence Agency in the 1980's to conduct effective covert action in support of United States' foreign policy objectives. The basic assumption in this discussion is that by 1978, the CIA's capabilities to conduct covert action had eroded to the point that it was virtually incapable of responding effectively to the covert action missions and tasks assigned to it by the National Security Council and the President. The reasons for this were both evolutionary and contemporary, and have been extensively discussed in the course of the Senate and House investigations of CIA's past covert action operations, the published reports that have emerged from these investigations, as well as in published works by former CIA employees and others outside of government concerned with the problems of past and future United States' covert action. In the view of this writer, the process of rebuilding and revitalizing covert action in the CIA will be a long-term affair. It will involve, at a minimum:

• The formulation of clear and resolute policies on foreign regional and country problems perceived to be an immediate and long-term threat to United States national security interests.

• The selection and recruitment of additional qualified American personnel, foreign agents, and cadre to manage and carry out covert action operations keyed to foreign policy objectives.

• The expansion and improvement of covert action training programs for employees (and agents) of the Directorate of Operations (DDO), and employees of other CIA directorates concerned with the support of covert action operations.

• An increase in intelligence resources in areas of anticipated covert action, and an improvement in the organizational interface among the intelligence collectors, analysts and covert action planners.

• A substantial increase in the funding levels for covert action staff personnel, foreign agents and organizational resources.

217

Background

Any discussion of the future of US covert action, and in particular the allocation of resources to this mission, must of necessity take into consideration past CIA covert action history, doctrine and methodology. Much has been written or otherwise disclosed on the nature and extent of CIA's past covert action operations in the paramilitary, political and propaganda fields. There is, therefore, no need to dwell at length on these operations *per se,* except as a general backdrop for a discussion of the erosion problem and future resource requirements.

Briefly, in the fields of covert political influence and non-attributable propaganda operations, the CIA from the early 1950's through the mid-1960's relied principally on "fronts" and other mass organizations. These operations were managed and directed by the DDO (formerly the Deputy Directorate of Plans—DDP) Covert Action Staff (CAS). They involved the establishment by CIA of a broad range of action instrumentalities or "fronts" (e.g., Radio Free Europe) and/or subsidies to existing organizations (e.g., The Asia Foundation) in the United States and abroad concerned with labor, youth and students, book publishing, radio and printed media.

A changing national mood on covert action in the 1960's manifested by aggressive and critical investigative reporting by the media on the CIA's covert action role, particuarly its involvement with American organizations and institutions, led to the termination of these relationships following the Katzenbach report in 1967. Despite this development, the CIA retained at that point an adequate staff of covert action specialists and substantial foreign agent and institutional resources. However, the handwriting was already on the wall, and the downward spiral in CIA's covert action resources had begun and would proceed at an accelerated pace.

It soon became apparent that most of the CAS residual foreign organizational assets would not survive exposure because of their long use, relatively high visibility, and the consequent threat of exposure by continuing investigative reporting by the media, publication of books and articles by disgruntled former employees of CIA and congressional investigations of CIA. For all practical purposes, the twenty-year epoch of CIA's use of organizational or institutional "fronts" as a principal means of conducting covert actions ended. The number of personnel assigned to the CAS was significantly reduced and the covert action budget reached its lowest point in the Agency's history. Without any significant foreign institutional resources, CIA was forced to rely mainly on residual agent resources to conduct its political action and propaganda operations. It was this situation which led to the use of the term covert action "infrastructure," which took on a sinister meaning during the course of congressional investigations of CIA's covert action operations. In fact, the "infrastructure" was nothing more than a catalogue of the total field resouces of CIA that could, on a selective basis, be used for covert action tasks.

The criticism of CIA, and covert action in particular, intensified in the post Vietnam and Watergate periods, and during the ensuing congressional investigations of CIA. This atmosphere, and in particular the enactment of the Hughes-Ryan Amendment contributed significantly to the continuing erosion of CIA's covert action capabilities and resources. There was also a diminution of covert action initiatives. Previously cooperative foreign liaisons and foreign agents were reluctant to take on covert action assignments. Area divisions and field stations became increasingly unwilling to accept covert action tasking because of fear of legal complications of the Hughes-Ryan Amendment, fear of compromise and consequent public exposure, lack of any significant capability, and reluctant or hostile Ambassadors. During this period the CIA was also under increasing pressure to reduce its staff personnel and its budgetary requirements. The combination of these factors resulted in a significant further reduction of CIA's covert action resources. Under pressure to reduce spending, many covert action projects were terminated, and many experienced covert action specialists either left the Agency or were reassigned to other tasks. By 1978, CIA's capabilities to respond to covert action tasking were minimal.

Finally, it should be noted that the intent of relating the foregoing chronology of events is not to point the finger of blame at any administration or member of CIA. These developments took place under four Presidents, four Directors of CIA and five DDOs. What happened to CIA's covert action capabilities during this period was a sign of the times, a manifestation of national discontent with certain United States foreign policies, and a changing national mood concerning the role the United States should play in international affairs. Viewed from within CIA, the paramount problem was survival of the Agency in face of a virtual firestorm of criticism rather than the viability of one particular mission. While no clear consensus emerged from this national debate, one fundamental fact is clear: the CIA remains charged by legislation and Executive Order with the responsiblity for United States covert action. It should also be abundantly clear to any informed and responsible observer of foreign affairs that the United States will, in the 1980's and beyond, continue to be faced with formidable challenges to its national security interests in unstable areas of the world, and from its foreign adversaries, particularly the Soviet Union. Events in Iran and Afghanistan since 1978 are typical of the types of foreign developments that have confronted the United States in the past, and in which covert action was successfully undertaken. One would hope and assume that the impact of these developments has not been lost on the Congress, the NSC and CIA managers, that the erosion of CIA covert action resources has been stopped, and that action to rebuild and revitalize the DDO covert action capabilities is under way in earnest.

Obtaining the Necessary Means

In the final analysis, a national determination to respond aggressively to foreign challenges to United States national security interests, manifested by clear and resolute foreign policies, will determine the future of covert action. However, in the short term a number of steps can be taken now by the Director of Central Intelligence (DCI) that will insure that the CIA is adequately staffed and equipped to perform its future covert action missions. These include:

• *Establish the CAS as an independent staff element of the DDO.* If the CIA is to effectively revitalize its covert action mission, the Covert Action Staff (CAS) must be bureaucratically positioned to have a strong voice in the management of covert action. The CAS should concern itself exclusively with the DDO's covert action operations, and should not be merged with other incompatible or unrelated staff functions for administrative convenience. At a minimum, the CAS should have an equal voice with the area divisions of the DDO in allocating budgetary and personnel resources to covert action.

• *Put the area divisions of the DDO back into covert action planning.* Covert action operations in the field cannot be managed and directed by a staff element not in the line of command. Those former employees of CIA and others familiar with the turbulent history of CIA covert action operations will recall the internecine warfare between the Office of Policy Coordination (OPC), charged independently with carrying out covert action in the 1950's, and the Office of Special Operations (OSO), then responsible at that time for intelligence operations. Even after the OPC and OSO were merged into a single clandestine service under the DDP (now DDO), residual friction between the CAS and the area divisions continued to be a problem. The fact is that the DDO area division chiefs are, next to the DDO himself, the most powerful officers in the directorate. In a bureaucratic struggle between a staff chief and a division chief, the latter will inevitably win. If the CIA is to commence the process of rebuilding its field covert action resources, the area divisions and field stations must accept a large measure of the responsibility for doing this. Area division parochialism should not be allowed to dictate the development of global covert action capabilities. Lacking a concept of global propaganda and confronted with a choice between keeping or terminating a covert action asset for which there may not be an immediate and priority need, area division and station chiefs, under budgetary or other pressures, will usually opt for termination. At a minimum, covert action staff positions in all of the area divisions should be established; and each field station in its mission directive should receive specific and detailed instructions on covert action tasking including the development of political influence and propaganda resources, when such action is indicated by current needs or anticipated in forward planning.

• *Re-examine and revise the DDO's staff personnel and career planning procedures along the following lines:*

(a) Establish a fixed quota for new employees having the necessary professional skills and qualifications and, in particular, the motivation for covert action assignments.

(b) Institute a planned and systematic program for assigning additional qualified and experienced on-board personnel to covert action positions at the staff, division and station levels, and to the Agency training establishment. Begin a program for inter-directorate assignments to covert action positions in the DDO of personnel having an interest in, and qualifications for, covert action operations such as DDI analysts, and DDS&T specialists to assist in developing technical deception operations.

(c) Develop reliable criteria for the selection and psychological testing of new personnel to screen for recruitment qualified "activists" for covert action assignments.

(d) Recruit mature personnel with a proven track record in applicable covert action skills. On-the-job training of unqualified or inexperienced on-board personnel for this purpose is time-consuming and often unproductive. An officer with prior practical experience as a working journalist or with other media experience will make a better propagandist. Similarly, personnel with working experience as political party organizers or in trade union management and organizing are obviously better qualified to handle projects in these areas. In-house training is not an adequate substitute for practical experience.

(e) Develop a long-term program to hire, on a career basis, foreign nationals with the necessary skills and experience to act as case officers for covert action projects abroad, particularly in those countries where an American officer cannot operate effectively for political or security reasons.

(f) Undertake a critical review of the DDO training programs and courses in covert action with a view toward updating and expanding the training establishment covert action curriculum, and providing for external training in specialist skills. Institute a mandatory policy for providing all new personnel assigned to the DDO with comprehensive covert action training, and on a selective basis periodically up-date the covert action training of on-board personnel slated for covert action positions. The number of hours of covert action training at the basic and advanced levels should be substantially increased to include instruction in both operational and managerial skills. Emphasis should be on extensive study, and critique of case studies of past covert action operations (successful and unsuccessful), covert action "war-gaming" of current and anticipated national security problems susceptible to covert action exploitation, and practical classroom experience in writing propaganda materials, preparing associated guidance, and in the preparation of covert action projects, and Special Coordination Committee (SCC) submissions.

• *Establish a formal CIA reserve organization of retired or otherwise inactive former CIA officers with proven abilities and skills, who could be recalled to temporary duty when a rapid expansion of CIA's personnel resources is necessary to help staff intelligence and covert action programs in response to future national security crises.* While CIA may do this now on an *ad hoc* basis, this procedure is not an adequate substitute for a formal organization consisting of a pool of officers who have declared themselves willing to serve the Agency and who, as part of an organized reserve, can be kept motivated through periodic briefings and training to sustain their interest and update their knowledge and skills.

• *Allocate sufficient financial resources to commence the process of rebuilding and revitalizing the DDO covert action mission.* Many of the suggestions made here can be implemented at no additional financial costs by organizational changes and a more balanced allocation of personnel and funds to covert action. The proposals for additional new personnel and programs can be started with an initial investment of several million dollars with a modest and gradual increase in funding keyed to future covert action planning and tasking.

• *Improve the interface between the CIA covert action planners, the intelligence collectors, the analysts and policy planners.* Contrary to the "rogue elephant" theory that past CIA covert actions were conceived in a vacuum and carried out without proper policy approval and oversight, covert action was in the past, and is now, an integral part of the overall intelligence process. The fact is that intelligence collection drives analysis, analysis drives policy and policy drives covert action. However, interface in the past between the concerned CIA elements has been less than perfect. Covert action planners are largely out of the intelligence collection loop in that they do not participate in the process of formulating intelligence requirements. Any effort, for example, to collect psychological vulnerability data on situations or people is usually rebuffed or given such a low priority that nothing is done, or the information collected may be inadequate for the purpose. Efforts at covert action operational tasking are no more successful. Attempts by the CAS to develop long-term covert action assets in countries having no immediate covert action tasking or priority are largely ignored. The interface between the covert action planners and the DDI analysts serving the policymaking elements of government were, for many years, non-existent or at best unsatisfactory. DDI comments on covert action submissions, with few exceptions, were mainly negative or at best so cautionary they contributed little to the decisionmaking process. Similarly, CAS contributions to national estimates were perfunctory or, if substantive, largely ignored. The reasons for this situation are varied and complex but can be summarized as stemming from narrow professional perceptions and organizational parochialism. The latter problem is not peculiar to the DDI, DDO or even to CIA. It pervades the entire intelligence community. Although this situation has improved in recent years, it should be mandatory that all covert action proposals going to the SCC be sent to the DDI for coordination and comment. Similarly, all national estimates drafted by the DDI should be sent to the CAS (and other concerned elements of DDO) for comment. This arrangement will provide the opportunity for a better interface between the covert action planners and the DDI analysts.

• *Establish within the CAS a forward-planning project review and evaluation element staffed by experienced and qualified covert action specialists, area specialists from the DDO divisions and, on a rotational basis, analysts from the DDI, within the following responsibilities:*

(a) Developing covert action programs responsive to current and anticipated foreign national security objectives and issues.

(b) Preparing the covert action comments on national estimates that impact on ongoing and planned covert action programs.

(c) Formulating requirements for the collection of covert action intelligence and operational information, and the resources necessary to carry out planned covert action programs.

(d) The review and evaluation of ongoing covert action programs and operations of the CAS and the area divisions. The division of these responsibilities between the CAS and the DDO plans staff, to the extent they exist, is not an effective arrangement.

(e) Preparation of the CAS budgetary submissions and the review of area division submissions as they relate to covert action.

(f) The preparation of CAS and review of divisional SCC submissions.

(g) Acting as the focal point for responding to and/or coordinating on all Congressional inquiries and required covert action reporting to the Congressional oversight committees.

• *Prepare a comprehensive and forward-looking analysis of national security problems confronting the United States in the 1980's with clearly-articulated and firm policy objectives for sustained covert actions on current and anticipated problems.* Previous national estimates, and the related NSC issuances providing action guidelines, were the driving force behind most successful CIA covert action programs throughout the 1950's and 1960's. In the future, CIA should not be left to its own perceptions in developing foreign covert action resources. Forward planning for covert action should be based on a global strategic assessment and comprehensive analysis of the major military, political, economic and psychological problems confronting the United States in the foreseeable future. Such an assessment should also include related collection requirements and specific options for covert action responses. A global strategic assessment along these lines, approved by the President and endorsed by the Congress, should provide a firm and realistic basis for rebuilding CIA's covert action resources.

• *Develop means whereby private American organizations and institutions capable of supporting United States political and psychological objectives abroad can be provided with overt financial assistance from the government.* Perhaps no aspect of past CIA covert action, with the exception of its ill-advised involvement in assassination plots, has generated more controversy than its covert use of American organizations and institutions. Nevertheless, non-governmental organizations and institutions did make a significant contribution to past covert action programs. While it seems highly unlikely, short of a major national security crisis or wartime situation, that the CIA will be permitted to use such organizations in the future, it is worth considering alternative arrangements whereby non-governmental entities could be given overt government financing for foreign programs supporting United States foreign policy goals. Such arrangements are not unprecedented in the United States. Some other governments also do this: for example, the Federal Republic of Germany channels funds overtly, through a private foundation, to worthwhile organizations and programs serving its foreign policy interest. To a certain extent the British Council in the United Kingdom also serves this purpose. It is reasonable to assume that a number of American non-governmental organizations and institutions operating abroad, or otherwise capable of favorably influencing foreign attitudes toward and perceptions of the United States, may be willing to accept an overt government subsidy which would free them from concerns with intelligence contamination and possible embarrassment or loss of profit stemming from covert relationships. For example, governmental funds could be made available to American publishers to print foreign language books of propaganda value that would not ordinarily be considered profitable to publish. Financial assistance might also be provided to an organization composed of responsible Cuban Americans to establish a "Radio Free Cuba" to broadcast to the Cuban people and to the peoples of other Latin American countries threatened by Cuban-sponsored subversion.

• *Create a Psychological Strategy Board to advise the President on United States overt and covert political and psychological strategy and objectives, and to act as an independent review authority on planned and on-going covert action operations.* A Psychological Strategy Board composed of prestigious Americans would minimize the possibility for future covert action abuses and excesses, and would be a step toward achieving a degree of national consensus on the purpose, nature and scope of United States covert action. There is also a need for better coordination and orchestration between overt and covert propaganda. For example, it is not unusual for the overt instrumentalities of the government, such as the United States Information Service or the Voice of America to undercut covert propaganda by disseminating information contradicting the covert campaign. The formulation of clear strategic objectives governing both overt and covert informational activities should help minimize this problem and provide for more effective orchestration of the over-all propaganda capabilities of the United States in these fields.

• *Establish a National Intelligence Institute for the purpose of im-*

proving intelligence training and education within the intelligence community. The issue of "parochialism," or the negative effect that narrow professional perceptions have on the collection of intelligence, its interpretation and analysis, and the nature of United States responses to national security developments abroad, has been commented on to some extent in previous publications of the Consortium for the Study of Intelligence. Suffice it to say that parochialism has also plagued CIA covert action efforts in the past, and will continue to do so in the future unless there is a better understanding of these operations in CIA and throughout the intelligence community. The decision to approve or disapprove a covert action operation is based on staff positions taken by biased or ill-informed members of the intelligence community advising their representatives sitting on the SCC and NSC. Since parochialism is a community-wide problem, improved training and education at the national level should help mitigate it. A National Intelligence Institute, under the aegis of the DCI, would be similar in purpose to that of the armed services war colleges, that is it would provide senior officers of the intelligence community with a broad education in the over-all role of United States intelligence, and a functional understanding of the role of individual community agencies and of the methodology of intelligence collection, counterintelligence, analysis, covert action, etc. In addition to minimizing the problem of intelligence community parochialism, a National Intelligence Institute, staffed by senior and competent intelligence officers and other qualified persons from the private sector, could also contribute to the process of achieving a degree of national consensus on the nature and scope of American intelligence activities in the future.

Discussants

Senator Malcolm Wallop: As one who will bear a part of the responsibility for rebuilding America's capability for covert action, I can only wish that all who share that responsibility knew and cared as much for this matter as Mr. Purcell evidentally does.

My point of departure must be Mr. Purcell's observation that the decline in our capabilities for covert action took place under four Presidents, four directors of CIA, and five DDO's. Congress took a hand also, but a much smaller one than is often assumed. At its worst, Congress passed the Hughes-Ryan Amendment, the most significant feature of which was not the requirement for reporting to Congress, but the requirement that the President (and therefore lots of people in the chain of command below him) certify that a given action was essential to national security. Forced to choose between doing without covert action or going on the record favoring it, most officials have chosen to do without. Covert action declined both before and after Hughes-Ryan because lots of people within the Executive Branch, most of them within CIA as Mr. Purcell points out, chose to do without covert action either for bureaucratic reasons, because they believed it unnecessary, or because, moved by scruples, they did not ask diligently enough whether or not it was necessary.

Today I would guess that a poll of the Senate would reflect the American people's just conviction that this country's influence in the world has declined dangerously, and that it must be restored by the most efficacious mixture of overt and covert means. Congress was not primarily responsible for reducing covert action to its current state, and Congress will not object to building it up to the necessary levels. In fact, Congress will almost surely urge that it be done. But, and here's my point, there is sure to be resistance to doing this from career officials in CIA and the State Department—if only because of inertia. In addition, we can be certain that few in the Executive Branch whose responsibility it will be to build and use a real capability for covert action will know much about how to do it, and will probably not be expert in the ways in which covert activity can supplement foreign policy. Much remains to be done to educate lots of people, and to replace others, before we can begin to do the things Mr. Purcell suggests.

Let me clarify two elements of the practical problem. The first concerns the lack of strategic thinking among what we might call the policymaking class in this country. Unless people at the very top undertake serious geopolitical planning and commitment, it is difficult to imagine them insisting on a serious effort to build up a capability to further those plans by covert action. But history does not contain many examples of self-satisfied groups of leaders previously unacquainted with strategic planning and who voluntarily subject themselves to its discipline. Today although there is something of a rebirth of strategic thought in the country, that rebirth has not yet reached the top of our government. When will it do so? I am afraid that serious strategic thinking, along with the will power to live by the results of such thinking, will permeate this country's decision-making structure only when the people at the top personally come to fear the real possibility that this country could lose a major war.

The second concerns the familiar tendency among those who wish American intelligence well, but who do not know it well, to rely on "the experts" in the bureaucracy or those recently retired from it. Of course, much expertise and wisdom is to be found there, indeed Mr. Purcell's insights obviously come from long experience in the CIA. But it's also clear that a substantial, perhaps even preponderant, portion of the higher management at CIA would argue against Mr. Purcell's recommendations in the abstract, and almost surely would oppose his concrete proposals as threats to current bureaucratic arrangements and budgetary priorities.

Clearly, it is no trivial matter to reverse a course of thoughts and actions which has developed under four Presidents, four directors of CIA, and five DDO's. The reasons for revising it immediately and completely are evident in our daily newspapers, and can be expected to become more painfully evident in the coming decade. This, however, is scant cause for satisfaction. Recall the old adage concerning diagnoses and cures: in their early stages diseases are easy to cure but hard to diagnose, while when they become easy to diagnose, diseases are much more difficult to cure.

Congressman Les Aspin: For the last few years, covert actions by the US intelligence community have faced a long drought. With the advent of the Reagan Administration, many anticipate that the drought has ended and the golden age will soon resume. It is, therefore, opportune to consider the ingredients of covert action planning that have made for success and failure in the past.

Some commentators argue that the logical conclusion from any such analysis is that the United States ought not to use covert actions under any circumstances. According to this view, any benefits we may derive from covert actions come at the expense of the good name of the United States and its ability to exercise influence and leadership in the world community.

Others argue that this is a nasty world, that covert action is as old as diplomacy itself, that Russian "dirty tricks" predate the existence of the American Republic itself, and that, therefore, we must play the game by the rules accepted by the old world and free the US intelligence agencies to meet Soviet intrigue with American intrigue.

Both propositions suffer from an excess of zeal and good intentions. Covert actions should not be approached on a simple yes or no basis. The United States has been, is now, and will continue to face decisions about launching covert actions. The key questions have been, are now, and will continue to be how workable is a proposed action and how apt is it for that situation, not should we ban covert action on some moral precept or should we "unleash" the intelligence agencies to act as they see fit.

Therefore, my comments here address operational questions: the points that the new president, any president, ought to be asking as covert action proposals cross his desk.

The President must remember that, like the automobile industry, "The Company" may be selling a product from which the steering wheel is liable to fall off. But unlike automobiles, covert actions, once sold, can rarely be recalled. Before buying into a proposed covert action, therefore, the President ought to go over a short checklist, which might look something like the following.

Is it based on good intelligence? The prerequisite of any good covert action is good intelligence. That should go without saying. Unfortunately, it is a point that has been ignored in the past to our regret. For example, in planning the Bay of Pigs operation in 1961, the intelligence community assumed that the small scale invasion would serve as a catalyst for an uprising of the Cuban people. That turned out to be a bad assumption, and the blame for accepting it must fall not only on the intelligence agencies, but also on President Kennedy. The President must beware of the hubris that periodically infects the clandestine services, the assumption that they are capable of carrying out whatever they put down on paper. Because of the perpetual desire to restrict the number of persons with knowledge of a planned covert action, vital expertise can often be shut out, even when that expertise may lie in the overt side of the CIA itself. If the covert action plans are grounded in broad sweeping assumptions, the President had best check to make sure the steering wheel is afixed tightly. He must ask probing questions and be prepared to reach outside the intelligence community to see if there is good reason for accepting those assumptions. Checking assumptions, incidentally, would not normally require tipping anyone off to the nature of the planned covert action.

Does it harmonize with avowed public policy? Democratic states are ill equipped to handle programs that require double think and double speak. If we embark upon a covert action that runs contrary to our avowed public policy, as in the case of Chile, we increase the risk of error as well as of exposure. Nothing is more likely to whet the whistle of a potential whistle blower than to find an administration preaching one thing publicly and practicing another covertly. And we should be glad of that. I am not suggesting that we should explicitly declare our intention to overthrow a government, but we must avoid the opposite extreme of declaring our support for an institution we are bending all efforts to overthrow. Perhaps we should turn the popular term "plausible deniability" on its head and aim for "plausible admissibility," the idea that if a covert action ever does come to light, it ought not to appear as a glaring contradiction of all that has been said and done in public but as a reasonably consistent extension of it.

Is the proposed covert action simply "social engineering" out of touch with society? This President, especially, should beware of intelligence community proposals to dabble in social engineering. If and when we commit ourselves to the unqualified support of a dictatorial regime, we are commiting ourselves to aiding and abetting that regime in putting a cap on simmering social issues. These problems cannot be kept on the back burner indefinitely; eventually they will boil over, scalding us along with the Somozas of the world. Attempting to restrain social pressures is just as much social engineering as efforts to promote human rights. If we are going to engage in social engineering through covert operations, then we ought to make sure we are going with the grain and not against it.

Was the plan thrown together overnight in response to a sudden crisis? Covert actions launched under emergency conditions face additional hazards. It takes time to get our assets in place. When we scramble our plan is more likely to be poorly thought out, our people are more likely to be poorly trained and the possibility of error will increase. Furthermore, in an emergency situation, facts are not always at hand and the players may be changing daily. The state of play is generally fluid. You cannot lay out careful plans for dealing with a fluid situation. Covert action is a blunt instrument for dealing with emergencies. The most successful covert operations are generally rather small and not particularly sexy when looked at individually. They provide neither dramatic successes nor drastic catastrophies. They make very poor screenplays. The best ones, in fact, involve simply the steady development of contacts, influence and access, making friends by doing small favors. There can be a tremendous payoff from this mundane sort of covert action. As Harry Rositske has suggested, the most effective use of clandestine officers is often to help ambassadors carry out the equivalent of machine politics on an international scale by increasing US influence through a network of loyalties nourished on a succession of favors.

Is the intelligence community trying to run a war? Major paramilitary operations, such as the one we ran in Laos, have been out of the question for the last several years. They ought not to be revived. There is no way a CIA mini-war can be kept secret, no matter how remote the corner of the globe. Let's leave war to the JCS.

Those are a few fundamental questions that any president should ask before checking the approve box on a proposed covert action. As the President poses those questions, I would suggest that he keep in mind the fact that covert action is basically a tactical weapon of specialized character. We have used it most often to combat communist influence at close quarters. It is a weapon of denial. Where it succeeds, it commonly denies not only communist advance but other advance as well. Despite the flaws in conception and execution of the Carter Administration's human rights policies, that program recognized something the Reagan Administration may be prone to forget. America, under both Democratic and Republican presidents, seeks a stable world. But this should not be confused with a static world. It is not enough to use covert action to defeat insurgency and tame leftist "isms" around the world if we ignore the fact that other societies are as prone to change as our own. Sometimes we really ought to be shaking up our own best friends. Postponing social change only breeds violence. If our skills and those of our friends enable them to postpone social change for very long, the eruption can come with a speed and decisiveness that overwhelm not only our friends but ourselves as well. Such was the case with the Shah in Iran and Somoza in Nicaragua. We treated these friends too well and were only too willing to help insulate them from changing reality.

It is not enough for a President to turn to his covert operatives and ask them how they can help us oppose trends that harm US interests. He must also ask how we can use our assets to build and support our vision of a progressive world.

Congressman C. W. Bill Young: My remarks are on the subject of the assets in the trenches. Secret meetings back here in Washington or in whatever their headquarters are important. But without the proper assets in the trenches, we will never get the job done. We have some of the most fantastic technology that the human mind can think of for the collection of intelligence, but I am one of those who believes that given all of that, without the proper human intelligence in the trenches, as Mr. Purcell's paper discusses, the job will not get done. And those assets out there do need our help. They need to know that what they are doing is supported by the people of this country and by our government. For a very long period of time, they haven't felt that. Morale among these people is lower than at head-quarters. I have spent a lot of time visiting with them in the field in many parts of the world, and I have listened to some of their com-plaints and problems. They are no less dedicated today than they were five years ago or ten years ago or twenty years ago, but they feel they lack the support of their government or of their people.

I believe that things are changing for the better in the media, in the Congress, and in the administration. I might say that I am very comfortable with the approach the new administration seems to be taking on intelligence. But, when intelligence people in the field, especially in a hostile environment, expect their name to be exposed in somebody's book or in some newspaper column, they just are not quite as willing to take the risk that they really have to take if they are going to do the job right.

For an asset to be effective in the field, he has to have collaborators, people who play the game with him, whether they are part of another country's intelligence service or private citizens. But I can say with-out hesitation or fear of contradiction that such collaborators are much deterred by our Freedom of Information Act. Without this cooperation, our field intelligence people are simply not getting the voluntary information and material that they need.

Representatives of one of the world's best intelligence operations came to Washington and visited with members and staff of the Congressional Committees on Intelligence, mainly to find out what we intend to do about the Freedom of Information Act. Are we to continue it in such a way that they themselves will fear exposure if they cooperate with us? Just what are we going to do?

I believe that the Freedom of Information Act should be amended to guarantee that not only our own people, but foreigners who help us, are not going to be exposed because of quirks in the American legal system. Of course, the problem of protecting our people is larger than that of the law.

We have to be extremely careful about what happens back here in Washington. I have visited with one man who is in a non-declared hostile assignment. He told me that the competitive adversary ser-vices in that same area knew that he was coming before he did. He felt that somebody in the State Department had let the word out somewhere that he was going to have that new assignment. Because his cover was blown before he was even physically present the country, he was going to have to be reassigned.

The collection of information, whether it is through ELINT or SIGINT or HUMINT, is very important if we are going to have covert activity. We have to have cooperation between those who collect and those who perform covert activities. But we also need a plan. We can't just pick out a problem area and suddenly send a covert action team in there and expect them to be effective. Covert action personnel have to be ones who know their way around, who have their own sources, their own communications, their own contacts, so that they can be effective.

I think Iran is a good example. We needed some strong covert activity in Iran starting on November 5, 1979. Because we didn't, 52 Americans remained hostages for over a year. Why could we not have put in a covert team? First, they would be known, they would be new kids on the block. Everyone would be suspicious. Why are they here? Who are they? They would be watched. We should have had assets in the Khomeni entourage from the beginning. We should have been able to influence some of the decisions that Khomeni made. Recently in other countries we have done such things and done them fairly effectively, but we didn't in Iran.

When the day comes that the world, and specifically the American people, can be told what took place in the rescue of the Americans through the Canadian Embassy, then I think you will realize more directly what I am saying. Covert activity can't be improvised on the spot. You must plan ahead. But if there is no plan, if there are no people in place, if there are no assets where they need to be, we have a serious problem in fulfilling our mission.

One final thought. Fidel Castro is heavily involved in what has been happening in Central America and the Caribbean area—Nicaragua, El Salvador, Guatemala and Honduras. President Carter and I had some very distinct differences on what the situation there is, but as the situation develops, I think it will become more and more obvious that President Carter was in error.

If we had been informed about Castro's plans and intentions, we would have a much better idea about things that are happening in Nicaragua and El Salvador and Guatemala, and Honduras. But we terminated much of our intelligence gathering related to Cuba. We turned off our technology aimed at Cuba. We didn't debrief people who had been to Cuba and returned, or those who had been in Cuba and got out. When 130,000 Cubans hit American shores, they came so fast and so furiously that there was just no opportunity to effectively perform any intelligence collection, to do any screening, or to make sure that some of those people weren't Cuban intelligence personnel working directly for Fidel Castro.

Mr. Purcell stresses the importance of the people in the trenches. The point that I am making in response is that those people have got to have back-up, they must have the support of their government, and they must have the support of the American people. And they have to know that they have it.

I am very optimistic about the future of our nation's security in this hostile world. I am convinced that as a result of the elections of 1980, we are going to rebuild the military and that we will have a foreign policy that has as its prime objective the advantage of the United States. I am satisfied that we are going to have an administration and a Congress that recognizes that intelligence is a very, very important part of this entire equation.

General Discussion

Mr. Purcell prefaced the discussion by arguing that it would be wrong to spend too much money on covert action too quickly. Good covert action, he said, follows good policy, and good policy should result from good intelligence collection and good analysis. He had left CIA because the Carter Administration had continued to ask CIA to perform covert acts while reducing the Agency's ability to perform them, and because the CIA's senior ranks passed on both the cuts and the requirements. Above all, we need good judgment about long-range foreign policy and the will to build up the means to carry it out.

A congressional staffer praised Mr. Purcell's suggestion that intelligence analysts ought to comment on the possibilities for covert action in their area and that specialists in covert action ought to comment on estimates on how to translate possibilities into plans for action. However, in the CIA, covert action specialists are excluded from the estimates process, and have difficulty making good careers. They should be given their own career element inside CIA. He urged the new administration to be more mindful of common sense than of the CIA's recent folkways.

Two former intelligence officers spoke favorably of a proposal to create an American counterpart of the British Council, or of the "foundations" run by West Germany's political parties but financed by the West German government. These semi-private, wholly overt entities channel money, advice and support to a variety of political causes around the world. The AFL-CIO has also done this sort of thing on a small scale for years, but there is now no way for Congress to provide it with support except through cumbersome grants through AID. They urged that an American bipartisan "board" be created, financed from both public and private sources, and that political action be done openly if at all possible.

Another former intelligence officer asked to what extent the academic community might now be willing to help support covert action. An academic replied by citing the case of a professor at a major university whose colleagues denied him tenure after they learned he had been in contact with the CIA. According to the ethics of the AAUP, he said, professors should not be associated with clandestine intelligence. However, the academic noted, the climate is changing. An intelligence officer agreed that academic participation in various kinds of intelligence activities would be likely. He cited the Defense Intelligence School and the several war colleges, which have never had trouble attracting academics. Another academic agreed. There are hundreds of good institutions, and thousands of unemployed academics.

A former intelligence officer asked the participants from the Congress about the prospects for congressional action to improve the environment for covert action. There was a consensus that Congress is likely to pass legislation to protect names of intelligence personnel as well as sources and methods. However, a congressional staffer pointed out that Congress has never been the major impediment to covert action. Instead, in recent years the CIA itself has been the major obstacle. He suggested that if one were to ask the CIA's supergrades to vote on whether a greater percentage of the CIA's budget shall be devoted to developing staff specialists and assets for covert action, the vote would be overwhelmingly negative. Covert action, he said, did not decline primarily because of Congressional initiatives but because a revolution took place within CIA. Two former intelligence officers suggested that the new administration could and should undo that revolution by serious "housecleaning."

A former intelligence official raised the topic of the intelligence community's organization. The 1947 National Security Act gave the Director of Central Intelligence (DCI) three jobs: presidential advisor on intelligence, manager of the intelligence community and manager of the CIA. No DCI, he said, has even done all three jobs well. He suggested that consideration be given to splitting them. A Congressional staffer answered that because collection and political and paramilitary action is such an absorbing job, anyone who has it should not be burdened with unrelated tasks. Clandestine collection is a related task, but managing analysts, determining the community budget and policy, and advising the President on intelligence certainly are less unrelated tasks. Another former official replied that if DCI's have not fulfilled all their responsibilities, it is because Presidents have failed to give them adequate support. The arrangements embodied in the 1947 National Security Act are basically adequate. A former government official suggested there was deep and growing frustration with the ineffectiveness of CIA, and said that although talk of abolishing CIA and establishing a real covert agency seems "far out" this could be done.

The discussion then turned to the political context of covert action. A former official argued that the overall purpose of American policy should be to persuade the Soviet Union, by the use of all means, to abandon its imperial drive, withdraw to its own borders, and allow its citizens more liberty. A former foreign intelligence official criticized the United States for having a defensive foreign policy. Rather, the US should have an offensive strategy aimed at bringing the Soviet system to collapse. Instead, we have sought on an *ad hoc* basis to hurt the Soviet Union, but not too badly. When a crack appears in the Soviet system, we give the Soviets time to repair it and to start their offensives afresh. Thus, many foreigners who have helped the US against the Soviet Union have felt betrayed. An academic replied that words like "offensive" and "defensive" don't mean much, that strategy is strategy. We could give access to our radios to a hundred irredentist groups, but we should not start anything we are not prepared to back up. Another academic maintained that while American policy has not actually sought the destruction of the Soviet system, that system is full of self-destructive tendencies. These are working themselves out. We should prepare ourselves to take advantage of these situations. A former intelligence officer added that, in his experience, the CIA was usually too cautious, to the point of inaction in planning covert action against the Soviet Union.

A former intelligence officer said that talk of exploiting Soviet vulnerabilities has the flavor of Alice in Wonderland, because we now have so few assets and so few people capable of making plans. There was widespread agreement with his final proposition that even if the opportunities are there, the capabilities are not.

Consortium for the Study of Intelligence

Origin and Purpose

During the past decade, there has been a flood of material dealing with intelligence, particularly American intelligence and its relationship to national security and U.S. foreign policy. Some of this information has been made available in the writings of former intelligence officials. Other major sources include Congressional documents resulting from oversight activities, and documents released under the Freedom of Information Act.

As a result it has become increasingly possible to undertake objective, scholarly and unclassified research into the intelligence process and product, and to examine their relationship to U.S. decision making.

In light of these new circumstances, a group of social scientists from several academic institutions decided in April, 1979, to create a CONSORTIUM FOR THE STUDY OF INTELLIGENCE (CSI). Its membership includes political scientists, particularly specialists in international relations and U.S. foreign policy, historians, sociologists and professors of international and constitutional law.

CSI set for itself the following purposes:

(i) To encourage teaching on both the graduate and undergraduate levels in the field of intelligence, as it relates to national security, foreign policy, law and ethics.

(ii) To promote the development of a theory of intelligence—What is it, and what is its place in American national security policy? Comparative analysis with the practice and experience of other nations will be emphasized.

(iii) To encourage research into the intelligence process itself—analysis and estimates, clandestine collection, counterintelligence, and covert action; and to determine the feasibility of measuring efficiency or setting standards of efficiency so that the product can be improved.

(iv) To study the tensions between intelligence activities and the democratic and constitutional values of our society, and to seek the development of principles and methods for reconciling the two.

For various cultural and political reasons, the study of intelligence has too often been regarded by academicians as *ultra vires*. Their self-exclusion from the subject has inhibited an understanding of this significant instrument of the modern nation-state.

Colloquium on Covert Action

December 5-6, 1980

Washington, DC

List of Participants

Gen. Giuseppe D'Ambrosio
Deputy Director, SISME;
Professor of Military
Institutions, Catholic University
of Milan

Mr. Daniel C. Arnold
Former Chief, Evaluations,
Plans & Design Staff, DDO,
CIA

Mr. Frank R. Barnett
President, National Strategy
Information Center

Mr. John Barron
Senior Editor,
Reader's Digest

Dr. Arnold Beichman
Freelance Writer; Professor of
Political Science

Dr. Richard Bissell
Managing Editor, ORBIS

Mr. Ladislav Bittman
Formerly with the
Czechoslovak Intelligence
Service

Dr. Adda B. Bozeman
Professor of International
Relations, Sarah Lawrence
College

Mr. Richard Burt
The New York Times

Dr. Ray S. Cline
Executive Director,
Georgetown Center for
Strategic & International
Studies; Former Deputy
Director for Intelligence, CIA

Dr. Angelo Codevilla
Professional Staff Member,
Senate Select Committee on
Intelligence

Mr. Eugene Douglas
Director, International Trade
and Government Affairs,
Memorex Corporation

Dr. John J. Dziak
Senior Soviet Specialist, DIA

Ms. Suzanne Garment
Associate Editor of the
Editorial Page, The Wall Street
Journal

Dr. Stephen P. Gibert
Professor of Government; and
Director, National Security
Studies Program, Georgetown
University

Mr. Richard H. Giza
Professional Staff Member,
House Permanent Select
Committee on Intelligence

Dr. Roy Godson
Associate Professor of
Government, Georgetown
University; Research Associate,
National Strategy Information
Center

Mr. Kenneth E. deGraffenreid
Professional Staff Member,
Senate Select Committee on
Intelligence

Mr. Jonathan Hall-Tipping
Former Head of British Defense
International Liaison Staff of
Washington, DC

Mr. Samuel Halpern
Former Executive Assistant to
the Deputy Director for Plans,
CIA

Dr. Samuel P. Huntington
Professor of Government,
Harvard University

Mr. Donald Jameson
Former Covert Action
Specialist, Soviet Division,
DDO, CIA

Mr. Roger Kaplan
Program Officer, Smith-
Richardson Foundation

Mr. Thomas K. Latimer
Staff Director, House
Permanent Select Committee on
Intelligence

Mr. Hubert Leonard
M. J. Murdock Charitable Trust

Mr. William Lewis
Trustee, Space Studies
Institute, Princeton, New
Jersey

Mr. Charles M. Lichenstein
Counsel to the Public
Broadcasting Service

Mr. John M. Maury
President, AFIO; Former Chief,
Soviet Russia Division, DDP,
CIA

Hon. Franco Mazzola
Undersecretary to the President
of the Council of Ministers, and
General Coordinator of the
Italian Security Services

Mr. Cord Meyer
Syndicated Columnist; Former
Assistant Deputy Director for
Plans, CIA

Hon. J. William Middendorf
Former Secretary of the Navy

Professor John Norton Moore
Director, Center for Oceans
Law and Policy, University of
Virginia Law School

Mr. Robert Moss
Author; Columnist

Mr. Lionel H. Olmer
Director of International
Programs, Motorola, Inc.

Mr. Michael O'Neil
Chief Counsel, House
Permanent Select Committee on
Intelligence

Mr. Donald J. Purcell
Former Chief, Covert Action
Staff, CIA

Mr. Alfred S. Regnery
Legislative Counsel to Senator
Paul Laxalt

Mr. Herbert Romerstein
Professional Staff Member,
House Permanent Select
Committee on Intelligence

Gen. Edward L. Rowny
Former JCS Representative to
SALT Negotiations

Mr. Allan Ryskind
Editor, Human Events

Dr. Mark Schneider
Professional Staff Member,
Senate Select Committee on
Intelligence

Dr. Paul Seabury
Professor of Political Science,
University of California at
Berkeley

Mr. Jerry Seib
The Wall Street Journal

Mr. Theodore G. Shackley
Former Associate Deputy
Director for Operations, CIA

Dr. Abram Shulsky
Professional Staff Member,
Senate Select Committee on
Intelligence

Ms. Annette Smiley
Professional Staff Member,
House Permanent Select
Committee on Intelligence

Mr. Paul A. Smith, Jr.
Editor, Problems of
Communism

Mr. Daniel R. Southerland
Christian Science Monitor

Professor W. Scott Thompson
Associate Professor of
Government, Fletcher School of
Law and Diplomacy

Mr. Hugh Tovar
Former Chief, Covert Action
Staff, CIA

Dr. Frank N. Trager
Director, National Security
Education Program, New York
University; Director of Studies,
National Strategy Information
Center

Mrs. Helen Trager
Author

Mr. P. L. Thyraud de Vosjoli
Former Chief of Station,
SDECE

Mr. Edwin Warner
TIME, Inc.

Mr. John Warner
Former General Counsel, CIA

Gen. Vernon A. Walters
Former Deputy Director of
Central Intelligence

Dr. Allen Weinstein
Professor of History, Smith
College

Mr. Lee Williams
Former Chief of Station, CIA

Mr. Richard Wilson
Department of Organization,
AFL-CIO

Hon. C. W. Bill Young, M.C.
Member, House Permanent
Select Committee on
Intelligence

INTELLIGENCE REQUIREMENTS FOR THE 1980's

Roy Godson, *Series Editor*

Volume One *1979* *revised 1983*	Elements of Intelligence
Volume Two *1980*	Analysis and Estimates
Volume Three *1980*	Counterintelligence
Volume Four *1981*	Covert Action
Volume Five *1982*	Clandestine Collection
Volume Six *1986*	Domestic Intelligence
Volume Seven *1986*	Intelligence and Policy

Volumes one through five are published by the National Strategy Information Center, Washington, D.C. and New York, N.Y.

Volumes six and seven are published and distributed by Lexington Books, Lexington, Massachusetts.